ANALYTIC AESTHETICS

For Damon, Aelia and Eden
in their quest for
truth, beauty and the good

Analytic Aesthetics

RICHARD SHUSTERMAN

Basil Blackwell

First published 1989

Basil Blackwell Ltd
108 Cowley Road, Oxford, OX4 1JF, UK

Basil Blackwell Inc.
432 Park Avenue South, Suite 1503
New York, NY 10016, USA

British Library Cataloguing in Publication Data

Analytic aesthetics.
1. Aesthetics
I. Shusterman, Richard M.
111.85

ISBN 0-631-16253-4

Library of Congress Cataloguing in Publication Data

Analytic aesthetics/[edited by] Richard Shusterman.
p.   cm.
Includes index.
ISBN 0-631-16253-4
1. Aesthetics, Modern—20th century.   2. Analysis (Philosophy)
3. Arts—Philosophy.   I. Shusterman, Richard.
BH201.A63 1989
111'.85—dc 19

Typeset in 10 on 11½ pt Times
by Colset Private Limited, Singapore

Printed in Great Britain by
T.J. Press (Padstow) Ltd., Padstow, Cornwall

Contents

List of Contributors

Charles Altieri is Professor of English and Comparative Literature at the University of Washington. Author of *Act and Quality: A Theory of Humanistic Understanding* (1981) and of *Self and Sensibility in Contemporary American Poetry* (1984), he has recently completed a book on *Abstraction in Modernist Painting and Poetry* due to appear in 1989. He is currently writing a collection of essays on what he calls *Expressivist Ethics*.

Pierre Bourdieu is Professor of Sociology at the Collège de France, Paris, and at the Ecole des hautes études. He is the author of many books, among which translated into English are *Outline of a Theory of Practice (1977), Distinction: A Social Critique of the Judgement of Taste* (1984) and (with J. C. Passeron) *Reproduction in Education, Society, and Culture* (1977).

Catherine Z. Elgin is the author of *With Reference to Reference* (1983) and (with Nelson Goodman) *Reconceptions* (1988). Her next book, a work in epistemology, is tentatively entitled *Philosophy Without Foundations*. She is currently Visiting Associate Professor of Philosophy at Princeton University.

Nelson Goodman is the author of *The Structure of Appearance* (1951), *Fact, Fiction, and Forecast* (1955), *Languages of Art* (1968), *Problems and Projects* (1972), *Ways of Worldmaking* (1978), *Of Mind and Other Matters* (1984), and (with Catherine Elgin) *Reconceptions* (1988). He masterminded the multi-media work, *Hockey Seen*, directed the Harvard Summer Dance Center, and founded Project Zero, a research program in arts education. Goodman is Professor Emeritus of Philosophy at Harvard University.

Joseph Margolis is Professor of Philosophy at Temple University. Author of numerous books on a wide variety of philosophical topics, he has written *Art and Philosophy* (1980) and edited *Philosophy Looks at the Arts*, which is now in its third edition (1987). Margolis has just completed a trilogy entitled *The Persistence of Reality* (1986, 1987, 1988) and recently served as President of the American Society for Aesthetics (1987–8).

Christopher Norris is Professor of English at the University of Wales in Cardiff. His books include *William Empson and the Philosophy of Literary Criticism* (1978), *Deconstruction* (1982), *The Deconstructive Turn* (1983), *The Contest of Faculties* (1985), *Jacques Derrida* (1986), *Paul de Man* (1988) and *Deconstruction and the Interests of Theory* (1988). He has also edited volumes on Shostakovich, George Orwell and post-structuralist criticism.

Anthony Savile teaches philosophy at Kings College, London University. He is the author of *The Test of Time* (1982) and *Aesthetic Reconstructions* (1987).

Roger Scruton is Professor of Aesthetics at Birkbeck College, London University. He is the founding editor of *The Salisbury Review* and has published fourteen books, including *Art and Imagination* (1974), *The Aesthetics of Architecture* (1979), *The Meaning of Conservatism* (1980), *Fortnight's Anger* (1981), *Sexual Desire* (1986), and *A Land Held Hostage: Lebanon and the West* (1987). He is currently finishing a book of short stories and a libretto for an opera.

Richard Shusterman is Associate Professor of Philosophy at Temple University. He is the author of *The Object of Literary Criticism* (1984) and *T.S. Eliot and the Philosophy of Criticism* (1988). Having completed the editing of this volume on *Analytic Aesthetics* (1989), he is currently writing a book on pragmatist aesthetics.

J. O. Urmson is Professor Emeritus of Philosophy at Stanford University and Emeritus Fellow at Corpus Christi College, Oxford. He is author of *Philosophical Analysis* (1956), *The Emotive Theory of Ethics* (1968), *Berkeley* (1982), and *Aristotle's Ethics* (1988).

Nicholas Wolterstorff is Professor of Philosophy at Calvin College (Michigan) and at the Free University of Amsterdam. He has published extensively in ontology, aesthetics, and recently in epistemology. His two books in aesthetics are *Works and Worlds of Art* (1980) and *Art in Action* (1980).

Acknowledgements

This book grew out of a special issue of *The Journal of Aesthetics and Art Criticism*, which John Fisher, the retiring editor of the journal, asked me to guest-edit. It was entitled 'Analytic Aesthetics: Retrospect and Prospect' and was published late in 1987. Because of constraints of space and publication deadlines, I could not include much of the fine material I had hoped to present in that volume. The present collection aims at further deepening our understanding of analytic philosophy and aesthetics by including four new essays (by Joseph Margolis, Christopher Norris, Anthony Savile, and J. O. Urmson) specially written for this book. Moreover, the essays by Altieri, Bourdieu, Elgin and Goodman, Scruton, and Wolterstorff have been somewhat revised, and I have provided a substantially revised and enlarged introductory essay.

I wish to thank John Fisher for his initial invitation, continued support, and permission to republish, and I gratefully acknowledge the skilful help of Terri Kettering, his editorial assistant. Alfred A. Knopf and Faber and Faber graciously permitted me to reprint several lines from Wallace Stevens' 'An Ordinary Evening in New Haven'. Temple University's Institute for Aesthetics and Department of Philosophy were supportive in a number of ways; Nadia Kravchenko and Brian Conolly provided welcome word-processing assistance; and Jaime Stover helped me dance through the proofs and index.

I should not forget to acknowledge Eddy Zemach, the teacher whose contagious enthusiasm first immersed me in analytic aesthetics and whose writings and conversations on the subject have been an enduring stimulation to me; nor should my gratitude to the contributing authors, however obvious, go without mention. This book is dedicated to my children and to our mutual acknowledgement.

1

Introduction: Analysing Analytic Aesthetics

Richard Shusterman

I

In the sense of the toastmaster's bromide, analytic aesthetics needs no introduction. It is familiar to all students of aesthetics, having dominated Anglo-American philosophy of art since the mid-century when it was enthusiastically heralded by an earlier and very influential Basil Blackwell anthology, *Aesthetics and Language*.[1] Moreover, though its early heady optimism has given way to sober awareness of its problems and limitations, and of the compelling appeal of rival theories inspired by continental philosophies, analytic aesthetics needs neither a final assessment nor a post-mortem verdict. It is still very much alive, as the essays here collected will witness. What analytic aesthetics does require, and what this volume aims to provide, is an interim account of its career: what it has been and achieved (and failed to achieve), where it presently stands and how it should best go on.

To say that analytic aesthetics is well known does not at all mean that we know very well what exactly it is or even who precisely count as analytic aestheticians and in which of their writings. That it is still alive does not mean it has not been radically transformed from what it originally was and aimed to be. What, then, is analytic aesthetics? What, if anything, particularly characterizes it, and in what way can we speak at all of a distinctive analytic movement, method, or even style in aesthetics? How much and in what manner does analytic aesthetics differ from its antecedents and rivals? Has it lived up to the hopes of revolutionary reform which informed many early analytic attempts at demolishing the projects and theories of traditional aesthetics? How has its own programme been pursued and modified over the years; where and why has it proved inadequate; how may it be improved; and can it point to any achievements of which philosophy can be proud?

To explore these questions and to stimulate their further exploration I

have collected nine new essays (and this Introduction) written specifically
to address the issues of analytic aesthetics.[2] But the stakes here are higher
than the fate of a particular philosophy of art. Our assessment of analytic
aesthetics is motivated not by mere historical curiosity about its past, nor
simply by doubts about its own future, but more urgently by concern for
the entire future of philosophical aesthetics. If so-called continental
theory is strongly challenging the analytic hegemony in Anglo-American
aesthetics, this seems less a reason for dismay than a welcome promise of
wider and more fruitful aesthetic dialogue. Indeed to promote such dialogue this collection includes papers from theorists (like Altieri, Bourdieu
and Norris) who are outside and critical of the analytic tradition, but
know it well enough to engage it in an illuminating way. Similarly, several
of the analytic contributors pay serious attention to Marxian and poststructuralist thinkers (as in Savile's critical but appreciative treatment of
Adorno on truth and beauty). The deeper and more troubling problem is
not *which* philosophy of art but *whether* philosophy of art has a future.
For there are influential currents of thought (issuing from analytic as well
as Marxian and poststructuralist sources) which not only see us as entering
the age of post-analytic philosophy but as straddling the threshold of a
post-philosophical culture. Moreover, no longer merely condemned in
Marxist circles as being associated or 'complicitous' with politically
oppressive ideology, aesthetics is now accused (by an analytic aesthetician
like Danto) as an oppressive ideology in its own right and one shockingly
and long directed at subjugating and disenfranchising art itself.[3] In the
light of such fundamental challenges, how should we conceive the future
role of the philosophy of art, and what function, if any, do the special
techniques, strategies and problems of analytic aesthetics have here?

Such questions are easier to ask (and to multiply) than to resolve, and
the reader should not expect the essays that constitute this volume to
supply conclusive or even collectively consistent answers to them all.
Indeed, some of the essays only treat these metaphilosophical questions
obliquely by considering what analysis can (or cannot) do for a particular
problem like style, musical meaning, interpretation, or the relation of
beauty to truth. Nor do the essays even provide a uniform and unchallengeable definition of analytic aesthetics. But it seems unreasonable to
expect such a definition. This is not only because analytic aesthetics is a
complex (and perhaps somewhat confused) field, nor simply because (as
Urmson notes) the definition of any philosophical field is a philosophical
problem itself and therefore shares the resolute irresolution of philosophy. Analytic aesthetics seems most unlikely to provoke unanimity
of definition because it remains a developing and valued tradition of
thought, and as such its very nature (hence also its formative past) will be
essentially contested by its participant practitioners in their struggle to
appropriate and develop it in the different ways they find most fruitful. If
we are pleased that analytic aesthetics is still alive, we should be content

that its definitive critical history and final analysis remain unwritten.

But though the essays here collected are short on convergent, unchallengeable conclusions on the nature, value and role of analytic aesthetics, and on its precise past and likely future, they none the less provide considerable illumination and stimulation for further inquiry toward possibly better answers. For in reading these essays, the reader is apt to discover (as I discovered) that he or she has a somewhat different view of analytic aesthetics, and such disagreement is the best stimulus for formulating, sharpening and revising one's own views on the subject. In that spirit, then, I shall neither summarize the ensuing papers and their complex interrelations of agreement and dispute; nor shall I attempt a hopeless synthesis or thankless critique of them all. Instead, to provide a tentative orientation and introductory provocation, I offer my own brief (hence sketchily argued) account of how analytic aesthetics and its career may be understood.

II

A fundamental and problematic issue in understanding analytic aesthetics is determining its scope. The question is whether to construe this notion as including all the aesthetic writings of twentieth-century analytic philosophers (as Wolterstorff seems to) or whether analytic aesthetics should be more narrowly construed (as Urmson would have it) to exclude projects of constructionist definition and conceptual reform even when these are performed by eminent and solidly analytic philosophers like Nelson Goodman. Indeed, some construe analytic aesthetics still more narrowly as a specific programme (originating in the late forties and reaching full force by the late fifties and through into the sixties) which involved only some of the analytic philosophers who wrote on aesthetics and, even of those, only some of their writings.[4] Of course, the narrower the scope the easier it is to provide precise accounts and convincing generalizations about analytic aesthetics. But the broader approach has the undeniable advantage of giving analytic aesthetics greater variety, vitality and richness. Certainly we want at least to start with a conception of the field that is wide enough to include the aesthetic writings of Goodman, Danto and Wollheim, even if their more reformatory and speculative aesthetic doctrines make them less paradigmatically analytic aestheticians than the likes of Weitz, Isenberg or Sibley. And certainly we cannot exclude Wittgenstein's aesthetic views, although they predated what most would call the age of analytic aesthetics. For these views became extremely influential, even if it was his general philosophical approach which was initially most formative of analytic philosophy of art.

This is not to say that the aesthetic theory of any solidly analytic philosopher will count as analytic aesthetics. The case of G. E. Moore is very instructive here. By even the narrowest construals of analytic philosophy, Moore counts as a (perhaps *the*) paradigmatic analyst; and his most famous book analyses in considerable detail such aesthetic issues as organic unity, beauty and the emotive and cognitive components in the appreciation of art and natural beauty.[5] Yet strangely, Moore is never considered an analytic aesthetician, not even a prototype of analytic aesthetics; and indeed his aesthetics has been almost totally ignored. Thus, even Arnold Isenberg, in trying to make an early case for analytic aesthetics, falsely assumes Moore's inattention to aesthetics when he laments that 'none of the leaders of the analytic movement, such as Moore and Russell, have ventured into a field [i.e., aesthetics] that was not shunned by Bacon, Hobbes, Locke, Hume or Kant.'[6] Why analytic aestheticians have been so blind and unreceptive to Moore's aesthetic theory is best explained by contrasting his views to their typical positions, a contrast which may further clarify what is more distinctive of analytic aesthetics. But to do this I must first try to sketch what the most typical features and themes of analytic aesthetics seem to be.

1   As its name clearly testifies, analytic aesthetics is a consequence (though perhaps not a mere epiphenomenon) of the twentieth-century analytic approach to philosophy introduced by Moore and Russell and continued by Wittgenstein and others through the various phases of logical atomism, logical positivism and ordinary-language analysis. Probably all analytic philosophers would agree with Russell's claim that analysis rather than the construction of philosophical systems is the major aim of philosophy.[7] But there has not only been considerable disagreement and unclarity about what precisely should be analysed (concepts, meanings, propositions), there was also the problem, acutely formulated in Langford's famous 'paradox of analysis' of how, in general, any formulated *analysans* could be perfectly accurate to its *analysandum* and still be informative.[8] Yet because of their confidence in the general superiority of the analytic approach and their evident pride in its success in other areas, analytic aestheticians tended to dismiss (if not entirely ignore) these difficulties as ultimately manageable and in no way precluding objectivity and agreement as to what constitutes a good analysis in particular cases.

However, a further problem is that there are at least two quite different modes of analysis. One is reductively breaking down a concept, fact, or putative entity into more basic components or properties which are its necessary and sufficient conditions. Such analysis was usually pursued for metaphysical reductions (e.g., objects into sense-data, the average man into a quotient of real men). But there is also a form of analysis aimed not at reductive definition but simply at clarifying vague and problematic notions employed in some area of discourse, distinguishing such a notion's complexities and different uses, even if failing to emerge with a precise, univocal definition of its essential conditions. Since aesthetic concepts seem among the vaguest, this second form of analysis has dominated analytic aesthetics; and it might be argued that analytic aesthetics only got off the ground after this form evolved from the first.[9] As Urmson notes, we can explain and justify our describing both procedures as analytic in terms of a common genealogy and a common aim of clarification rather than critical reform.

But this limitation of aim is not shared by yet another analytic mode which likewise evolved out of first-generation analysis: the Carnapian procedure of rational reconstruction. If clarificatory analysis reveals our aesthetic concepts as troublingly vague, why not proceed to make them better and more precise. Goodman takes this constructivist line in his definitions of musical and literary works of art, which Urmson here criticizes and takes to be a departure from analytic aesthetics as it should be understood.[10] But Urmson's own idea that analysis is confined to clarification without criticism seems itself somewhat a departure from Russell's initial view that analysis 'consists in criticizing and clarifying notions', where we aim at 'passing from those obvious, vague, ambiguous things, that we feel quite sure of, to something precise, clear, definite'.[11] As the Carnap–Strawson exchange[12] makes clear, the very concept and project of analysis reveals a basic tension between precisionist definition through conceptual critique and construction and, on the other hand, the faithful and accepting clarification of our ordinary-language concepts. This tension, as we see, is reflected in analytic aesthetics. Urmson is surely right to allow room for both approaches, but one could add that this room should be found under the concept of analytic aesthetics. For whatever uniformity we gain by excluding Goodman's influential work and methods from analytic aesthetics is offset by impoverishment of the field.

2 Clearly, then, analytic aesthetics cannot properly be understood without reference to the various analytic methods and achievements first established in other branches of philosophy. But no less essential for its understanding is a grasp of the background of aesthetic theory against which it sharply and successfully rebelled. Such theory was highly transcendental and idealistic in tone, and largely dominated by the romantic idealist aesthetic of Croce with its distinction-demolishing essentialism that all art is simply expression and that there are no substantial classificatory (e.g., genre) distinctions to be made between different expressions, every expression being completely unique. The vigorous burgeoning of analytic aesthetics in mid-century owed as much to the perceived failures and woolly dreariness of Crocean idealist expressionism and other romantic essentialisms (e.g. the Bell–Fry theory of 'Significant Form') as to the perceived achievements of the analytic method.[13] But if analytic aesthetics developed by challenging romantic essentialism and expressionism, it did not altogether rid itself of romantic tenets, such as the uniqueness, gratuitousness and autonomy of works of art. Wolterstorff's essay highlights the residual romanticism of analytic aesthetics.

3 Anti-essentialism about art[14] and the quest for clarity (especially
through close concern with language) are perhaps the most common and
distinctive features of analytic aesthetics; and though distinguishable they
are clearly related. The murky confusion of traditional aesthetics was
imputed to its assumption that the arts shared a common essence which
once discovered by the aesthetician could also serve as an absolute standard for aesthetic judgement. Pointing out how the various arts are very
different and that their subsumption under our common concept of art
was not effected till the eighteenth century[15], the analysts argued that the
essentialist presumption led traditional aesthetic theories to ignore,
conflate or homogenize obvious differences between the arts and to speak
in terms that are so vague, muddled and general as to conceal all those
differences behind a mist of confusion by means of an empty and ambiguous formula of essence. Thus Passmore (as also Hampshire, Kennick,
Gallie and Weitz) saw the woolly dreariness of aesthetics 'as arising out of
the attempt to impose a spurious unity on things, the spuriousness being
reflected in the emptiness of the formulae in which that unity is inscribed':
expression, representation, Significant Form, beauty.[16] In the aim of
greater clarity and more meaningful theories, Passmore went so far as to
suggest that 'there is no aesthetics and yet there are principles of literary
criticism, musical criticism, etc.' and that general aesthetics should be
abandoned for 'an intensive special study of the separate arts, carried out
with . . . much respect for real differences between the works of art
themselves'.[17] Such concern with the close study of the separate arts and
their criticism was everywhere endorsed by analytic aesthetics and points
to another important feature which distinguishes it markedly from most
traditional philosophical aesthetics. But some would argue that analytic
aesthetics has not yet gone far enough in the direction of analysing particular works of art.

Two puzzles might be raised with respect to analytic aesthetics' typical
bias against essentialist definition and frequent fear to generalize about
art. First, if we make the apparently obvious assumption that 'art' is not
what Moore would call a simple unanalysable concept like 'good' or
'yellow', it would follow from the Moorean notion of analysis that
art should admit of some essentialist definition. Secondly, if the anti-
essentialist drive toward particularism and preoccupation with the
uniqueness of works of art (best captured in Hampshire's remark that
'when in Aesthetics one is travelling from the particular to the general,
one is travelling in the wrong direction'[18]) is pushed to its logical conclusion, there is not much difference between such particularist anti-
essentialism and the Crocean essentialism analysts so scorned. Both
assume that uniqueness is an essential property of an artwork; it is only
that Croce gives the further explanation that such uniqueness follows
from art's being expression, since what has been truly 'expressed is not
repeated'.[19] Fortunately, however, most analysts implicitly realized that

no matter how much we deny real essences, there must be some point and validity in generalizations about art and its criticism, even if they are best made about specific art forms or genres rather than about art as a whole. Hence, as Passmore recommended, we find much analytic effort concentrating in particular arts and their criticism.

4 Indeed, analytic aesthetics typically saw itself as fundamentally a second-order discipline engaged in the clarification and critical refinement of the concepts of art and art criticism. It neither presumed to offer new manifestoes about what art should be nor revolutionary criteria about how art should be evaluated. It instead sought a more logical and systematic account of the principles of art and criticism as actually reflected in the practice of good critics. And since such practice was distinctly verbal, this perfectly fit analytic philosophy's special concern with language. It also neatly corresponded with analytic philosophy's role regarding what seemed to be its main concern and paradigm of a worthy first-order discipline – science. As science described nature, art criticism (understood widely to include art history and theory) described art; what science was for analytic philosophy in general (preponderantly concerned with logical and epistemological foundations for scientific knowledge), art criticism – the careful, systematic and potentially even scientific study of the different arts – was for analytic aesthetics. Without art criticism as a serious first-order cognitive discipline for analysts to clarify, logically sharpen and ground, there would be much less room or reason for analytic aesthetics to depart from traditional revisionary flights into the essence of beauty or 'the aesthetic'. What helps explain both its anti-essentialism and sudden burst of vigor in the late forties and early fifties is that by this time art criticism, music criticism and especially literary criticism were already established as serious and separate academic enterprises with scientific or at least cognitive pretensions.[20]

It is thus not at all surprising that analytic aesthetics burgeoned well after general analytic philosophy had already reached (and perhaps passed) its prime. Second-order analytic method had to wait till it found the aesthetic counterpart of science in academic art criticism. Literary criticism seemed to represent the most developed of such 'scientific' critical disciplines, and not surprisingly analytic aestheticians most frequently and closely concerned themselves with it. (Consider Beardsley and Weitz, probably the two most influential figures in the fifties and sixties: Beardsley's most influential essay was co-authored with a literary critic [Wimsatt], while Weitz was himself something of a scholar and practitioner of literary criticism.[21]) It should therefore be no more surprising that with poststructuralism's challenge of the scientific study of texts, and more generally of the systematic and principled accumulation of knowledge of artistic meanings, the appeal of analytic aesthetics has significantly waned. But even if the perceived dissimilarities of science and art criticism would eventually scuttle its grand metacritical programme, analytic aesthetics was primarily and most promisingly perceived as the philosophy of art criticism. Of course, an apparently larger project, 'the philosophy of art and art criticism', was sometimes expressed. But since, in second-order fashion, art was to be studied through its criticism, philosophy of art effectively collapsed into the philosophy of art criticism. There are, of course (as the Altieri and Elgin–Goodman essays suggest), serious limitations with this conception of aesthetics as metacriticism; and there are also internal tensions which trouble it. But before considering these latter, we should note two large-scale and problematic consequences which followed from seeing aesthetics as the philosophy of criticism.

5   One consequence is obviously an overwhelming preoccupation with art rather than natural beauty. (There was no first-order aesthetic discipline of nature criticism in the fifties, though ecological hindsight suggests perhaps there should have been.) Of course, beyond Kant and certainly since Hegel, it is hard to find aestheticians who gave as much attention to nature as to art. But in analytic aesthetics the bias toward art and neglect of nature is particular pronounced. The point is too obvious to belabour, but one example is Wollheim's castigating Kant and Bullough (and by extension many others) for trying to understand the aesthetic attitude by means of examples from nature, when, for Wollheim, the only central, non-derivative case of the aesthetic attitude is regarding a work of art under the concept of art.[22] Perhaps this prejudice was further fuelled by analytic philosophy's special concern with language. Its linguistic turn in aesthetics is evident in the relentless titling of books and articles in the form 'The Language(s) of Art (Criticism, Fiction, Painting, Poetry, Music, Metaphor, etc)'. Language obviously involves intention and mind. To study the language(s) of nature and natural beauty might well have seemed naively animistic or more sinisterly theological to secularly enlightened analysts. Preoccupation with art and its criticism did not mean that analytic aesthetics totally ignored more traditional and general aesthetic topics such as defining the aesthetic attitude or aesthetic experience. But it most typically tended to challenge or undermine them, as in Dickie's radical critique of these notions.[23]

Analysis and its preponderant concern for art have been nearly fatal to the traditional idea of the aesthetic. It is true that a number of early analytic efforts were devoted to a more general foundational quest to define the aesthetic and clearly distinguish it from the non-aesthetic (e.g., in terms of a special aesthetic dimension, attitude, experience, judgement, or logically distinct breed of concepts). But all these attempts proved unsatisfactory.[24] Moreover, they seemed deeply problematic and misguided in the face of developments in twentieth-century art which vigorously opposed assimilation of art into the aesthetic. The notion of 'aesthetic', etymologically and historically wedded to sensory perception (and traditionally suggestive of form and pleasure), hardly seems reconcilable with the artworks of Duchamp and so many others whose appreciation requires more than what the senses can discern. Though frequently felt and somehow recognized, this tension between art and the aesthetic was usually swept deftly under the carpet by ignoring natural beauty and tacitly identifying the aesthetic with what relates to art and its criticism. But Goodman and Danto, probably the most influential analytic aestheticians of the past two decades, have come to recognize and explicitly denounce the traditional concept of the aesthetic as a misleading repressive ideology which trivializes art as mere sensuous pleasure with no essential cognitive dimension. And Goodman's revisionary account of the aesthetic is purely and explicitly in terms of the characteristic symbolic functioning of the various languages of *art*, where aesthetic value is construed simply as cognitive efficacy in the functioning of symbol systems so characterized.[25]

6   A second apparent consequence of analytic aesthetics' self-construal as a second-order discipline of metacriticism was a strong tendency to avoid evaluative issues, generally by relegating them to the first-order level of criticism itself. The philosopher of art was to analyse the evaluative judgements of critics and to clarify and critically examine their supporting reasons or premises. But it was not his role to contest their expert verdicts. He might try to extract and formulate from their practice some evaluative standards, but he was not expected to offer original ones of his own. What made it even worse for evaluation was academic criticism's own great reluctance to evaluate. Since it aspired (as a university-based discipline) to some sort of scientific status, and since the then reigning dogma held science to be value-neutral, academic criticism essentially confined itself to finding facts and new interpretations; and it could be scathing (like Northrop Frye) in rejecting evaluation as 'meaningless criticism' and 'leisure-class gossip'.[26]

Thus, though the influential analyst Charles Stevenson insisted that interpretation and evaluation could not be clearly separated in criticism, and though Beardsley offered not only canons of evaluation but a theoretical grounding for them in an account of aesthetic experience, analytic aesthetics gave far less attention to value than did traditional aesthetics.[27] Indeed, not only did it spend proportionally more time on other topics (like interpretation, the definition of art, representation, expression, fiction, the ontological status and identity of artworks), analytic aesthetics often seemed to want to skirt the question of evaluation altogether as being too traditionally muddled and fruitlessly intractable and misleading. This is starkly expressed in Wollheim's explicit refusal to discuss the question in his *Art and its Objects*, and even more bluntly in Goodman's continuing refrain that excessive concentration on the question of 'excellence in art has been partly to blame for the lack of excellence in aesthetics'.[28] Moreover, even those analysts who did discuss this topic typically insisted (against Harold Osborne) that artistic evaluations could be accurately made and justified without relying on or appealing to aesthetic theory.[29]

But perhaps the most striking sign of analytic aesthetics' discomfort and shrinking disengagement from the issue of evaluating art is its very distinctive attempt to distinguish a non-evaluative, merely classificatory, sense of 'art' from the more characteristic evaluative or honorific sense of 'art' as something at least prima facie valuable. Most analysts initially held with Weitz that the aesthetician's task was not to define art but to describe the logic of its concept. While Gallie suggested that what helps make art an essentially contested concept and therefore apparently impossible to define is its ineliminable evaluative dimension, Weitz made much of sharply distinguishing descriptive and evaluative senses of the concept.[30] Though he held art undefinable in either descriptive or honorific sense, the conceptual wedge that Weitz helped drive between them led some to think that analysis could factor out and ignore the so-called evaluative sense and concentrate philosophical efforts on understanding 'art' in its purely descriptive or classificatory content. Here objectivity and definition might succeed since there would apparently be no values to obstruct and obfuscate precise logical analysis.

We find precisely this move in Dickie's influential institutional definition of art, which defines an artwork only in the classificatory sense: to wit, as an artefact given the status of a candidate for apppreciation by some agent acting on behalf of a social institution called the artworld.[31] But what real value or substance can such a definition possibly have? For, as its proponents admit, the strictly classificatory judgement 'This is art' has virtually no use. Moreover, the substantive aesthetic issue which motivates such definitional quests, i.e., whether and how we should appreciate a particular artefact as a work of art, is merely deferred to the artworld and its evaluational decisions and definitions. The very notion of candidate for appreciation presupposes a background where art is evaluatively appreciated, and such evaluations (as Wittgenstein stressed[32]) take many more forms than traditional ascriptions of beauty: there is rightness, precision, importance, originality, etc. Art and (the contest of) value cannot in a holistic sense be separated, which is not to say that particular works of art cannot be bad or valueless.

7   This suggests another salient feature of analytic aesthetics – its neglect of the socially charged context of art. In trying to define art in purely non-evaluative terms and in assuming the validity of entrenched evaluations without questioning their social import and motivation, analytic philosophy did not only ignore something very important. It also misleadingly suggested that art could be properly understood without having to understand (and take a stand in) the contested field of culture. In this

arena, the struggle over aesthetic valorization both reflects and bears on the struggle for larger social stakes in a very complex field of individuals and class fragments competing for social legitimation and distinction. There are reasons beyond the artworld for 'art' being an essentially contested concept. Analytic philosophy's blindness to the complex and contested social context of art, criticism and even its own aesthetic theorizing is paradoxically most striking (as Bourdieu here points out) in its very attempt to define art in terms of a social institution.

8   A somewhat similar point might be made about analytic aesthetics' lack of emphasis on history, characteristic of analytic philosophy's general ahistorical approach to problems.[33] Such a point would, however, require significant qualifications and exceptions. Certainly Wittgenstein, Wollheim and Danto have emphasized the historicity of art and its appreciation; and some analysts have done serious scholarship in the history of aesthetics.[34] But there is nothing in mainstream analytic aesthetics to match the grand historiosophical or genealogical approach which has been central in continental philosophy of art since Hegel. The only thing at all like it is Danto's recent (and avowedly Hegelian) theory of art's original philosophical subjugation and subsequent evolution into philosophy which Danto sets out in *The Philosophical Disenfrancisement of Art*. But this book is clearly very remote from analytic aesthetics as typically practised and ordinarily understood. Moreover, it must be stressed that art's history is seen by Danto (and by analytic aesthetics in general) as autonomous and relatively isolated from history's socio-economic factors and struggles.[35] Analytic aesthetics will seek to justify both this 'isolationist' historical perspective and its own general penchant for the ahistorical, piecemeal treatment of particular problems narrowly defined and logically purified as being necessary means for adequate clarity and focus. Marxian critics will instead interpret and condemn such perspectives as ideological reflections of the social fragmentation, isolation and reification engendered by late capitalism. Analysts will counter by demanding that such charges and concepts be themselves clearly and precisely defined. This is a debate which must be introduced but not pursued here.

9   Instead, having touched on what I think are the major themes of analytic aesthetics, we may return to consider the problem of G. E. Moore. Though neglected as an aesthetician, Moore had a substantial influence on aesthetics through three very different routes. His influence on Bloomsbury aesthetics was deep and wide ranging but is most clear in the Bell–Fry aesthetic of Significant Form, which reflects Moore's view on the intuition of intrinsic value in terms of organic unity, as well as some of his views on language and unanalysable concepts. Secondly, he influenced I. A. Richards by inciting him to disagreement, most significantly in Richard's seminal doctrine that full appreciation of literary

works does not require belief in their truth. Moore felt that truth added to the aesthetic value of a work or any object. Thirdly, Wittgenstein, like Richards, also seems to have developed his aesthetic views partly by disagreement with Moore, particularly with Moore's preoccupation with the judgement-form and predicate of beauty as containing the key to understanding aesthetics.[36] Such concentration on beauty departs sharply from the typical analytic perspective. But is there any convergence between Moorean and analytic aesthetics, and where else do they diverge?

Very briefly then, we can say that Moore shared (and partly inspired) analytic aesthetics' quest for clarity and its dedication to careful and rigorous conceptual analysis through close attention to language and its ambiguities. In *Principia Ethica* he thought that beauty could be analysed and defined in terms of the (unanalysable) notion of good, but he later put both beauty and goodness on the same level, as basic forms of intrinisic value. However, even when he thought that beauty could be analysed and defined, Moore held that its definition (based as it was on undefinable goodness) could never generate any general, essential, discursively formulable criterion of beauty.[37] To attempt such an essentialist definition would be to commit what Moore called the naturalistic fallacy. This anti-essentialist, particularist approach to aesthetic judgement was common to much analytic aesthetics, as was the idea Moore championed of aesthetic value being some sort of non-natural and non-instrumental value, something intrinsically and ultimately good in itself. Here Moore (and analysis) represent aesthetic autonomy and stand opposed to the Hegelian notion of beauty and art as a mere historical stage to be superseded in the development of *Geist*. Indeed, Moore represents the extremity of that sort of blindness to the wider historical and social contexts and determinants of art and art-appreciation which is characteristic of most analytic aesthetics. The aesthetic value of objects is determined for Moore by the intuitive grasp of the individual observer who must employ a 'method of absolute isolation', introspectively assessing whether and how much value the objects would have 'if they existed *by themselves*, in absolute isolation' and then moving on to determine 'what comparative value seems to attach to the isolated existence of each'.[38]

Moore's most marked differences with analytic aesthetics are three. He was concerned entirely with the question of value, and pursued it by narrow and single-minded concentration on what he regarded as the paradigmatic aesthetic value concept – the beautiful. This contrasts not only with analytic aesthetics' de-emphasis on evaluation, its frequent avoidance or explicit repudiation of this matter as a topic for aesthetic theory, but also with its crucial recognition that there are a vast variety of predicates in which our aesthetic evaluations of both art and nature are couched. Secondly, in clear opposition to apparently all other analysts, Moore gave pride of place to natural beauty rather than art. With what might seem a blind philosophical bias for reality coupled with extraordinary aesthetic (if not also philosophical) naiveté, Moore argues that 'beauty in Nature should be held superior to an equally beautiful landscape [painting] or imagination', simply because the former is real and thus beauty is further beautified by truth.[39] Moore's downgrading of art (though only *vis-à-vis* natural beauty) is perhaps symptomatic and certainly consonant with his total disregard of art criticism. This is the third feature where Moore's theory diverges radically from analytic aesthetics, which conceived itself largely, indeed primarily, as the philosophy of art criticism.

10 Let us then return, in conclusion, to the problems of analytic aesthetics' self-conception as metacriticism. It confined philosophy's understanding of art and the aesthetic to what criticism understood or sought to understand, thereby inhibiting philosophy from using its aesthetic inquiries to achieve philosophical illumination in epistemology, philosophy of mind and philosophy of language, or indeed from using its philosophical arsenal in these areas to formulate its own criticism of artworks. But apart from such problems of limitation of scope (lamented here by Altieri and Elgin and Goodman), there were problems of consistency intrinsic to the very project of clarifying the language and logic of criticism. Two basic tensions were at work here: the first between the ideals of descriptive accuracy and critical reform, the second between the different language-games or logics in critical practice.

Analytic aesthetics as a clarificatory second-order account of first-order critical practice assumed (and had to assume) that this practice (at least as practised by established critics in the discipline) was both worthwhile and productive of acceptable results which it was not the analyst's job to question. His or her role was simply to elucidate the logical form of proper critical practice and perhaps formulate and sharpen it into clear principles which critics might use if they felt they had gone astray or were unresolvably deadlocked on a particular question. The job was to provide a clear map or picture of a very complex and vague terrain, intuitively familiar to critics who were its best explorers but had no skill in precise cartography. But if critical practice was confusingly vague and yet essentially acceptable, what should the analyst's job of clarification be? Should it simply make that practice more clear to us by tracing all its complex vagaries or should it make the practice itself more clear by criticizing such ambiguities and recommending somewhat different and clearer concepts, standards or procedures? Descriptive accuracy versus prescriptive clarity was analytic aesthetics' insoluble dilemma. As Wittgenstein pointedly posed it, 'won't it become a hopeless task to draw a sharp picture corresponding to the blurred one? . . . And this is the position you are in if you look for definitions corresponding to our concepts in aesthetics or ethics.'[40] It seems equally hopeless to recommend a definite reform to render critical practice less ambiguous (as Beardsley did in his anti-intentionalism and three objective canons) and then to pretend that this is not so much a substantial reform as the analytic discovery of what all good critics were really doing all along when they were doing things right.[41] Yet Beardsley's reformatory 'analyses' were probably those most stimulating and influential for critics and theorists both within and outside the analytic tradition. And a more explicitly constructivist and pragmatist analyst like Goodman (who is also less committed to metacriticism) can flatly insist that analysis of antecedent practice and concepts is just a springboard for critically constructive efforts to improve or replace them. It therefore seems likely that analytic aesthetics will move in this more pragmatist and activist direction, especially since recent critical practice has taken some surprising new paths which most analytic theorists will not wish to follow or accept as critical paradigms to which analysis as accurate second-order reflection must be faithful.

This suggests the second source of tension in the metacritical programme of analysis – the plurality of contested critical practices. In accord with philosophy's traditional search for general, fundamental and unifying principles, much analytic effort was devoted to uncovering the underlying logic behind the complex variety of critical practices; for example, to reveal *the* basic logic of interpretation at work in the seemingly different interpretive practices of different critics (and to do the same sort of thing for evaluation). Analysts sought to do this by close examination and accurate description of what good critics actually do when interpreting, but they arrived at very different and inconsistent accounts of interpretive logic. The reason is simply that there is no basic or essential logic of interpretation, but instead different logics (and not merely various methods) of interpretation. Different critics play different interpretive 'games' with different logics implicit in and structuring the games they practise. These different games reflect and serve different aims; and their fundamental logical variance is concealed by their never being explicitly formulated and further by their sharing much the same terms – 'the poem', 'the right interpretation', 'the meaning', 'justification' – but using them in often very different senses. The cause of the controversy and divergence of analysis of interpretive logic is that analysts are analysing different logics which they take as paradigmatic and from which they generalize for all interpretation.[42]

But if analysis is the clarificatory project of accurately describing the actual logic employed in criticism rather than normatively prescribing the logic that should be employed, then the analytic aesthetician has a problem. He is not justified in defending his theory of interpretive logic by rejecting all the entrenched interpretive practices which do not fit his paradigm on the grounds that they are not 'true' interpretation or that they do not satisfy the true or proper ends of interpretation. For the true nature and ends of interpretation are essentially contested by critics, and thus to determine such issues would be to legislate or recommend not neutrally to analyse. The idea that there is or must be one essential or proper interpretive logic (whether objectivist, relativist, non-cognitivist etc.) which underlies all good criticism was perhaps a vestige of essentialism that analytic aesthetics had great trouble shedding. For the faith that such a logic was there to be discovered and subsequently employed to ground and grade academic criticism was what gave that project of analysis its whole point and appeal.

Of course, an analyst could maintain the ideal of neutral objective analysis by accepting the plurality of critical practices (even those he finds most unsavoury) and faithfully analysing their variant logics. Their different aims, strengths and limitations would be indicated, but no transcendental philosophical privileging would be provided; and the variant practices would be left to prove themselves by the power and appeal of their achievements. This path of analytic purism seems to converge with radical deconstruction in concluding that there is no philosophically privileged right way for criticism. But such a posture of rigorous neutrality is arguably itself a scientistic prejudice involving gross self-decption. For philosophy's abnegation of normative judgement as to how texts and artworks *should be* understood for the sake of representing accurately how they *are in fact* understood seems to betray the issue that really matters to us, and instead pursues an old analytic dream of discovering and mirroring the true structure of facts, here the logical structure of criticism.

Pragmatists would argue that this dream rests on the dubious assumption that the nature of criticism (or art) is simply there to be discovered rather than to be made and remade. They would insist that it is partly a philosopher's responsiblity to see that it is made right and not just left to professional critics. Analytic aestheticians like Goodman and Margolis have displayed clear pragmatist leanings (albeit mainly in their non-aesthetic writings). Moreover, some analysts like Scruton show great zeal in polemically confronting structuralist and poststructuralist critics and theorists on the issue of how art should be understood and experienced. It might then seem likely that analytic aesthetics will take a more activist and interventionist role in the contest over the nature of art and art criticism rather than simply clarify or logically explicate, with implicit acquiescence, what the prominent critics see fit to do.

But if it pursues this direction, or if it takes some of the other directions recommended by the contributors to this volume, will it still remain analytic aesthetics? Or will it be something new, something analytic only in its style, terminology and the authors it cites? The answer to this question depends not only on the future but on how analytic aesthetics should be understood. I hope the following essays will help us to a better understanding.

NOTES

1 William Elton (ed.), *Aesthetics and Language* (Oxford, Basil Blackwell, 1954). A later trove of influential analytic papers is collected in Cyril Barrett (ed.), *Collected Papers in Aesthetics* (Oxford, Basil Blackwell, 1965). The present collection may be seen as continuing a Basil Blackwell tradition in covering the field of analytic aesthetics. Other important papers reflecting the growth and change of analytic aesthetics can be found in the three editions of *Philosophy Looks at the Arts*, edited by Joseph Margolis (the first from New York, Scribner, 1962; the second and third from Philadelphia, Temple University Press, 1978, 1987).

2 Four of the essays are published here for the first time. The others originally appeared in a special issue of *the Journal of Aesthetics and Art Criticism*, 46 (1988) which I guest-edited, but they have been somewhat revised here. For more precise details see my Acknowledgements.

3 See Arthur Danto, *The Philosophical Disenfranchisement of Art* (New York, Columbia University Press, 1986) for his argument that aesthetics, since Plato, constitutes philosophy's self-promoting ideology aimed at disenfranchising art by theoretically subjugating it to and ultimately transforming it into philosophy.

4 See Anita Silvers, 'Letting the Sun Shine In: Has Analytic Aesthetics Made Aesthetics Clear?', *Journal of Aesthetics and Art Criticism*, 46 (1988), 137–49.

5 G. E. Moore, *Principia Ethica* (Cambridge, Cambridge University Press, 1903).

6 See Arnold Isenberg, 'Analytic Philosophy and the Study of Art', *Journal of Aesthetics and Art Criticism*, 46 (1988), 125–36.

7 See, for example, Bertrand Russell, 'Logical Atomism', in D. Pears (ed.), *Russell's Philosophy of Logical Atomism* (London, Fontana, 1972), 162.

8 See C. H. Langford, 'Moore's Notion of Analysis', in P. A. Schilpp (ed.), *The Philosophy of G. E. Moore* (Evanston) Ill., Northwestern University Press, 1942), pp. 319–42. Moore's response is on pages 660–7.

9 Though most frequently Moore, Russell and Wittgenstein are *all* cited as influences and exempla, it is clearly the work of the later Wittgenstein (reinforced by the somewhat similar methods of Ryle and Austin) which ignited analtyic aesthetics in the fifties. Explicit testimony of this can be found in Elton, *Aesthetics and Language*, pp. 1n., 11–12.

10 See Nelson Goodman, *Languages of Art* (Oxford, Oxford University Press, 1969), pp. 177–221.

11 See Bertrand Russell, 'Logical Atomism', and 'The Philosophy of Logical Atomism', in Pears (ed.), *Russell's Philosophy of Logical Atomism*, pp. 162, 33.

12 See P. F. Strawson, 'Carnap's views on Constructed Systems versus Natural Languages in Analytic Philosophy', in P. A. Schilpp (ed.), *The Philosophy of Rudolph Carnap* (LaSalle, Ill., Open Court, 1963), pp. 503–18. Carnap replies on pages 933–40.

13 One of Isenberg's central arguments in recommending analytic aesthetics is simply that since other aesthetic philosophizing has left things in such a muddle, analytic aesthetics – as committed to clarity – deserves a chance to

prove itself and could hardly make matters worse. See Isenberg, p. 128.

14 Beardsley, however, might seem an exception to this, since he regards works of art as constituting a special 'function-class' of objects most suitable for producing aesthetic experience, where aesthetic experience is treated in an essentialist manner. See Monroe Beardsley, *Aesthetics: Problems in the Philosophy of Criticism* (New York, Harcourt, Brace, 1958), pp. 524–30. Danto also seems to embrace some sort of essentialism; see his *The Transfiguration of the Commonplace* (Cambridge, Mass., Harvard University Press, 1981), pp. viii, 28. I should further note that analytic aesthetics in fact displayed two kinds of anti-essentialism – weak and strong. The weak held that if we follow Wittgenstein's advice 'to look and see' we just will not find any essence of art, while the stronger view held that art could not possibly have any essence because of art's adventurous character and the open nature of its concept. This distinction is nicely elucidated in T. J. Diffey, 'Essentialism and the Definition of Art', *British Journal of Aesthetics*, 13 (1973), 103–20.

15 Analysts were particularly fond of making this point by reference to the historical research of P. O. Kristeller's 'The Modern System of Art', *Journal of the History of Ideas*, 11, 12 (1951, 1952).

16 J. A. Passmore, 'The Dreariness of Aesthetics', in Elton (ed.), *Aesthetics and Language*, p. 44. See also Stuart Hampshire, 'Logic and Appreciation' and W. B. Gallie, 'The Function of Philosophical Aesthetics' in the same volume; W. E. Kennick, 'Does Traditional Aesthetics Rest on a Mistake', *Mind*, 47 (1958), reprinted in Barrett (ed.), *Collected Papers in Aesthetics*; and Morris Weitz, 'The Role of Theory in Aesthetics', *Journal of Aesthetics and Art Criticism*, 16 (1955), 27–35.

17 Passmore, 'Dreariness of Aesthetics', pp. 50, 55.

18 Hampshire, 'Logic and Appreciation', p. 169.

19 Benedetto Croce, *Aesthetic* (London, Macmillan, 1922), p. 150.

20 This dependence on the separate 'scientific' study of the different arts is also a reason why the mid-century analytic aestheticians were especially hard on Croce, whose essentialism was coupled with a virulent anti-scientism about the understanding of art. For more on this see Richard Shusterman 'Analytic Aesthetics, Literary Theory and Deconstruction', *Monist*, 69 (1986), 22–38.

21 Consider, for example, not only Weitz's scholarly and compendious *Hamlet and the Philosophy of Literary Criticism* (London, Faber, 1964), but his excellent study of Eliot's poetry, 'T. S. Eliot: Time as a Mode of Salvation', first published in the *Sewanee Review* in 1952 and reprinted in B. Bergonzi (ed.), *T. S Eliot: Four Quartets* (London, Macmillan, 1969), pp. 138–52. The Beardsley-Wimsatt essay I refer to is of course 'The International Fallacy', reprinted along with their other influential paper 'The Affective Fallacy', in W. K. Wimsatt, *The Verbal Icon* (Lexington University of Kentucky Press, 1967), pp. 3–39.

22 See Richard Wollheim, *Art and its Objects* (Harmondsworth, Penguin, 1975), s. 42.

23 See George Dickie, 'The Myth of the Aesthetic Attitude', *American Philosophical Quarterly*, 1 (1964), 56–66; and 'Beardsley's Phantom Aesthetic Experience', *Journal of Philosophy*, 62 (1965), 129–36.

24 For more detail on this, see Richard Shusterman, 'Deconstruction and Analysis: Confrontation and Convergence', *British Journal of Aesthetics*, 26 (1986), 310–24.

25 See Danto's *The Philosophical Disenfranchisement of Art*, xiv–xv, 1–21; and Nelson Goodman, *Languages of Art*, pp. 248–64; and *Of Mind and Other Matters* (Cambridge, Mass., Harvard University Press, 1984), pp. 138–53.

26 See Northrop Frye, *The Anatomy of Criticism* (Princeton, NJ, Princeton University Press, 1957), p. 18.

27 See C. L. Stevenson, 'On the Reasons that Can Be Given for the Interpretation of a Poem', in Joseph Margolis (ed.), *Philosophy Looks at the Arts* (New York, Scribner, 1962), p. 124; and Beardsley, *Aesthetics*, pp. 524–43.

28 See Wollheim, *Art and its Objects*, s.65. I should note that though this section is unchanged, Wollheim adds a brief essay on evaluation in the second edition of his book (published by Cambridge University Press in 1980). The Goodman citation is from his *Problems and Projects* (Indianapolis, Bobbs–Merrill, 1968), p. 121. See also his *Languages of Art*, pp. 261–2: 'Excessive concentration on the question of excellence has been responsible, I think, for constriction and distortion of aesthetic inquiry. . . . And a criterion of aesthetic merit is no more the major aim of aesthetics than a criterion of virtue is the major aim of psychology.' The theme is continued (albeit in a more moderate vein) in *Of Mind and Other Matters*, pp. 164–6.

29 According to Kennick, the very assumption that a definition of art is used or needed when properly evaluating art represents the second grave mistake (after essentialism) on which traditional aesthetics rested. See Kennick in Barrett (ed.), *Collected Papers in Aesthetics*, pp. 1–21. For a detailed account of the views of other analysts (e.g., Hampshire, Isenberg, Macdonald, Sibley) who denied that evaluation was or should be guided by any general theory, see Richard Shusterman, 'Evaluative Reasoning in Criticism', *Ratio*, 23 (1981), 142–59; and 'Wittgenstein and Critical Reasoning', *Philosophy and Phenomenological Research*, 47 (1986), 91–110.

30 See Weitz, 'Role of Theory in Aesthetics'; and W. B. Gallie, 'Art as an Essentially Contested Concept', *Philosophical Quarterly*, 6 (1956), 97–114.

31 See, for example, George Dickie, *Aesthetics* (New York, Bobbs–Merrill, 1971), pp. 98–108. In response to numerous criticisms, the theory has gone through a number of revisions since first advanced in G. Dickie, 'Defining Art', *American Philosophical Quarterly*, 6 (1969), 253–6. The latest version is found in Dickie's *The Art Circle* (New York, Haven, 1984). Perhaps the most sustained and powerful case against the whole idea of defining art in a purely classificatory sense is in B. R. Tilghman, *But is it Art?* (Oxford, Basil Blackwell, 1984).

32 Ludwig Wittgenstein, *Lectures and Conversations on Aesthetics, Psychology and Religious Belief*, ed. by C. Barrett (Oxford, Basil Blackwell, 1970), p. 3.

33 Consider, for example, Goodman's glib and global dismissal of past aesthetic theory as hopelessly misguided and obsolete, its relation to his own contemporary aesthetics being that of the horse and buggy to the motor car (*Of Mind and Other Matters*, p. 198).

34 Apart from Beardsley's history of aesthetics [*Aesthetics from Classical Greece to the Present* (New York, Macmillan, 1966)], we can point to important historical studies in eighteenth-century aesthetics by Peter Kivy, *Reid's Lectures on the Fine Arts* (The Hague, Nijhoff, 1973) and *The Seventh Sense: A Study of Frances Hutcheson's Aesthetics* (New York, Franklin, 1975).

35 For Danto the factors or imperatives directing art's evolution and history are

those of 'its own internal development' (*The Philosophical Disenfrancisement of Art*, pp. 97–111, 203–4, citation from p. 204); and Roger Scruton similarly insists, against Marxian views, that art history be viewed as having the 'autonomy constitutive of a genuine independent subject' in *The Aesthetic Understanding* (London, Methuen, 1983), p. 167.

36   For Richards' admission of Moore's great but reactive influence, see the interview in his *Complementarities: Uncollected Essays*, edited by J. P. Russo (Manchester, Carcanet, 1976), pp. 257–258. Wittgenstein's critique of Moore (*Lectures and Conversations*, p. 2) shows Wittgenstein to be one of the few analytic aestheticians to emphasize that the very meaning of art and aesthetic judgement is mainly a function of its complex role and social embeddedness in a particular historical age or culture, a role which can change through more general socio-cultural change. One should also note that Moore had a major role in the dissemination and influence of Wittgenstein's later aesthetic views (which Wittgenstein had left unpublished) by publishing his own account of them in *Mind* (1955). This account, in an essay entitled 'Wittgenstein's Lectures 1930–33', is reprinted in Moore's *Philosophical Papers* (London, Allen and Unwin, 1959), pp. 252–324.

37   'It appears probable that the beautiful should be *defined* as that of which the admiring contemplation is good in itself.' But 'there can be no single criterion of beauty', since it, like goodness, must be intuitively perceived in terms of the particular organic unities which manifest it (*Principia Ethica*, pp. 201–2). For his later view see G. E. Moore, *Philosophical Studies* (London, Routledge Kegan Paul, 1922), p. 253. For more detailed discussion of Moore's theory of organic unity and its relation to aesthetics, see Richard Shusterman, 'Organic Unity: Analysis and Deconstruction', in Reed Way Dasenbrock (ed.) *Redrawing the Lines: Analytic Philosophy, Deconstruction and Literary Theory* (Minneapolis, University of Minnesota Press, 1989).

38   Moore, *Principia Ethica*, pp. 187–8.

39   *Ibid.*, pp. 194–7; quotation from p. 196.

40   Wittgenstein, *Philosophical Investigations*, para. 77.

41   Beardsley, *Aesthetics*, pp. 17–29, 454–70.

42   See Richard Shusterman, 'The Logic of Interpretation', *Philosophical Quarterly*, 28 (1978), 310–24.

2

The Methods of Aesthetics

J. O. Urmson

When I was an undergraduate at Oxford in the thirties there was no provision whatsoever for instruction in or the study of philosophical aesthetics, nor do I remember that anyone found this surprising. In so far as we were aware of aesthetics we thought of it as a poor relation of moral philosophy, as moral philosophy was then practised. If, with G. E. Moore, one claimed to intuit goodness in moral contexts as a non-natural property, then presumably one would consistently claim to intuit beauty in aesthetic contexts in the same way. If one was a subjectivist in morals one consistently located beauty in the eye of the beholder. One could be more sophisticated than that, but the point is that the answer to the aesthetic question tended to be treated as a mere consequence of the answer to the moral question, needing no serious independent thought. If asked what further questions arose in aesthetics beyond the question of the nature of beauty I should certainly in those days have been stumped for an answer. I do remember making an unaided attempt to read Croce's *Aesthetic*, but what little I could understand seemed to me to have little to do with what I vaguely expected to find discussed.

J. A. Passmore's well-known paper 'The Dreariness of Aesthetics', published in *Mind* in 1951, in which he surveys the history of that period and beyond, confirms my impression of the way things then were. It starts with the sentence: 'British philosophers, with some few exceptions, pay little attention to aesthetics'; and on the next page we read ' "What beauty is" is normally supposed to be the main theme of aesthetics itself'.[1] Comparably with my difficulties with Croce, Passmore writes of a bad translation of Maritain's *Art and Poetry* that 'so used are they to reading nonsense in books on aesthetics that even when the translator piled nonsense on nonsense they were unperturbed'; 'they' are the critics of the book in the learned journals.

So there is a two-fold explanation of the neglect of aesthetics in those days in Britain and, though to a lesser extent, in the United States. On the one hand the subject seemed to be very jejune; on the other hand those who did write on the subject tended to be unintelligible. If the reader should exclaim that we were quite wrong to think the subject to be so narrow and jejune, I reply that I agree with him entirely. If he wishes further to claim that it was also our fault that we did not appreciate the pearls of wisdom that Maritain and others so vainly scattered in our porcine haunts, I need more convincing. But I am in any case attempting to describe, not to defend, the attitude towards aesthetics which was common in the first half of the twentieth century in such milieus of which I was aware.

What, within my experience, led to the development of the sort of work in aesthetics in which I have been interested was also two-fold. First, we began to realize that there were very many interesting questions in aesthetics other than the traditional question 'What is beauty?' The differences between the arts, temporal and non-temporal, performing and non-performing, the nature of realism in art, the relation of score to musical performance and of script to dramatic performance are a few random samples of the type of questions I have in mind. These questions, it is clear, could not be regarded as mere analogues of more important issues in moral philosophy.

Secondly, we came to realize how inadequate 'What is beauty?' was as a formulation of even the traditional question of aesthetics, a formulation which was totally inadequate to cope with the issues involved. I remember a brief conversation between O. K. Bouwsma and George Paul round about 1950 that went something like this:

Bouwsma   Paul, would you say that *War and Peace* was a good book?
Paul   Yes, I would.
Bouwsma (slyly)   Paul, would you say that *War and Peace* was a beautiful book?
Paul   No, I would not.
Bouwsma (somewhat disappointed)   Nor would I.

Such moments as these began to remove the blinkers from our eyes.

At the same time, J. L. Austin was telling us that in any case we should forget for a while the situations in which the word 'beautiful' might be appropriate (beautiful sunsets and melodies) and concentrate our attention on such problems as the difference between dumpy and dainty milk-jugs (an example on which his Saturday morning group spent some time). Briefly, we were led to realize that there was a vast vocabulary of terms used in aesthetic contexts and that 'the philosophy of beauty' was a very inadequate and far too narrow account of the field of philosophical aesthetics.

So much for a semi-autobiographical account of how some like-minded people, including myself, came to take an interest in philosophical aesthetics. Briefly we were attracted by a realization that there were questions in aesthetics beyond the rather moth-eaten topic of beauty and the eye of the beholder, and the recognition that these questions could be tackled by the same down-to-earth methods and in the same plain English which we had learned to use in other areas of philosophy.

What I have been referring to would presumably be called analytic aesthetics. But what are the defining features of analytic aesthetics? It is surely obvious that we cannot profitably discuss the relationship of analytic aesthetic to other types of philosophical aesthetics without first raising that question.

The notion of analysis in philosophy was first influentially introduced by Kant with his terminology of analytic and synthetic judgements, and he used it in a way that was clearly analogous to its use in chemistry. We take some concept, such as that of an effect, and find that it is compounded of the concepts of being an event and of having a cause rather as water is found to be a compound of hydrogen and oxygen. Russell and his colleagues reintroduced the term 'analysis' with the same chemical implications; they called themselves logical atomists and spoke of their task as being the analysis of molecular propositions into their atomic constituents; they diverged from Kant not in their use of the term *analytic* but in taking the subjects of their analysis not to be terms like 'effect' or bachelor,' but propositions such as 'This is a tomato' or 'The spirit of the age is restless' which were thought to be compounds of atomic propositions.

The notion that conceptual systems and the natural languages which embody them can be treated as edifices where all our concepts are built up out of a set of simple concepts (or simple ideas) and its sister notion that all the propositions expressible in a language were either logically simple or reformulable as a complex of such simple propositions have long since died. When they died the use of the term 'analysis' with the old chemical associations died with them. The question therefore arises how the continued use of the expression 'analytic philosophy' could be justified. The continuity can be in part explained, though not justified, in purely historical ways; those philosophers who had advocated analysis in the old way continued to be called analytic philosophers even though their methods had changed. But there is, I believe, a justification. The old-style analysts had started from some datum which they found in the current conceptual and linguistic apparatus. They did not invent the concept of an effect or of a bachelor, but found them in common employment; they did not propose the use of such propositions as 'This is a tomato' and 'The spirit of the age is restless', but came upon them in common speech. Taking these propositions or concepts as data, part at least of the point of their analysis was to clarify these data and make them more intelligible. At least some of what has since been called analysis has shared these methods and goals; it has continued to take the concepts and propositions which it found in use and to treat them as data to be examined and clarified, not as candidates to be criticized, tested and perhaps rejected. Such continuity seems an adequate justification of treating this work as being of the same character as traditional analysis and calling it by the same name.

One thing which is surely without justification is to treat the notion of analysis as being more or less synonymous with that of empiricism. The traditional analysis of 'effect' into 'event having a cause' is no less analysis if one believes that the concept of cause is a simple a priori concept than if one believes that it itself has a complicated Humean analysis. Further, however empiricist in spirit Hume's chapter on miracles may be, for example, it is mainly concerned with questions of the justification of certain beliefs which it would be quaint to call analytical.

Another thing that cannot be done is to define analysis in terms of the questions it undertakes to answer, at least if we individuate questions by their verbal form. This point can best be made clear by illustration.

The whole of Book I of R. G. Collingwood's *The Principles of Art*[2] is devoted to the question 'What is a work of art?', which I take to be, beyond controversy, a question that has often been raised in what we should unhesitatingly call analytic aesthetics. I now quote from page 151 of that work:

> Let us recapitulate and summarize our attempt to answer the question, what is a work of art? What, for example, is a piece of music?
>
> 1 In the pseudo-aesthetic sense for which art is a kind of craft, a piece of music is a series of audible noises. The psychological and 'realistic' aestheticians, as we can now see, have not got beyond this pseudo-aesthetic conception.
> 2 If 'work of art' means work of art proper, a piece of music is not something audible, but something which may exist solely in the musician's head.
> 3 To some extent it must exist solely in the musician's head (including, of course, the audience as well as the composer under that name), for his imagination is always supplementing, correcting and expurgating what he actually hears.
> 4 The music which he actually enjoys as a work of art is thus never sensuously or 'actually' heard at all. It is something imagined.
> 5 But it is not imagined sound (in the case of painting, it is not imagined colour-patterns, &c.). It is an imagined experience of total activity.
> 6 Thus a work of art proper is a total activity which the person enjoying it apprehends, or is conscious of, by the use of his imagination.

Now if we were to suppose that Collingwood was trying to elucidate the concepts of 'piece of music' and 'work of art' as they are naturally employed by ourselves or anyone we know we could only conclude that he exhibits a degree of incompetence without parallel in philosophical literature. This is clearly not his aim. Perhaps 'series of audible noises', given in the clause numbered (1), is thought by Collingwood to be something like an analysis of the normal concept (contemptuously called 'pseudo-aesthetic' by Collingwood), though as such it would be more plausible as an account of a performance. So if we are to regard Collingwood as the very gifted man that he certainly was we cannot suppose that he is answering an analytic question, even though his question 'What is a piece of music?' is formulated in words often used to ask an analytic question.

If we are to benefit from reading Collingwood or be in a position to criticize him we need to know what other than analysis is his goal, for unless we know this we can have no criterion of success in his type of endeavour. If Collingwood is to be subjected to adverse criticism it must be initially of his failure to make clear what these criteria are. Only when we know the answer to that question can we ask whether his project is worthwhile – unless of course we claim to know a priori that only analytic aesthetics is legitimate. It is clearly not self-evident what question is being asked when on says 'What is a piece of music?' unless it is the analytic one, though it clearly is used in diverse ways.

So this initial illustration from the writings of Collingwood is designed to make three main points. In the first place, one cannot identify an analytic question from its verbal form since Collingwood is clearly using the verbal form 'What is a piece of music?', which might well be used to ask an analytic question, for quite other purposes. Anyone with any experience of philosophical aesthetics will know that this is not an isolated or exceptional example. In the second place, one cannot know whether Collingwood's account of what a piece of music is is correct, or even whether it is appropriate to ask whether it is correct, until one knows what criteria of success, if any, are applicable to his enterprise. Thirdly, one cannot know whether his enterprise is worth undertaking and what purpose it serves until one knows what criteria of success are relevant to the enterprise.

My difficulty with Collingwood is that he does not tell us clearly what criteria of success are relevant to his enterprise, and they are not self-evident. I should be inclined to hazard the guess that Collingwood believes that if one composes a piece of music or attends to a piece of music (as ordinarily conceived) one has an experience or conscious activity of self-expression, that this is what is important in composing or appreciating music, so that hearing the sounds is merely a causal adjunct to what really matters. On this interpretation Collingwood is making a judgement of importance which he makes in deviant fashion by transferring the name 'piece of music' to something more important than the thing called a piece of music in vulgar parlance. I am not sure that this is a correct account of what Collingwood was doing, and I am sure that Collingwood would contemptuously repudiate it. But if I am wrong I have no idea what would be right.

My second illustration is from the writings of Nelson Goodman. Nobody would count Collingwood as a typical analytic philosopher, but many would so count Goodman, and indeed much of his work may no doubt be correctly so called. Let us now consider, however, his answer to the question 'What is a score of a piece of music?' which he gives in his *Languages of Art*.[3] Goodman's account of a score is very well known by all who are likely to attend to this essay and has the complete clarity which one can always confidently expect from Goodman. I shall therefore not undertake to paraphrase or explain it here.[4] It is entirely clear that Goodman's account of a score neither is, nor is intended to be, an elucidation or analysis of the everyday notion of a score. Goodman himself says of his account in a footnote to page 128 that 'This is by no means true of everything commonly called a score'. He goes on to give an account of a performance as requiring full compliance with a score and immediately goes on to say 'This is not to say that the exigencies that dictate our technical discourse need govern our everyday speech. I am no more recommending that in ordinary discourse we refuse to say that a pianist who misses a note has performed a Chopin Polonaise than that we refuse to call a whale a fish, the earth spherical, or a grayish-pink human white' (p. 187).

So, once again, we are obliged to ask what are the criteria of success in Goodman's enterprise. At times it seems that he is attempting to make our language more serviceable for he justifies his strict use of 'score' and 'performance' by saying that 'this is one of those cases where ordinary usage gets us quickly into trouble' (p. 186). But appearances here must be deceptive since Goodman wants us to continue with ordinary usage, which would be unkind of him if he really thought that so doing would quickly get us into trouble. Nor, so far as I know, has anyone employing the words 'score' and 'performance' as in ordinary usage found himself wondering whether he was listening to Beethoven's Fifth Symphony or to 'Three Blind Mice'. Moreover, while anyone sufficiently instructed is aware that it is inaccurate to call the earth spherical and false to call a whale a fish and conventional to call a greyish-pink human white, in ordinary discourse, it is obviously totally correct in ordinary discourse to call a performance of the Fifth Symphony with one fluffed note a performance of that work.

The trouble into which we fall with ordinary discourse which Goodman has in mind cannot, it seems, be practical. Goodman is alive and can speak for himself, and I shall not attempt to give an account of his criteria of success for him. But clearly he is neither trying to analyse ordinary speech, nor to offer an alternative to ordinary speech of greater practical utility but rather to construct a language satisfying certain theoretical requirements such as the one that 'a good definition always unequivocally determines what objects conform to it' (p. 129). If something like this is what Goodman is doing then it is clear that what he is doing is no adequate substitute for the analysis of ordinary concepts and that such analysis does not begin to perform the task that Goodman has in mind. It would surely be very silly to ask which of these projects is the correct one for a philosophical aesthetician to undertake; they can live alongside each other. I do not believe that Goodman would want to do what I do and I do not want to do what he does (nor have I the capacity to do so). But that is no good ground for mudslinging.

So much for my two illustrations, designed to show that not all questions in philosophical aesthetics expressed in the form 'What is an X?' are analytic in character, and that when they are not so analytic it is necessary to know what other goals they have and what criteria of accuracy and merit are applicable to them. It is also clear that Collingwood's questions are quite different in character from Goodman's though in neither case am I sure how to characterize them.

I have so far been talking as though it were quite evident what analytical questions were like and what criteria of accuracy and merit were applicable to them. This is, beyond doubt, false, for two quite different reasons. The first is that the term 'analytical', like so many terms of art in philosophy, has no agreed meaning. Thus we English speakers all agree pretty closely about what counts as a pig, or a chair or a tomato; if there is disagreement it will almost certainly be agreed that it is a marginal case where the decision could reasonably go either way. But with regard to analysis, some thoroughly competent philosophers may well count as a clear case of analysis something which others will regard as clearly other than analytical. Thus there may well be aestheticians who would claim that the account of musical scores and performance in Goodman's *Languages of Art* is a clear case of analytic aesthetics, while I have used it as an illustration of non-analytic aesthetics. If there are such, my disagreement with them is surely not philosophical nor decidable by rational argument; we simply speak two different dialects of philosophical English.

The other difficulty in characterizing analytic aesthetics is that all philosophical enterprises are puzzling and hard to characterize accurately and illuminatingly, and analytic aesthetics is a philosophical enterprise. 'What is analytic aesthetics?' is itself a philosophical problem. But I do not think that the philosophical problem of the nature of analytic aesthetics is significantly different from the question of the nature of analytic moral philosophy, or political philosophy or of any other branch of philosophy, and so I do not propose to go deeply into the question in a paper which is directed centrally to aesthetics. I therefore content myself with a few remarks all of which, I fully realize, require further elucidation and, perhaps, refinement.

The goal of analytic aesthetics is, as I understand it, to elucidate some portion of some conceptual apparatus, usually that implicit in the natural language that we speak, which is treated as a datum to be elucidated, not as a proposal to be criticized. There will naturally be some higher goal which motivates the attempt at elucidation, perhaps to remove some philosophical perplexity, as Russell was motivated to produce his theory of descriptions as a solution to his perplexities about the golden mountain and similar objects or perhaps pure intellectual curiosity, which is presumably what led Austin to examine the cluster of concepts including *instrument, tool, implement* and the like. The accuracy of a piece of analysis will be determined by whether it covers everything that falls under the relevant concept and nothing more. Taken, absurdly, as analysis, Collingwood's account of a piece of music could be decisively refuted by pointing out that it makes good sense to say 'Yesterday I heard a piece of music' and Goodman's account of a performance by pointing out that it makes perfectly good sense to say 'Yesterday I heard a performance of Beethoven's Fifth Symphony which included three wrong notes'. That is why it would be ridiculous to regard these accounts as analytical.

As to the form and method of analysis, there is very little that one can say except that analysis takes many forms and any that achieves its end of conceptual elucidation is legitimate. No doubt, originally analysis was conceived as being the provision of definitions (A work of art is a . . .) or equivalences ('He performed a piece of music' means the same as ' . . .'). But that is surely no longer the case. I myself would certainly regard O. K. Bouwsma's famous paper 'The Expression Theory of Art' as analytic, though it contains no significant definitions or equivalences.[5]

If this certainly brief, certainly inadequate, probably inaccurate and possibly rebarbative account of analytic aesthetics is at least more or less on the right track, it is surely clear that analytic aesthetics is an indispensable part of philosophical aesthetics and equally clear that it is not the whole of philosophical aesthetics.

Conceptual analysis has always played a major role in philosophy from the time of Plato and Aristotle. The only innovation in recent times is that analytic questions are now more commonly than in former times treated on their own and for their own sake rather than as subsidiary to other issues and that we now attempt to treat them more accurately and more exhaustively than of old. That there is a place for conceptual analysis in aesthetics is surely obvious. We need not complain if Collingwood denies that any art is representational,[6] given the general character of his work, nor if Goodman denies the possibility of representation in music, given his revisionary definitions of performance, score, representation and denotation. But it surely remains as a worthwhile enterprise in philosophical aesthetics to ask what we mean by representation in the ordinary sense of 'representation' and other keys words. Surely it is a legitimate task of philosophy to attempt to gain an explicit understanding of all the key terms we use in relation to the arts, and I, for one, would agree with Austin that it is prudent to make sure that one has such an understanding of these terms before one discards them as useless in favour of some philosophical idiolect.

But it is equally clear that there are many questions that are traditionally and properly regarded as important in philosophical aesthetics which are not analytic. David Hume, for example, held the view that those things which look to have the character required by their practical function are aesthetically pleasing and those things without such an appearance are not. He says for example: 'A building, whose doors and windows were exact squares, would hurt the eye by that very proportion; as ill adapted to the figure of a human creature, for whose service the fabric was intended'.[7] That is surely a legitimate speculation in philosophical aesthetics, and if it is false then its contradictory will be a truth. The same can be said of Hutcheson's claim that 'the Figures that excite in us the Ideas of Beauty, seem to be those in which there is *Uniformity amidst Variety*'.[8] Hutcheson and Hume are founding fathers of philosophical aesthetics and we should not attempt to cast them out as illegitimate.

It is, of course, easy to go on giving indisputable examples of non-analytic problems in aesthetics, just as it is easy to give examples of analytic questions that are central to aesthetics. To ask, therefore, whether the right way to do aesthetics is analytical or non-analytical seems to be rather on a par with asking whether china manufacturers should make cups or plates, the answer to which is that, while individual manufacturers may legitimately specialize, we must hope that the industry as a whole will continue to produce both cups and plates.

However, while I can read analytic aesthetics with pleasure and profit, and can read the non-analytic theories of Hutcheson and Hume with pleasure and profit, there is a great deal of non-analytic aesthetics which, when I force myself to read it, I do so with great distaste and reluctance and totally without profit. No doubt, part of the explanation of this is merely personal taste, perhaps mere narrowness of personal taste. In so far as that is the case the matter can be of no interest to anyone save myself. But while I have no doubt that this is part of the explanation I do not think it is the whole of it. It might be of interest to more than myself to consider what some of these adverse features are, always remembering that we are not involved in an attack on non-analytic aesthetics, but only in detecting some diseases to which it is liable.

First, and less importantly, many writers on aesthetics are fatally attracted to the use of unnecessarily long sentences, containing unnecessarily long words, and often words that are neologisms or used in new senses, as if the resources of the English language were insufficient to convey their thoughts. John Passmore drew attention to this long ago and things have not improved since. Equally unimportantly, it is irritating to be offered unnecessarily far-fetched illustrations; in the visual arts we are instructed to recall the entablature in the church at such and such a village in southern Albania, or in music we are given a polyrhythmic and bitonal example in obsolete clefs where a couple of bars of *Three Blind Mice* would have done equally well. Again unimportant, but again irritating, is the common attitude of contemptuous superiority to those who are not in their coterie. This attitude, and some defects already noted, can perhaps be illustrated by Adorno's statement that 'nobody can understand Wagner's *Meistersinger*, for instance, who does not register, like Nietzsche, the narcissistic self-portrayal of positivity in this opera, i.e. the moment of untruth'.[9] The same author tells us that 'Beethoven's symphonies in their most arcane chemistry are part of the bourgeois process of production and express the perennial disaster brought on by capitalism'. Again, in his contempt for those who believe that the function of art is to give pleasure, Adorno tells us that 'if you ask a musician if he enjoys playing his instrument, he will probably reply: "I hate it" '. Well, I have just two books on instrumental playing by me: one says 'you may, even when playing quite by yourself, be too carried away by the musical pleasure of what you are doing to listen critically to small technical faults'; the other says that 'enjoyment is the be-all and end-all of amateur playing'.[10] There is something unsatisfactory in making a point with one illustration; but Adorno is not a mere secondary figure and those who read in aesthetics will very easily find parallels elsewhere, and in abundance.

However, the main difficulty with much, though by no means all, non-analytic aesthetics is, I think, the difficulty of determining to what controls it is intended to be subjected. It is often not clear how one determines whether what is said is accurate, true, or successful in attaining the goal of the author. Let us consider, for example, the question of taking pleasure in, or enjoying, the arts. Collingwood tells us, as do many other writers on aesthetics, that 'the function of art proper' is not to give pleasure or amusement; according to Collingwood the function of art proper is to express emotion. Hebbel, in his *Journal*, also agrees that the function of art is not to give pleasure but, differing from Collingwood, he tells us that the first and last aim of art is to render intuitively perceptible the process of life itself, to show how the soul of man develops in the atmosphere surrounding him. I do not wish to say that either, Collingwood or Hebbel is wrong, though clearly they cannot both be right; my problem is rather that I have no idea how to decide who, if anyone, is right.

If I were to object to Collingwood by pointing out that on hearing and seeing the scene in the *Magic Flute* where Monostatos and Papageno first meet and take each other to be the devil I enjoy it and even laugh out loud but am not aware of an act of self-expression, will he accept that as a refutation, or will he say that the scene in question is not 'art proper' or will he say that I react improperly to art proper? Do we have any clear idea of what Collingwood might possibly regard as tending to refute his view? Does Hebbel really think that in writing that scene Mozart had as his first and last aim to make intuitively perceptible the process of life itself, and, if not, does he count that as a refutation of his theory?

One can easily see that sometimes a singer is expressing his emotions and that some episodes in some novels make one aware of aspects of life that one had failed fully to appreciate; one can thus at least seem to grasp something that Collingwood and Hebbel had in mind. One can also learn a little, though not much, about the methods of ancient agriculture by reading Vergil's *Georgics*, and Vergil explicitly says that the aim of the *Georgics* was to give instruction to farmers, revealing no desire to amuse, to express emotion or to reveal deep truths about life. But I, for one, simply do not know how the various authors who have written on the topic think that the true function of art can be determined, how 'art proper' can be distinguished, or how it could be determined that art had any specific and invariable function.

I do not wish to say that the writings of even those aestheticians against whom I think that these complaints hold are worthless. One can often find in them very perceptive passages. In a way it would be easier if this were not so, for then one could simply disregard them. The problem is, of course, not specific to aesthetics; one meets very similar problems with the Hegels, the Heideggers and the Sartres in the realms of metaphysics. Matter, for example, is (or is not) a basic reality we are told, and we would be more grateful for the information if we knew how to confirm it. I am for free-thinking in aesthetics; we should not lay down the law about what questions should be raised in aesthetics, or how they should be tackled. It would be most unreasonable to demand that everything should be on the topics one would oneself choose or in the style one would oneself employ. But I am sure that a plea for maximum clarity and maximum simplicity would be in order and that if it were granted nothing of value would be lost.

NOTES

1   The paper is reprinted in W.Elton (ed.), *Aesthetics and Language* (Oxford, Basil Blackwell, 1954), pp. 35–55. Quotations in this paragraph are from pp. 36, 37, and 43n.

2   R. G. Collingwood, *The Principles of Art* (Oxford, Oxford University Press, 1934).

3   Nelson Goodman, *Languages of Art* (Oxford, Oxford University Press, 1969).

4   [Ed. – Briefly, for Goodman 'a score is a character in a notational system', where such a system must exhibit the following five features: syntactic disjointness ('no mark may belong to more than one character'), syntactic finite differentiation (it must be theoretically possible to determine which character a mark belongs to), unambiguity (identity and invariance of reference or compliance), semantic disjointness (no two characters should have common compliants) and semantic finite differentiation (the theoretical possibility to determine whether an object does or does not comply with a particular character). 'A system is notational, then, if and only if all objects

complying with inscriptions of a given character belong to the same compliance class and we can, theoretically, determine that each mark belongs to and each object complies with inscriptions of, at most one particular character'. I quote here from *Languages of Art*, pp. 135-6, 156, 177. All these requirements are explained by Goodman with greater detail, precision and clarity in pp. 127-57 of his book.]

5 The paper is reprinted in Elton (ed.), *Aesthetics and Language*, pp. 73-99.

6 Collingwood, *Principles of Art*, p. 43.

7 David Hume, *An Inquiry Concerning the Principles of Morals*, s. V, pt 1.

8 Francis Hutcheson, *Inquiry into the Original of our Ideas of Beauty and Virtue*, (Will and John Smith, London, 1725), p. 15.

9 Theodor Adorno, *Aesthetic Theory* (London, Routledge and Kegan Paul, 1984), p. 371. The following quotations in this paragraph are from pp. 342 and 19 respectively.

10 See, respectively, Evelyn Rothwell, *Oboe Technique* (Oxford, Oxford University Press, 1962), p. 60; and A. Rowland-Jones, *Recorder Technique* (Oxford, Oxford University Press, 1963), p. 123.

3

Philosophy of Art after Analysis and Romanticism

Nicholas Wolterstorff

It is beyond dispute that the glory of twentieth-century analytic philosophy is not revealed in the field of philosophy of art. If one is on the lookout for analytic philosophy's greatest attainments, one must look elsewhere. Why is that?

Most of the major figures of analytic philosophy spent no time at all reflecting on the arts. As for the remaining ones, their reflections on art were rarely central to their philosophical work. The cultivation of analytic philosophy of art was left almost entirely to figures of the second and lower ranks. Mainly they applied to art lessons learned elsewhere. Nobody tried to apply elsewhere lessons learned in thinking about art – with the exception, perhaps, of those who applied lessons learned in thinking about poetic metaphor. The busy hive of analytic philosophy was never located in the field of philosophy of art. Why is that?

The answer cannot be that the priorities of the analytic philosopher mirrored the priorities of our culture; for in modern Western culture, art is no minor matter. So is it perhaps that what determines philosophy's attention to some component of culture is not prominence but crisis? Not that either; for in our century art has not lacked for crises. It must be something in the character of analytic philosophy which accounts for art's minority status there – or strictly, something in the *relation* of the character of analytic philosophy to the character of art, or to the character of our modern ways of thinking about art. Perhaps the fit is poor.

I

In a good many of his writings over the past decade or so, Richard Rorty has expounded the thesis that analytic philosophy, when it was still a movement and not merely a style, was a version of neo-Kantianism. That interpretation seems to me correct. Or at least what seems to me correct is that the 'ideal type' (using Max Weber's concept of *ideal type*) of analytic philosopher was a neo-Kantian with empiricist predilections.

Philosophers hold and defend theses. But deeper in their thought than the theses they hold and defend are the pictures and images which govern and guide their holding and defending. Analytic philosophy has been governed and guided by the image of a scheme of concepts applied to a content which is given, an image bequeathed to it by Kant. Kant regarded the content as 'intuition' – *Anschauugen*. Some analytic philosophers agreed. But others thought that what is given is not just our intuitions but also items in the world independent of our intuitions; and even more held that among our concepts are to be found some that apply not to our intuitions but to items in the world independent of our subjectivity. Kant also held that concepts *structure* intuitions and that experience is *constituted* by those structured intuitions: to experience a table is (under the appropriate circumstances) to *take* one's intuitions *as* a table; it is to *conceptualize* them *as* a table. Probably most analytic philosophers did not accept this structuring/constituting thesis concerning the working of concepts. But the conviction that in thinking and speaking we apply (some part of) our conceptual scheme to some content or other, has been common coinage – as was the Kantian conviction that ultimately the content is *given* to us and that we *provide* the concepts. The human mind exhibits a duality of receptivity and spontaneity. Thought – and perhaps even experience – represent the interplay of these two dimensions: receptivity and spontaneity, the structured given and the contributed, content and structure, awareness and concept.

Obviously there is much about our conceptual schemes and our intuitions that is contingent. But beneath the contingency there is – so argued Kant – necessity. There are connections of logical necessity among the concepts. In addition, it is necessary that human beings – or more generally, finite knowers – intuit space and time. And it is necessary that they conceptualize the intuitional given in certain ways. These modes of necessity constitute necessity's full scope. Beyond *de dicto* necessity, and *de re* necessity concerning the powers of intuiting and conceptualizing of finite knowers, there is no necessity. Further, *de dicto* necessity is not a feature of the metaphysical structure of things independent of finite knowers. It too has the status of being a limit on the powers of finite knowers: it is impossible for us to think of a proposition of the form *p and ~p* as true. The laws of logic are the rules of thought. All necessity, then, can be thought of as pertaining to how we think and experience. Necessity is the limit on human spontaneity. This, I say, was Kant's view. Within analytic philosophy there was a powerful impetus toward following Kant in this subjectivizing of necessity. Necessity represents the limits on thought, or language, or whatever.

This picture made available to Kant and the neo-Kantians an elegant way of delineating the task of philosophy among the 'sciences'. Philosophy deals with our conceptual scheme as such; the other sciences deal with the *application* of one and another part of that scheme. In philosophy, as Wittgenstein remarked, the scheme idles. More specifically, philosophy deals with the necessary structure of our conceptual scheme. Now necessity is ascertainable a priori; conducting experiments and taking polls is irrelevant to the discerning of necessity. Philosophy is thus an armchair enterprise. Philosophical knowledge is a priori knowledge. Rorty says that neo-Kantians regarded philosophical knowledge as apodictic (certain). It is quite true that some did indeed not only regard genuine philosophical knowledge as a priori, but as certain.

What questions do philosophers pose as they stand back to discern necessity in our conceptual scheme? Here one finds a sharp difference between Kant on the one hand and the analytic philosopher on the other. Kant's preoccupying concern was to establish that every conceptual scheme of human beings will necessarily contain certain specific concepts, such as existence, necessity and causality, and certain types of concepts, such as those of enduring objects and of qualities. In addition, he endeavoured to show that there is an ineradicable dynamic in the constitution of us human beings which leads us to think of the intuitions given to us as reality putting in its appearance to us, and which leads us to think of that reality along certain quite definite lines – this in spite of the fact that *knowledge* of that reality is in principle unattainable for us. These views on Kant's part contain and produce deep paradoxes. Of these, the analytic philosophers were well aware. Accordingly, they did their best to keep the Kantian preoccupations at arm's length. They simply avoided the question of the extent to which we human beings can do our thinking with alternative conceptual schemes – insisting only that any viable conceptual scheme will satisfy the laws of logic.

With the Kantian preoccupations thus renounced, what was it that remained for philosophers to do? Philosophers would concern themselves solely with the *internal* necessities of our conceptual schemes – with the necessary relations holding among concepts. They would offer necessary and sufficient conditions for the application of concepts. They would *analyse* concepts. Philosophy would be the Analytic of Concepts. Philosophy would be conceptual analysis. As such, philosophy would finally become scientific. Its days of wandering in the sloughs of indecisiveness would be over. It would now at long last join the other sciences in the algorithmic settling of disputes.[1] The great philosophical problems would either be solved or dissolved. At the core of the philosophical enterprise would be the activity of looking to see whether *p* does or does not entail *q*.

What would be the point of this enterprise? What values would conceptual analysis serve? Two things especially were emphasized. The cause of clarity would be served; never has there been a philosophical movement which so prized clarity. We do not discern the logic of scientific discourse, do not discern the logic of moral discourse, do not discern the structure of one and another sort of fact. These structures are obscured from us. Language, especially language outside of science, serves other purposes than to display for us the structure of the facts. One of the consequences of its service of those other purposes is that it conceals from us that structure. The task of the philosopher is to undo that concealment – to make the hidden manifest.

It was widely held, however, that this attempt to uncover the concealed would show that some of our language, instead of stating facts obscurely, states no facts at all. It is without sense: nonsense. Eventually analytic philosophers acknowledged that some of such language might none the less serve valuable human purposes. It might be useful for expressing our emotions, useful for marrying people, etc. But even then the conviction remained that some of it served no useful purpose whatsoever. Especially some of the talk produced by traditional philosophers was seen as *nothing but* nonsense – parading, however, under the guise of sense, hence obfuscation. Traditional philosophy contains 'metaphysics'. And so, just as in Kant, the problem of demarcation became central in analytic philosophy. Usually it took the form of trying to demarcate 'genuine science' from 'metaphysics'. For it was assumed without question that mathematics and the hard sciences are paradigms of sense. There, rationality rules. There, rationality is embodied. If, on one's analysis of rationality, the hard sciences prove not to be rational, that is to be taken as evidence against one's analysis of rationality and not as evidence against science's rationality. The central version of the problem of demarcation became that of trying to demarcate genuine science from the pseudo-science of metaphysics.

If one knew nothing directly of the movement itself, the image evoked by my description of analytic philosophy would probably be that of the philosopher wandering aimlessly in the field of concepts, analysing whatever strikes him as unclear. In fact, analysis was not a directionless enterprise. For one thing, it was above all three areas of thought and discourse that drew the attention of the analytic philosopher: scientific discourse, the discourse of individual morality, and discourse about knowledge and rationality. Secondly, in the first and last of these, especially, two deep assumptions determined the direction of attempts at analysis. Attempts at analysis were directed by pervasive adherence to foundationalism with respect to knowledge. Knowledge, it was assumed, has a foundational structure: some of what we know is known immediately and everything else that we know is known because we know it on the basis of that. What we know immediately, we are certain of. And we are certain of something because at that point we are directly aware of reality. This is *the given*. Secondly, attempts at analysis were directed by what may be called *concept constructivism*. All concepts, it was widely assumed, either apply to what we are directly aware of or are constructed out of such concepts by simple logical operations. The direction of analysis was foundationalist and constructivist.

II

Analytic philosophy as I have described it has now almost entirely disappeared. Images central to the project have been widely discarded; assumptions fundamental to it have come under attack and been widely rejected. Rorty, especially, has offered a narrative of the demise – a narrative which argues that analytic philosophy was deconstructed into pragmatist-Hegelianism. Shortly I shall discuss the Rortian narrative. But first, let us return to our question as to why it was that analysis never flourished in philosophy of art.

Ever since the early Romantics, it has been a commonplace that high culture in the West has a science side and an art/humanities side, and that these two co-exist in tension. C. P. Snow's well-known writings on the matter served to express, for our own times, a thesis already a century and a half old. Analytic philosophy emerged from the science side of our culture; almost all its great figures were trained in science or mathematics. It was about that side of culture that they were knowledgeable and it was in that side of culture that they were interested. Often they went so far as to express the conviction that the primary business of philosophy is to uncover the 'logic' of science. And, as already mentioned, many of them embraced the goal of making philosophy itself finally scientific. Analytic philosophy was to be 'scientific' philosophy. Hans Reichenbach in *The Rise of Scientific Philosophy* caught the spirit. In the Preface to that work he said that

> The present book . . . maintains that philosophic speculation is a passing stage, occurring when philosophic problems are raised at a time which does not possess the logical means to solve them. It claims that there is, and always has been, a scientific approach to philosophy. And it wishes to show that from this ground has sprung a scientific philosophy which, in the science of our time, has found the tools to solve those problems that in earlier times have been the subject of guesswork only. To put it briefly: this book is written with the intention of showing that philosophy has proceeded from speculation to science.[2]

Given these attitudes, it was entirely to be expected that the standard advice given to fledgling philosophers was: study more science and mathematics. Nobody counselled studying more art. Likewise it was entirely to be expected that graduate departments would be especially welcoming to those who already had extensive training in science and mathematics.

Beyond this, there was something plainly ill-fitting – so it would appear, at any rate – between the project of analytic philosophy and the reality of art. The goal of the analytic philosopher was to uncover the structure of our conceptual schemes. Now in fact science consists of a great deal more than conceptual schemes – more even than bodies of theories expressed with conceptual schemes. But at least theories and concepts are prominent in science. Art is different. Buildings, paintings, string quartets, sculptures, dances: How is the analytic philosopher to get a purchase on these? Where are the conceptual schemes? Where are the languages? In poetry, fiction and drama there is of course language, in the most straightforward sense. But the Romantic tradition had long warned that here language works differently, so differently that it is not even referential. In short, it is not evident that the philosopher committed to conceptual analysis has much of anything to do when it comes to art.

Two different strategies were adopted for coping with this difficulty. Of one, Monroe Beardsley was the most noted practitioner. Beardsley's strategy was to call attention to the difference between art and art criticism, and then to propose that aesthetics, instead of remaining the philosophy of art or the philosophy of the aesthetic dimension, should become the philosophy of art criticism. For in art criticism, one has that on which the analytic philosopher can practise his craft: a conceptual scheme. Thus Beardsley gave to his major book, *Aesthetics*, the subtitle: *Problems in the Philosophy of Criticism.*[3] He said, in the opening paragraph of the Introduction, that

> There would be no problems of aesthetics, in the sense in which I propose to mark out this field of study, if no one ever talked about works of art. So long as we enjoy a movie, a story, or a song, in silence – except perhaps for occasional grunts or groans, murmurs of annoyance or satisfaction – there is no call for philosophy. But as soon as we utter a statement about the work, various sorts of questions can arise.

And in summarizing his delineation of the field he said that

> In the course of this book, then, we shall think of aesthetics as a distinctive philosophical inquiry: it is concerned with the nature and basis of criticism – in the broad sense of this term – just as criticism itself is concerned with works of art.

Philosophical aesthetics, he said, 'deals with questions about the meaning and truth of critical statements.'

To conceive of aesthetics thus is to place it at a remove from the phenomena of art and the aesthetic. To all but the most hardened analytic philosopher, that will already give pause. But perhaps it is more important to observe that the foundationalism and constructivism which gave point and direction to the work of analysis in philosophy of science had little grip on the 'Beardsleyans' in aesthetics. For example, vast amounts of time and energy were devoted to devising analyses of the concept of *work of art*. For sheer boringness, the results of these endeavours have few peers. Something interesting might have turned up if philosophers had looked into the emergence of our (modern) concepts of *the arts* and *works of art*. When and where did these concepts emerge? Why? What intellectual and social purposes did they serve? Do those purposes remain viable? Have the concepts attached to the words 'an art' and 'a work of art' remained steady over the years or have they altered? If they have changed, why have they changed? All such historical inquiries would, however, be regarded by the neo-Kantian analytic philosopher as mucking around in the contingent. The analytic philosopher of art, like his fellow analytic philosophers, practised his craft with resolute ahistoricism – slicing into the conceptual scheme of art criticism at a certain moment in its history, never asking why that scheme had arisen and developed as it had, just attempting to offer analyses of the concepts critics use and uncover criteria for the warranted assertion of the statements they make, scarcely guided in his analyses even by the doctrine of foundationalism and constructivism.

There was, as I have mentioned, a second strategy for developing analytic philosophy of art – a strategy which expanded the notion of language and then treated works of art as examples of language, on this expanded concept. Of this strategy, Langer and Goodman have been the foremost practitioners – though it must at once be said that in their writings on art, neither one was a typical analytic philosopher. Langer argued that the language of art is an iconic language, and that works of art iconically express and communicate the dynamic dimension of the emotional life. Not surprisingly, she was attacked on the ground that an iconic language is not really a language at all. Goodman, by contrast, argued that the languages of art are entirely conventional, not at all iconic; conventionally established denotation was for him the central concept. The price he paid was to leave it thoroughly obscure how and what such things as pure music and abstract painting denote. In the field of music, Goodman devoted almost all his attention to the language of *scores* for music and said almost nothing about any supposed language of music. And in general, his contention that the arts present us with specimens of conventional (not iconic) language led Goodman to focus his attention on representational art and on notational systems for the arts, and to neglect what falls outside this net.

III

Though the foundationalism and constructivism which served to give direction to analysis in philosophy of science played little role in philosophy of art, it must not be inferred that philosophy of art in the analytic style was lacking in definite character. On the contrary, analytic philosophy of art has for the most part been a species of Romantic philosophy of art. In Beardsley's case, it is easy to see why: criticism, whose language

Beardsley set it as his task to 'analyse', has itself for the first part of our century been predominantly a species of Romantic criticism. But the same has been true for those not committed to the 'Beardsleyan' approach. For most of our century our ways of thinking about art have been shaped by the ideology of Romanticism.

I propose to make this thesis seem plausible – demonstration would require a book – by summarizing the account of Romantic art theory offered by Tzvetan Todorov in his book *Theories of the Symbol*.[4] To anyone acquainted with analytic philosophy of art, the Romanticism of it will then be evident.

The advantage of my following Todorov's discussion, sometimes even to using his very words, over offering my own account, is that the suspicion that I have slanted the account for the purpose of defending my thesis that analytic philosophy of art is a species of Romantic philosophy of art is thereby rendered groundless.[5]

Todorov opens his discussion by taking as paradigmatic the thought of an early Romantic, Karl Philip Moritz. The dominant theory of art before the Romantics was of course the imitation theory. Moritz introduced the radical innovation of changing the traditional subject of the verb 'to imitate'. It is not the *work* which imitates but the *artist*; and the artist imitates by producing works. What he thereby imitates is the creative productivity of nature. The born artist, writes Moritz, has to create as nature does. Others Romantics preferred to speak of *God* as that which the artist imitates – the artist has become a creator God', said Herder. And yet others moved fluidly back and forth between Nature and God as the artist's model in creativity.

A corollary of the view that the artist creates like unto God or Nature is that 'the accent no longer falls upon the relationship of representation (linking the work and the world), but upon the relationship of expression, the one that links the work and the artist.'[6] Romantic philosophy of art became preeminently a philosophy of artistic creation: creation is self-expression. And above all, what artists express is their emotions.

A second corollary is that 'In this new framework, the work of art has in common with nature the fact that each is a closed totality, a complete universe. . . . The resemblance no longer resides in the appearance of similar forms, but in the possession of an identical internal structure: the relationship of the constituent parts is the same, only the coefficient of the size varies. The work is not the image but the diagram of the world' (p. 154). The artwork is thus conceived as a microcosm of the great macrocosm. 'Like the world, the work of art is a self-sufficient totality' (p. 155).

None the less, the Romantics regarded the work of art as signifying. Indeed, says Todorov, we might say 'that all the characteristics of a work of art are concentrated in a single notion, which the romantics will later call *symbol*' (p. 161). 'The nature of the beautiful object,' remarks

Moritz, 'consists in the fact that the parts and the whole become expressive and significant, one part always through another and the whole through itself' (p. 159).

But if the significance of the work lies in its organic unity, what does it signify? What else indeed but itself, somehow? Again, Moritz: 'An authentic work of art, a beautiful poem, is something finished and completed in itself, something that exists for itself, and whose value lies in itself, and in the ordered relationship of its parts. . . . – He who can ask, after reading them, "What does the *Iliad* signify? What does the *Odyssey* signify?" must be little moved by Homer's lofty poetic beauty – All that a poem signifies is found in itself' (p. 162). As Todorov remarks, 'Signification in art is an interpenetration of the signifier and the signified; all distance between the two is abolished' (p. 162). Todorov records some of the intense struggle of the Romantics to explain and articulate this notion of the symbol.

Running throughout Romantic theory of art is the notion of the autonomy of the work. Creation as self-expression and the autonomy of the work are the two deepest themes in Romantic aesthetics. In turn, the doctrine of the autonomy of the work had two sides. We have been looking at one side: the significance of the work of art lies entirely in its interior relationships. It is a hermetic totality. But there is another side: the work of art is *useless*. It has no purpose, no reason for being, outside itself. Works of art are not for doing things with. Works of art are not for accomplishing something with. They are not to be soiled with the grime and sweat of human toil. They are intransitive.

These two phases of autonomy, of the work as bearing its significance within itself and of the work as useless, were closely linked in the minds of the Romantics. Says Moritz: the concept of uselessness 'is all the more easily and all the more closely linked with the concept of beauty, to the extent that this latter also needs no purpose, no reason for being, outside itself, but possesses its entire value and the goal of its existence in itself' (p. 155). Of course this is just to declare the fact of a connection, not to explain it. Moritz, in his attempt to specify the connection, says that 'Where an object lacks external utility or purpose, these must be sought in the object itself, if this object is to arouse pleasure in me. . . . To put it in different terms; seeing a beautiful object, I must feel pleasure uniquely for its own sake; to this end, the absence of external finality has to be compensated for by an internal finality; the object must be something fully realized in itself' (p. 157). 'The autonomy of a totality is a necessary condition of its beauty' (p. 159).

These two Romantic themes – of creation as self-expression and of the work as autonomous – have also been the great themes of analytic philosophy of art, though the latter, indeed, has much outweighed the former in importance. The slogans still echo: intentional fallacy, affective fallacy, implied narrator, disinterested contemplation, uselessness.

IV

But works of art are not useless – so I have argued in some of my work in philosophy of art.[7] They are some of the most useful things we human beings possess. We use music to lull babies to sleep and to accompany the hoeing of cotton. We use poetry to entertain children and to address the gods. We use representational painting to impress the public with the wealth of patrons and to celebrate the founding events of religions and nations. And so forth, on and on. Works of art are not piled up in closets of discard nor tossed on the trash heaps of inutility. They are to be found in the fabric of human action. They are used.

One response would be that though works of music may indeed be used to do such things as lull babies to sleep, if thus used they are not works of *art*. Brief reflection, however, shows this response to have the consequence that probably nothing is a work of art. A more subtle and guarded response would be that works of music, when used to lull babies, are not functioning *qua* works of art. Strictly speaking this is, of course, not so much a response as a change of topic. The claim was made that works of art are useless. When it was observed that works of music, poetry, painting etc. are obviously *not* useless – it being assumed that these are works of art – the new point was made that the uses pointed to are not examples of treating the work *as* a work of art. But let us run with the change of topic.

What is this phenomenon of *functioning as* (being treated as) a work of art? Quite clearly, it is functioning as an object of perceptual contemplation. Many would say that it is narrower than this, that this is just the genus – that functioning as a work of art is a *species* of functioning as an object of perceptual contemplation. Perhaps so. But in any case, when treating something as a work of art occurs, then the work no longer serves merely as an instrument of some action but as an object of attention in its own right.

But then why isn't treating something as a work of art a way of *using* it? Isn't contemplating something perceptually, whatever be the benefit that one expects to ensue from such contemplation, a mode of using it? It would be a mistake to hang the Romantic theorist by the noose of ordinary usage. Of course it is a mode of use. But the Romantic theorist wishes to emphasize the difference between this use and other uses – the difference between attending to this object so as to make one's acquaintance with it, and using it as a medium. And beyond stressing the difference between this use and other uses, the Romantic wishes to emphasize the importance of this use. That is what he has in mind by saying that art is, or should be, useless.

A parting of the ways now confronts us. One can explore this use. Kant's *Critique of Judgment* was the first great example of such exploration. More precisely, Kant explored the somewhat more narrow phenomenon of perceptual contemplation conducted for the sake of aesthetic delight. Alternatively, one can turn in the other direction and explore the arts – something Kant did not much do. We have seen that such exploration, if it is to be at all faithful to art, must renounce the dogma of the uselessness of art, of the autonomy of art. Perceptual contemplation is a use. But more importantly, perceptual contemplation has rarely been either the sole intended, or actual, use of examples of the (fine) arts. Though our poets do indeed want us to notice their words, they also want to say things and want us to notice what they are saying. Though our painters want us to notice the design, many also want to represent things and want us to notice what they represent. The notion that all works of art are autonomous or were meant to be treated autonomously is the great Romantic illusion. The illusion lives on, among other places, in the failure to distinguish between aesthetics and philosophy of art. Humanity's art has nothing special to do with aesthetics. (And aesthetics has nothing special to do with art.)

All this is almost foolishly obvious when pointed out. The untenability of the other side of the autonomy doctrine is almost equally obvious. Creators of works of art do not merely struggle to devise organically unified images – they do not even merely struggle to devise organically unified images which are objective correlatives of their emotions. Wittingly and unwillingly they struggle to embody social, material and cultural realities within their works.[8] And poets do not merely create symbols whose only mode of signification is self-signification. In his 'Eleven Addresses to the Lord', John Berryman addressed God, and referred to God and to Polycarp and to the apostle John.[9] And writers of fiction do not merely create fictional narrators who then monologically say all that is said by the words of the text. Often writers themselves say what is said by the words of their texts – though of course in doing so they may engage in literary pretence. They may speak through poetic masks. We can, after all, pretend about ourselves.[10]

To make these points is to rehearse only some of the ways in which philosophers of art have tried to defend the thesis that works of art are autonomous, hermetic totalities – and to hint at only some of the reasons for thinking that the thesis, in almost all its manifestations, is false. Works of art do not all function autonomously nor are they autonomous totalities.

Why have we thought otherwise? Surely we have thought otherwise because we have been *schooled* to think otherwise. For most of us, that schooling occurs in the course of our induction into the attitudes and practices of our institution (social formation) of high art. Our institution of high art is oriented around the perceptual contemplation of art – and then, especially, around perceptual contemplation for the purpose of aesthetic delight. One enters the institution by learning how to listen to music, learning at the same time to overlook or denigrate the fact that music has many other ways of entering our lives than serving as the object of attentive listening; one enters it by learning how to look at paintings, learning at the same time to overlook or denigrate the fact that visual representation and design have many other ways of entering our lives than by serving as the object of attentive looking; one enters it by learning how to read poetry, learning at the same time to look past or demean the many other ways poetry has of entering our lives than by serving as the object of attentive reading. Romantic theory of the arts, I suggest, is best thought of as the ideology of our modern Western bourgeois institution of high art. The institutional realities of high art have combined with Romantic theories of art to produce that picture of art which has shaped analytic philosophy of art.

V

In *Literary Theory: An Introduction*,[11] Terry Eagleton remarks that

> one might very roughly periodize the history of modern literary theory in three stages: a preoccupation with the author (Romanticism and the nineteenth century); an exclusive concern with the text (New Criticism); and a marked shift of attention to the reader over recent years. The reader has always been the most underprivileged of this trio – strangely, since without him or her there would be no literary texts at all. (p. 74)

An implication of our discussion above is that the move from focus on the artist to focus on the work should not be viewed as a move out of the ambit of Romanticism. The same cannot be said for the move to focus on the reader. And Eagleton is by no means alone in suggesting that what unifies the disparate, polemical, contentious body of recent criticism and theory is focus on the reader. Jonathan Culler, for example, uses the same thesis to organize his *On Deconstruction: Theory and Criticism after Structuralism*.[12]

Or have we been fooled by appearances? Has recent theory not really moved out of the ambit of Romanticism? In many of the 'poststructuralists', the Romantic themes are still there – oriented now around the reader, however, rather than around the creator. The creative freedom of the reader has replaced the creative freedom of the author/artist as the centre of reflection. Indeed, for some theorists the reader has become little short of a free creative artist, with the text no more than an initiating occasion. It is less than clear that the reader's presence on stage for the last quarter century represents the end of Romanticism. And already voices are raised saying that it is time once again to bring the author/artist into the picture.[13]

Whirl is king: from artist to work to receiver and back again to artist. Surely it is time for us to break out, to start over, somehow to find a way of approaching art which no longer focuses successively on artist and work and receiver, but instead holds these all in view simultaneously – and does so in such a way as to answer the call, now increasingly heard, to take account of the social embeddedness of whichever of these one has in the centre of one's attention: artist, work, receiver.[14] I suggest that we approach art from the angle of the social practices of art. Let me explain, and in my explanation let me follow, fairly closely, Alasdair MacIntyre's explication of the idea of a social practice in his *After Virtue*.[15]

A practice is an activity of a certain sort – characteristically, an activity which involves the manipulation of material of one kind or another in one way or another. That material will usually reflect technological developments in society. Thus practices interact with technologies: technologies are themselves embedded in practices; but apart from that, practices require technologies and new technologies suggest new practices.

Secondly, a social practice is an activity which requires learned skills and knowledge. Some things we are born able to do; others, we naturally acquire the ability for doing in the process of maturation. Not so with the skills enabling practices. They must be learned, most of them, anyway. And to a large extent the skills and knowledge requisite are not just picked up on our own but taught us by others, sometimes by modelling, sometimes by explicit verbal instructions. In that way, among others, practices are inherently social.

Furthermore, in the case of a practice the new learner confronts a situation in which the requisite skills and knowledge are in good measure already being exercised by practitioners of the practice. When the knowledge and skills necessary for practice become complex, critics and consultants and professional teachers put in their appearance, and some of these will not themselves be practitioners of that practice. Some may themselves not even have the skills necessary for being practitioners. But in addition to all such instructors, there will be a body of practitioners of the practice which the new learner joins. Characteristically, the same will have been true, earlier, of those current practitioners.

Thus a practice is an ongoing activity into which new members are inducted. Practices have histories; they have traditions. As MacIntyre remarks

> To enter into a practice is to enter into a relationship not only with its contemporary practitioners, but also with those who have preceded us in the practice, particularly those whose achievements extended the reach of the practice to its present point. It is thus the achievement, and *a fortiori* the authority, of a tradition which I then confront and from which I have to learn.[16]

In that last sentence, MacIntyre alludes to the fact that when an activity is a practice, those who engage in the activity, along with those who teach the activity, will regard some performances of the activity as better than others. There will be standards of excellence operative within the activity whereby some people are judged to farm better than others, whereby some people are judged to skate better than others, etc. To be inducted into the practice is not just to pick up the skills and knowledge requisite for its performance but also to be taught the current standards of excellence for the practice. As MacIntyre puts it

> A practice involves standards of excellence and obedience to rules. . . . To enter into a practice is to accept the authority of those standards and the inadequacy of my own performance as judged by them. It is to subject my own attitudes, choices, preferences and tastes to the standards which currently and partially define the practice. . . . If, on starting to listen to music, I do not accept my own incapacity to judge correctly, I will never learn to hear, let alone to appreciate, Bartok's last quartets.[17]

The learning of the standards of excellence operative within a practice does not usually occur by way of learning formulated criteria of evaluation; the *formulation* of criteria is a difficult and sophisticated task. The learning in question occurs far more often by way of modelling and casual hints.

In thinking about the standards of evaluation operative within a practice, it is of prime importance not to think of them as an unshakable monolith. Often there will be critics of the current standards. Often different practitioners will operate with somewhat different standards. And in most practices, the standards will have changed over the course of history – sometimes subtly, sometimes dramatically. Such changes will often call forth new knowledge and new skills, and these in turn will often suggest new standards again. Innovations in knowledge, in standards and in skills, nourish each other; among these three there is a circular process of discovery and innovation. Practices alter and expand our human modes and degrees of achieving excellence.

The way we evaluate what goes on in practices is, of course, directly connected to what we find desirable in those practices. Here it is important to distinguish between goods *internal* to activities and goods *external*; and correlatively, between engaging in an activity for external goods, that is, goods which are only contingently attached to that activity and which can in principle be attached to a wide variety of significantly different activities (e.g., profit, fame, self-satisfaction), and engaging in an activity for *internal* goods, that is, goods which can only be achieved by engaging in this activity or ones closely similar. The internal goods in question may be either *products* of the activity or *experiences* which come our way in the course of engaging in the activity – in the case of farming, for example, they may either be foodstuffs or the pleasurable experience of working the soil.

Since we are not analysing the notion of a social practice for its own sake but for the sake of illuminating the social practices of art, let me content myself with pointing out one last feature of such practices, connected directly to the preceding point. In the course of the history of a practice, new internal goods may come to light and old ones become unattractive. A fundamental feature of social practices is this plasticity with respect to internal goods and goals, and indeed external. There is no such thing as *the* purpose of farming, of painting, of figure ice skating. There may, of course, be some abiding goals inherent in these practices; but what is just as important to observe is that the goals as a whole, of those who participate in practices, shift. MacIntyre's example of the point is a good one for our purposes. Consider, he says,

> the practice of portrait painting as it developed in Western Europe from the late middle ages to the eighteenth century. The successful portrait painter is able to achieve many goods which are . . . external to the practice of portrait painting – fame, wealth, social status, even a measure of power and influence at courts upon occasion. But those external goods are not to be confused with the goods which are internal to the practice. . . . Originally in medieval paintings of the saints the face was an icon; the question of a resemblance between the depicted face of Christ or St. Peter and the face that Jesus or Peter actually possessed at some particular age did not even arise. the antithesis to this iconography was the relative naturalism of certain fifteenth-century Flemish and German paintings. The heavy eyelids, the coifed hair, the lines around the mouth undeniably represent some particular woman, either actual or envisaged. Resemblance has usurped the iconic relationship. But with Rembrandt there is, so to speak, synthesis: the naturalistic portrait is now rendered as an icon, but an icon of a new and hitherto inconceivable kind.[18]

It will be obvious by now that the various arts-of-making which we classify as *fine arts* are examples of social practices – *paradigmatic* examples. Take, for example, the activity of painting: clearly this is an ongoing activity with a history and tradition which requires knowledge and skill for its practice. And though we no longer have a guild system for training new participants in the practice, none the less young would-be painters begin their careers by absorbing a good deal of the knowledge and skill – and yes, the goals and standards of evaluation – of those currently engaged in the practice. Nowadays fledgling painters almost always take painting courses taught by painters. Furthermore, the practice continues its uninterrupted course through profound changes in the knowledge, the skills, the standards of evaluation, and the goals of its practitioners, as well as through profound disputes and disagreements on goals and standards. The existence of those changes, disputes and disagreements is connected with the emergence of new internal goods and the disappearance of old ones, along, indeed, with the emergence of new external goods and the disappearance of old ones. What is characteristic of the practice of painting among us is the ebb and flow of new internal goods aimed at by our painters. A great innovator comes along, and suddenly new possibilities are opened up for this ancient practice of painting – whether now it be the practice of representational painting that we have in mind or the practice of abstract design painting.

My examples (and MacIntyre's) have focused on composition-practice. But it should be obvious that we find in the arts not only long-enduring compositional practices but also *reception*-practices, and in the so-called performing arts, *performance*-practices; and that the artist normally composes her work for insertion into those reception-and performance-practices – composes it for that, not just in the weak, readily acknowledged, sense that she is motivated by the desire that it function in such practices, but in the strong sense, that her desire that it fit into those practices loops back so as to guide her composing.

Consider, for example, the activity of reading poetry. Reading poetry is an ongoing historical activity which we teach novices to engage in. We induct them into the practice, mainly by way of school education. We teach them the requisite knowledge and skills for reading poetry; and we impart to them a feel for the difference between better and worse ways of reading, and of better and worse kinds of poetry. Further, we all recognize that there are goods internal to the reading of poetry, goods which can only be achieved by reading poetry; and anyone acquainted with the history of literary theory knows that the goods which readers have tried to achieve in reading poetry have varied widely across history. Today the goals and standards of reading are much contested. Literary theory of the past twenty-five years is the scene of the contest.

Indeed, not only have the goods pursued in the reading of poetry varied, and not only are they contested. We must recall here the point made earlier, that *reading* poetry is but one of many uses to which poetry can be and has been put. The social practice of receiving and using poetry is not today, and never has been, confined to reading. Poems are also recited to invoke rain from the gods, chanted in games, sung to entertain small children, etc.

VI

Philosophy of art after Romanticism must historicize Romanticism. Instead of accepting the Romantic claim that now, finally, art has come into its own and its essence has been revealed in thought, it must insist that Romantic practice and thought in the arts represent just one stage in those interlocking ever-changing social practices which are the arts. Romantic ideology is not the philosophy of the end time in art. It is a polemic, couched in essentialist and eschatological terms, in favour of certain ways of conducting the social practices of art and against other ways.

But though the way ahead for philosophy of art after Romanticism is to historicize Romanticism, it does not follow that the way ahead is to become a species of historicism – or, as Rorty calls it, of pragmatism. To see what else it might become, we must glance now at the fall of analytic philosophy. Rorty has offered a narrative of that fall, but another, quite different, narrative is also possible. To set the stage, let us briefly rehearse Rorty's narrative, as offered in his *Philosophy and the Mirror of Nature*.[19]

Analytic philosophy, says Rorty, cannot be written without one or the other of such related distinctions as the necessary and the contingent, the analytic and the synthetic, the structural and the empirical, the philosophical and the scientific. 'If there are no intuitions into which to resolve concepts (in the manner of the *Aufbau*) nor any internal relations among concepts to make possible 'grammatical discoveries' (in the manner of 'Oxford philosophy'), then indeed it is hard to imagine what an 'analysis' might be' (p. 172). Accordingly, says Rorty, the story he wants to tell is 'how the notion of two sorts of representations – intuitions and concepts – fell into disrepute in the latter days of the analytic movement' (p. 168). In Rorty's narrative, Quine and Sellars become the central figures in the demise of analytic philosophy and the emergence of its successor – pragmatism.

The conviction that there is some sort of 'given' on which the mind imposes its concepts was never very firm in the analytic tradition, says Rorty. In 'Empiricism and the Philosophy of Mind', Sellars launched an all-out attack on what he called 'The Myth of the Given'; but this was just the culmination of a good many queries and hesitations. By contrast, the distinction between the necessary and contingent went unquestioned until the publication of Quine's 'Two Dogmas of Empiricism'.

Analytic philosophers did not follow Kant in his claim that some necessary truths are synthetic – that there are, in Kantian parlance, *synthetic a prioris*. For them, the necessary/contingent distinction coincided with the analytic/synthetic distinction. Indeed, many of them viewed these distinctions not only as coincident but as identical. The concept of the necessary just is the concept of the analytic; the concept of the contingent just is the concept of the synthetic. Though attempts to explain the analytic/synthetic distinction were many and diverse, there was something of a consensus around the conviction – now to use Quine's words – that *synthetic* truths are 'grounded in fact' and *analytic* truths are 'grounded in meanings independently of matters of fact'.[20] One of Quine's purposes in his essay was to attack this distinction as untenable. The conclusion he drew was that 'for all its a priori reasonableness, a boundary between analytic and synthetic statements simply has not been drawn. That there is such a distinction to be drawn at all is an unempirical dogma of empiricists, a metaphysical article of faith'.[21]

Rorty's narrative thus far points to the destructive consequences, for analytic philosophy, of Quine's and Sellars's work. The scheme/content picture must be surrendered and the conviction undergirding foundationalism – that some of our beliefs and assertions are certain and hence privileged because they report a reality to which we have direct access, viz., meanings and the intuitional given – must be given up. But Rorty continues his narration by pointing to what he sees as the positive, forward-looking element in this same work of Quine and Sellars. Here he treats them together: they both, on his interpretation, affirm 'epistemological behaviorism', or pragmatism. We do indeed regard various reports about our inner life as certain. But 'for Sellars, the certainty of "I have a pain" is a reflection of the fact that nobody cares to question it, not conversely' (p. 174). So too we regard 'All men are animals' and 'There have been some black dogs' as certain; and Quine thinks, says Rorty, that an anthropologist would not be able 'to discriminate the sentences to which natives invariably and wholeheartedly assent into contingent empirical platitudes on the one hand and necessary conceptual truths on the other' (p. 173). But this certainty too 'is a reflection of the fact that nobody cares to question it, not conversely'. According to epistemological behaviourism, says Rorty, 'rationality and epistemic authority' are not to be explained by reference to meanings and experiential givens, to which we have direct access. 'Quine thinks that "meanings" drop out as wheels that are not part of the mechanism, and Sellars thinks the same of "self-authenticating non-verbal episodes" (p. 174). Rationality and epistemic authority are to be explained 'by reference to what society lets us say, rather than the latter by the former'. And this, says Rorty, is the essence of epistemological behaviourism, or pragmatism. The rules of the language-game in which we participate allow us to say certain things under certain circumstances and not other things under those circumstances; warrant and entitlement are always and only by reference to some such rules. We can probe the historical origins of such rules, the relative usefulness of such rules, the relation of such rules to the structure of the brain, etc. But what we cannot do is 'ground' such rules in a reality which we apprehend.

> To be behaviorist in the large sense in which Sellars and Quine are behaviorist is not to offer reductionist analyses, but to refuse to attempt a certain sort of explanation: the sort of explanation which not only interposes such a notion as 'acquaintance with meanings' or 'acquaintance with sensory appearances' between the impact of the environment on human beings and their reports about it, but uses such notions to explain the reliability of such reports (p. 176)

> For the Quine–Sellars approach to epistemology, to say that truth and knowledge can only be judged by the standards of the inquirers of our own day is not to say that human knowledge is less noble or important, or more 'cut off from the world,' than we had thought.

It is merely to say that nothing counts as justification unless by reference to what we already accept, and that there is no way to get outside our beliefs and our language so as to find some test other than coherence. (p. 178)

Rorty's reading of the character and history of analytic philosophy is that once again the fundamental Kant/Hegel dialectic has come into play. At the end of the nineteenth century, Western philosophy was Hegelian in its general character, with pragmatism being the characteristically American manifestation of this. At the turn of the century this Hegelianism was overwhelmed with a new surge of neo-Kantianism, the great figure in the Anglo-American world being Russell, on the continent, Husserl, these having Frege as common patrimony.[22] But once again the Hegelian dynamic asserted itself, undercutting the assumptions of twentieth-century neo-Kantianism, appearing somewhat earlier on the continent than in the ambience of analytic philosophy, but appearing there too in the pivotal work of Quine and Sellars, so that once again there is a coalescence between European and Anglo-American philosophy. Once again our human conceptualizing is properly seen as historicized; once again the notion of there being limits on our conceptualizing and our thinking, these limits constituting necessity, is discarded. This time, however, instead of history being seen as the attempt of Hegel's Reason to realize itself, history is seen as the attempt of human beings to find *what works*.

This, I say, is Rorty's narrative of the history of analytic philosophy; call it the pragmatist–Hegelian narrative. But a different narrative, a *Realist* narrative, is also possible. The Realist agrees that classic analytic philosophy was a species of neo-Kantianism – a species which absorbed some of the major themes of John Locke. The Realist also agrees that the probing of some of the assumptions of analytic philosophy which took place at the hands of such as Quine and Sellars has led to the emergence of a mode of thought which is pragmatist–Hegelian in its orientation – plus, of course, leading simply to bewilderment in many. But the Realist contends that Rorty's narration stops too soon and is too myopic. Pragmatism is not the only successor to analytic philosophy. There is another sucessor: that other is Realism. The Realist refuses to participate in the dialectic of Kantianism and Hegelianism. He questions assumptions common to both. Analytic philosophy has split in two.

Locke held that though there are real essences, we know nothing of them. We know only of nominal essence. In other words, Locke held that though there is both necessity *de re* and *de dicto*, we know only of necessity *de dicto*. For example, though we know that something, to be gold, must be yellow and malleable, we do no know and cannot know, of any actual lump of stuff, whether or not it is essentially gold. Kant, as we have already seen, moved beyond Locke to deny that there is any *de re* necessity to be known (that, at least, was Kant's official position; in fact he appears to offer a vast anthropological essentialism). In this, classic analytic philosophy followed him. And the pragmatist-Hegelians have taken the last step of denying that there is any necessity at all.

Now Quine was well aware of the traditional claim that there is *de re* necessity; he professed, however, to find the notion unintelligible. He understood such claims as that cyclists must have legs – *must*, that is, to be cyclists; but the claim that someone *had* to be a cyclist, or *had* to be a person, or whatever, of such a claim he could make no sense. However, in his seminal papers of the sixties Saul Kripke proposed a way of making sense of necessity which included a way of making sense of *de re* necessity. Kripke resurrected the Leibnizian notion of possible worlds; and then suggested that a proposition is necessarily true if true in all possible worlds and that some property belongs to the essence of something if it has that property in all possible worlds in which there is that thing. Kripke himself did not offer an ontology of possible worlds; on that, there have subsequently been various suggestions. One of the simplest and least problematic is that of Alvin Plantinga.[23] Possible worlds are states of affairs, highly complex ones, so complex as to be complete, in the sense that, if some state of affairs S is a possible world, then for every state of affairs S*, S either includes or precludes S*.

In some of his later work Kripke went on to argue that not only do we know some of the essential properties of things, but that the project of natural science can be seen, in good measure, as the attempt to discover the essences of various natural kinds and of various stuffs – e.g., of water. This was the first blow to the old Kantian insistence that necessity is a priori and contingency a posteriori. But more generally, the characteristic Kantian blur between epistemology and ontology, when it came to matters of necessity, was undone. That blur was as essential to Quine the pragmatist as it was to Kant. For Quine took the notion of necessity to be the notion of what we would never give up; and then argued that probably, for everything which we believe, there is some circumstance or other under which we would give it up. The Realist holds, however, that all such epistemic notions as feeling certain of something, not being willing to give something up under any circumstances whatsoever, etc., are different from the notion of necessity. Of some propositions which are in fact necessary and with which we are acquainted we may be very uncertain; it would not take much at all to push us into giving them up. Indeed, some we may already have given up, to the extent not only of not believing them but of believing them false. There is nothing even puzzling about the notion of believing to be false a proposition which is in fact necessary. Furthermore, the Realist does not identify the necessary/contingent distinction with the analytic/synthetic distinction. *Qua* Realist, he does not even have a view on whether they coincide. Indeed, he can live happily with the consequence that nothing like the Kantian analytic/synthetic distinction can be made out. For the issue of whether it can be made out is just the issue of whether all *de dicto* necessity is analytic or whether some is synthetic. But the attention of the Realist is not focussed on species of *de dicto* necessity. It is not focussed on *de dicto* necessity at all. His contention is rather that in addition to *de dicto* necessity there is *de re* necessity, and that with some of this *de re* necessity we are acquainted. Indeed, he regards *de dicto* necessity as being, at bottom, a species of *de re* necessity. For *de dicto* necessity consists of propositions being essentially true – i.e., being true in all possible worlds in which they exist. Thus Quine's 'Two Dogmas of Empiricism', which the Pragmatist sees as decisive, the Realist sees as misguided – as spinning out the consequences of assumptions which ought to be discarded rather than elaborated.

There is a long tradition, going back at least to Plato, which holds that it is the business of the philosopher to discover and contemplate the structure of the realm of necessity, that such contemplation is of higher worth than anything else we human beings can do, and that it can serve to direct our lives in the world. After first subjectivizing necessity, Kant, in his own way, perpetuated this tradition. The sort of Realist I have in mind rejects it. Of course it is true that that Platonic picture of the philosopher's task is *compatible* with modal realism. It is not, however, *compelled* by it; and it should, in my view, be rejected. The Realist is happy to embrace, along with the pragmatist, Sellars' rough and ready formula for the task of philosophy: To discuss how things, in the most general sense of the term, hang together, in the most general sense of the term. What in part distinguishes the Realist is his conviction that to speak with any amplitude of how things hang together, we will have to speak of necessity *de re*. Necessity and essence are features of reality. The new Realist wishes to break that ancient bond between the necessary and the important. It is more important to discover the contingent social practices of art than to find the essence of art – if, indeed, art has an essence. The new Realist breaks as firmly as does the pragmatist with the Platonic/Kantian notion that philosophers are confined to being students of necessity.

We have seen that the Realist breaks with the Kantian notion that necessity marks the bounds on human intuiting, conceptualizing and judging. He breaks with this notion not by following the pragmatist-Hegelian line of saying that there are no such limits, but rather, by being a Realist concerning modality. But there is another rejection exercised by the Realist which goes perhaps even deeper.

Kant held that we have no intellectual intuitions – no awarenesses other than sensory awarenesses – sensory, of course, comprising for him inner sense as well as outer sense. Kant's way of construing concepts fits this contention – concepts are not apprehensions of predicables but modes of organization of intuitions. Intuitions are given to us; we provide the concepts. More specifically, we impose modes of organization on the disparate intuitions. The outcome of this creative blending of the given and the imposed is knowledge. Here, then, is the origin of that picture which has so powerfully dominated analytic philosophy: the picture of scheme and content, of organizing structure and intuitional given. The pragmatist-Hegelian has various reasons for rejecting this picture. Perhaps the deepest is that he find it incoherent. What is this stuff to which the conceptual scheme is applied? Kant thought that whatever conceptual scheme we applied would always and necessarily have the same fundamental structure. Others have spoken of alternative conceptual schemes. Either way, says the pragmatist, the picture is the same: that of applying a conceptual scheme to some stuff. But any way of thinking of that stuff already involves the use of a concept. Kant spoke of it as intuitions. That is already to conceptualize it – namely, as intuition. Others preferred speaking of the scheme as applied to the world. But world too is a concept. The whole idea of a world out there, or of intuitions in here, waiting to be conceptualized, is hopelessly incoherent. Better to scrap the whole idea – it would be world and intuitions well lost. We must allow to sink into us the full force of the fact that we cannot get outside our concepts – or if one prefers, our language. Philosophers suggest 'that there is some way of breaking out of language in order to compare it with something else. But there is no way to think about either the world or our purposes except by using our language.'[24] We dwell – all of us together – in the prison house of language – or of concepts. That is the image which irresistibly comes to mind when the pragmatist speaks. Of course the pragmatist would reject the image. For we cannot think of anything as being outside this prison. And what kind of prison is a prison with nothing outside? No prison. Better to use images of freedom. The inescapability of language is the inescapability of freedom. We must learn to live with pure contingency. Pragmatism

> is the doctrine that there are no constraints on inquiry save conversational ones – no wholesale constraints derived from the nature of the objects, or of the mind, or of language, but only those retail constraints provided by the remarks of our fellow-inquirers. . . .

> I prefer this . . . way of characterizing pragmatism because it seems to me to focus on a fundamental choice which confronts the reflective mind: that between accepting the contingent character of starting-points, and attempting to evade this contingency. To accept the contingency of starting-points is to accept our inheritance from, and our conversation with, our fellow-humans as our only source of guidance. . . . Our identification with our community – our society, our political tradition, our intellectual heritage – is heightened when we see this community as ours rather than nature's, shaped rather then found, one among many which men have made . . . James, in arguing against realists and idealists that 'the trail of the

human serpent is over all,' was reminding us that our glory is in our participation in fallible and transitory human projects, not in our obedience to permanent nonhuman constraints.[25]

The Realist sees things differently. Though he too rejects the scheme/ content picture, he does so for a reason very different from that of the pragmatist-Hegelians. For him, the basic picture is not that of taking something as so-and-so – i.e., conceptualizing something as so-and-so; but rather, that of *recognizing* something as what it is – becoming acquainted with it. We do not just *take* some un-nameable protean stuff *as* a duck. We recognize the duck before us to be a duck – sometimes, anyway. The Realist rejects the Kantian claim that we have no intellectual intuitions. He holds that there are predicables and propositions (states of affairs), and that, of many of these, we have a grasp. He thinks of concepts – some of them, anyway – as graspings of predicables. And he holds that some of the predicables that we grasp are instantiated and are known by us to be instantiated. Reality, though not made by us, is thus also not alien to us. Concepts are not mental representations screening reality from us. Neither are they modes of organization imposed on unorganized protean stuff. The image of conceptualizing some given stuff – doing something to it, taking it as so-and-so, imposing a mode of organization on it – is wrong, relevant admittedly for some of our contact with reality but not for all and not for what is most basic. The pragmatist-Hegelian does not remove what is wrong about this image by proposing that we scrap the notion of a stuff taken in various ways, and keep just the *takings*. The smile does not come without the cat. Neither does the Realist think of believings as inclinations to assert, which are governed solely by the rules of the social game – horizontally, as it were. He holds that when we believe, there is something which is the object of belief – a states of affairs. And he holds that some of the state of affairs which we believe to be the case are in fact the case. We are at home in the world – without having made it.
     So, at bottom, the reason the Realist does not see necesity as merely the limits on the ways we can take things, is that he does not regard the phenomenon of us taking things a certain way as at the bottom of things. We can take a design as either a duck or a rabbit. But what it really is, then, is a design – neither a duck nor a rabbit.
     Much more could be said by way of delineating and advocating the position which I have been calling Realism; but this must suffice.[26] Not one but two coherent philosophical visions have emerged from, and superseded, analytic philosophy in its senescence. One is the pragmatism which Rorty eloquently propounds – essentially one more manifestation of the Hegelian response to Kantianism. The other is Realism, which refuses to participate in the Kant/Hegel dialectic and instead rejects assumptions shared alike by Kantians and Hegelians. Pragmatists and

Realists agree in rejecting the picture of a scheme of necessities imposed on a given of contingencies. They agree in rejecting the notion that the philosopher is a specialist in necessity. They agree that philosophy is not apodictic. And though the Realist, *qua Realist*, is not opposed to classical foundationalism and concept constructivism, he is, in my judgement, well advised to share the pragmatist's opposition to these. But from there on, they part ways. For the Realist holds that there is a reality 'out there', a reality which includes necessity, to which we can be faithful or unfaithful in our beliefs – not just a social game whose shifting rules we can follow or not follow. Indeed, he regards rules, along with the persons who obey or defy them, as also part of the reality 'out there' to which, in our beliefs, we can be faithful or unfaithful.

VII

The world within which the social practices of art are played out includes, as the Realist sees it, necessity and possibility and impossibility – and properties and actions and kinds and states of affairs. Down through the ages, for example, one of the things done with works of art – with some, not all – is world-projection. Never will the projected world of a work of art be our actual world – that is to say, never will it be that possible world which is the actual world. The actual world is too vast for projection. And usually what the artist projects is not even, in its totality, *part* of the actual world. Usually, in its totality, it is a merely possible state of affairs; and sometimes, in its totality, an impossible state of affairs. The writers and tellers and presenters of fiction project worlds.

In the course of fictionally projecting a state of affairs, the fictioneer will often refer to countries, persons, events etc. which do or did exist. Customarily in those cases, the world of the work will include states of affairs which cannot occur without those entities existing. In that way, the world of the work is anchored to those entities. The world is not a self-contained, hermetically closed, phenomenon. But in addition to this, the writer will delineate for us *types* of entities – person-types, country-types, city-types etc. Some of these are the fictional characters of fiction.

I think an adequate ontology of types will yield the conclusion that writers do not create characters but select and delineate them – just as I think an adequate theory of states of affairs will yield the the conclusion that writers do not create states of affairs but take note of them and call them to our attention. What underlies the possibility of fiction is the human capacity for envisagement.[27]

On such a view as here alluded to, world-projection is not a way of world-making. But neither is it, as the old view would have it, a mode of imitation. If we reject Romanticism in the arts and approach art from the side of its social practices, and if the philosophy of art we then develop rejects the Kantian/Hegelian dialectic and adopts instead a Realist orientation, then we will see the social practices of art as dealing not just with actuality but with possibility and impossibility; and not just with particulars but with properties and actions and kinds. The fictioneer neither makes a world nor imitates a world, but selects from the vast realm of possibility and impossibility a segment thereof, a 'world', for us to consider. Among the many benefits of a Realist philosophy of art is that it offers us a cogent and powerful way of explaining what it is to project a world.

NOTES

1   Cf. Moritz Schlick, 'The Turning Point in Philosophy', in A. J. Ayer, (ed.) *Logical Positivism* (New York, The Free Press, 1959), p. 54: 'I refer to this anarchy of philosophical opinions which has so often been described, in order to leave no doubt that I am fully conscious of the scope and weighty significance of the conviction that I should now like to express. For I am convinced that we now find ourselves at an altogether decisive turning point in philosophy, and that we are objectively justified in considering that an end has come to the fruitless conflict of systems. We are already at the present time, in my opinion, in possession of methods which make every such conflict in principle unnecessary. What is now required is their resolute application.'

2   Hans Reichenbach, *The Rise of Scientific Philosophy* (Berkeley, Ca, University of California Press, 1963).

3   Monroe Beardsley, *Aesthetics: Problems in the Philosophy of Criticism* (New York, Harcourt, Brace & Co., 1958). The quotations in this paragraph are from pp. 1, 6 and 7.

4   Tzvetan Todorov, *Theories of the Symbol* (Ithaca, NY, Cornell University Press, 1982).

5   Two recent articles by Richard Shusterman ('Analytic Aesthetics, Literary Theory, and Deconstruction', in *The Monist*, 69 (1986) 22–38 and 'Deconstruction and Analysis: Confrontation and Convergence', in *British Journal of Aesthetics*, 26 (1986), 310–24 might be thought to make this thesis questionable from the very start. Shusterman there argues, cogently in my view, that the rise of analytic philosophy of art was in part a reaction to the aesthetics of Croce. Two points of clarification must be made, however. When I say that analytic philosophy of art is a species of Romantic philosophy of art, I mean that analytic philosophers of art have thought about art along basically Romantic lines, not that their philosophical style and presuppositions have been Romantic. Analytic philosophy of art, like analytic philosophy in general, was always a species of neo-Kantianism. Accordingly, and secondly, the reaction to Croce should not be seen as a rejection of Romantic ways of thinking of art but as a neo-Kantian reaction to a species of Hegelianism. (I follow Charles Taylor, in his books on Hegel, in not regarding Hegel as himself a Romantic but as reacting to various fundamental themes in Romantic ways of thinking generally.) Analytic philosophy rejected Croce's Hegelianism, and should be seen as one of the many moves

in the Kant/Hegel polarity; it did not reject Croce's Romantic picture of art –
though indeed it tended to emphasize different themes from the Romantics
than Croce emphasized.

6   Todorov, *Theories of the Symbol*, p. 154. Throughout the following discus-
    sion citations are given in the text by page number only.
7   See especially my *Art in Action* (Grand Rapids, Mich., Eerdmans, 1980), P. I.
8   See my 'The Work of Making a Work of Music' in Philip Alperson (ed.)
    What is Music?: *An Introduction to the Philosophy of Music*' (New York,
    Haven), 1988.
9   See my 'Art Texts Autonomous?: An Interaction with the Hermeneutic
    of Paul Ricoeur', in *Aesthetics: Proceedings of the 8th International
    Wittgenstein Symposium* (Vienna, Hölder–Pichler–Tempsky, 1984).
10 See my *Works and Worlds of Art* (Oxford, Oxford University Press; 1980),
    P. 3 s. X.
11 Terry Eagleton, *Literary Theory: An Introduction* (Minneapolis, University
    of Minnesota Press, 1983).
12 Jonathan Culler, *On Deconstruction: Theory and Criticism After Struc-
    turalism* (Ithaca, NY, Cornell University Press, 1982).
13 See, for example, Linda Hutcheon's review of Reiss, Said and Eagleton, in
    Diacritics, 13 (1983), 32–42.
14 See, for example, Edward Said's call, in the Introduction of *The World, the
    Text, and the Critics*, to set texts in the context of their generating social
    realities.
15 Alasdair MacIntyre, *After Virtue* (Notre Dame, Notre Dame Press, 1981).
16 Ibid., p. 181.
17 Ibid., p. 177.
18 Ibid., pp. 176–7.
19 Richard Rorty, *Philosophy and the Mirror of Nature* (Princeton, NJ
    Princeton University Press, 1979) p. 172. Throughout the following dis-
    cussion citations are given in the text by page number only.
20 W. V. O. Quine, 'Two Dogmas of Empiricism', in *From a Logical Point of
    View* (New York, Harper and Row, 2nd rev. edn. 1963) p. 20.
21 Ibid., p. 37.
22 Richard Shusterman's discussion in 'Analytic Aesthetics, Literary
    Theory . . .', pp. 22–38, makes clear that the same thing happened in philo-
    sophy of art. Croce was the great Hegelian; and the analytic reaction to him
    was typical in its charge of dreary woolliness. See especially the articles by
    Gallie and Passmore in W. Elton (ed.) *Aesthetics and Language* (Oxford,
    Basil Blackwell, 1954). It may be worth repeating that on my interpretation,
    the reaction to Croce did not represent a rejection of a fundamentally
    Romantic way of looking at art but the rejection of a Hegelian way of arti-
    culating the Romantic vision, in favour of a neo-Kantian, analytic, way.
23 See A. Plantinga, *The Nature of Necessity* (Oxford, Oxford University Press,
    1974).
24 Richard Rorty, *Consequences of Pragmatism* (Minneapolis, University of
    Minnesota Press, 1982), p. xix. Compare this passage, in ibid., p. xxxix: 'So
    the question of whether such a post-philosophical culture is desirable can also
    be put as the question: can the ubiquity of language ever really be taken
    seriously? Can we see ourselves as never encountering reality *except under a*

chosen description as, in Nelson Goodman's phrase, making worlds rather than finding them?'

25 Ibid., p. 166.
26 For more detailed discussions of the Realist/anti-Realist (pragmatist) debate, see my 'Realism as anti-Realism: How to Feel at Home in the World', in *Proceedings of the Catholic Philosophical Society* (1985) and 'Are Concept Users World-makers', in James Toberlin (ed.), *Philosophical Perspectives I: Metaphysics* (Atascadero, Ca, Ridgeview, 1987).
27 These ideas about projected worlds and fictional entities are developed in detail in my *Works and Worlds of Art*.

4

Style *As* the Man: From Aesthetics to Speculative Philosophy

Charles Altieri

Few topics are more appealing to literary critics than those inviting critiques of analytic philosophy, a discipline we fear and resent because it seems to waste powers we lack on subjects we like to think require our love of speculative vagueness. Therefore I want to use my essay in this volume to illustrate what I think are two fundamental limitations in (most) analytic work in aesthetics so that I can show how the critic's task too can be seen as philosophically significant. First, the analytic work tends to be stubbornly atomistic. It usually breaks aesthetic experience into a set of isolated problems, then approaches each problem as if it could be solved without much concern for its relations either to other aesthetic features or to more general philosophical paradigms. Secondly, this work often treats elements within a work of art as if they too could be easily isolated as constituents which could be given their importance by the set of philosophical themes that the inquiry projects. But the effect is both to cheapen the art and to blind the analysts to the possibility that the artwork's synthetic structure might make more challenging speculative use of what they confine to their own methodological parameters.

There is no better example of these problems, and of the cost they exact, than recent aesthetic theorizing on the concept of style. Most philosophers approach the concept by trying to define the specific semantic elements that can be said to constitute the style of a work, author or period. Such work is often quite sensitive to the limitations of taxonomy, and often quite acute in seeing the range of distinctions that the subject requires, as is evident in the anthology *The Concept of Style*.[1] At times the best analytic aestheticians, like Goodman, Danto and Scruton, even argue that what is at stake in such discussions are matters of expression and intentionality which resist the prevailing disciplinary commitments of analytic philosophy. But in my view there remains a striking dichotomy between the aesthetician's analyses and the effects which the stylistic devices have as elements given speculative focus and dramatic force by particular works of art. I do not expect philosophers to become new critics. But there seems to me something seriously lacking when that analytic work fails to ask how what the style is really doing might in fact reveal certain aspects of human agency which could then put pressure on our philosophical methods and our working concepts. Moreover when philosophers fail to honour the speculative dimensions of the artworks, they make it easy for literary critics to justify their disdain for any philosophy that is not fully attuned to the play of artistic imaginations. And that both leads criticism to some terribly embarrassing philosophical gestures and deprives it of a cogent language for describing the range of social roles that the arts can play.

History makes the point easy to illustrate. For if one looks to the ways that interpretive critics actually use concepts of style, one finds the ideas coming not from analytic philosophy or linguistics but from Paul de Man's deconstructive treatments of style as presenting an inescapable aporia between the performative and the descriptive dimensions of speech acts.[2] Yet de Man's speculative frameworks offers only the slightest concrete hold on the issues which one needs to distinguish about style, and it promotes a single set of oppositions more confining and considerably more self-righteous than any work of equal stature in analytic philosophy. None the less de Man thrives because he sees that style is first of all human action in language and therefore must be considered in terms of the dynamics of needs and desires which such actions brings into play. So the task facing literary criticism, and one central motive for worrying about these philosophical issues, is the need to find conceptual models for the full range and depth of such actions without being forced into de Man's rigid thematic dichotomies. Here I shall seek that aid by showing how the more clearly we see the problems in analytic aesthetics on the subject of style the better we find ourselves able to appreciate by contrast what is at stake in the reflections on expressive agency carried out in Wittgenstein's treatment of the 'as'.

I

I find Nelson Goodman's well-known essay on style the best locus for isolating the specific problems that characterize analytic aesthetics' treatments of the subject.[3] This is in part because Goodman himself does such a good job of identifying the difficulties others encounter, in part because Goodman's own extensionalist commitments highlight the areas where we need the modes of speculation he forbids. Therefore if I can show that Goodman is correct in his criticisms, but then severely reductive in what he puts in the place of the prevailing views, I shall be in a position to indicate both what we need for a fuller account of style and how those issues then become significant data for other more general philosophical questions about human agency.

Goodman's attack on other approaches to style worries less about the inadequacies of particular claims than about the fact that there seem to be too many plausible claims, each difficult to work out with the necessary specificity. Suppose we begin with the idea that style clearly has something to do with the way that something is said, with the 'how' rather than the 'what'. Then we must define the nature and force of that 'how', and serious troubles begin. At least three plausible 'contents' for the 'how' emerge. One can, for example, stress the ways in which style modifies the actual import of a given utterance because of what it adds or transforms about the claim. But there seems no theoretical way to determine when or how style does or does not allow synonymous formulations. In some cases the formal component is inextricably a part of the distinctive message; in others one can clearly accomplish the same practical effects in other ways. Second, we often attend to style less for its specific cognitive claims than for the expressive registers it brings to bear as signs of the author's emotive relation to that 'content'. But here too one encounters situations where sometimes the emotive dimension is inseparable from the effect and affect of the content, while at other times either there is no significant emotional supplement or what does get expressed can clearly be abstracted from the specific claim. Finally, there are features of style which resist all subjective expression in order to serve as direct examples of certain aspects of the work's message. Consider Pope's 'And ten low words oft creep in one dull line' ('Essay on Criticism', line 347). The expression literally demonstrates the point, so that the properties which the work actually possesses become in effect concrete testimony for its claims, regardless of any attribution we might make about the state of the author. This small example then stands metonymically for the assertions made about style by formalists like Clement Greenberg on the one hand and on the other by theorists like Roland Barthes, who are obsessed with the capacity of the medium of writing to displace all questions about the world or about expressive identity into the constructed play of literal signifying elements. But even these gestures towards a material textuality fail to provide secure interpretations of what will count as intrinsic properties. Such interpretations require some argument or some expressive register which we project beyond the literalness of the writing or painting.

Therefore we find ourselves with three basic categories for style – what goes into the saying, what is expressed, and what is exemplified – which breed certain basic theoretical oppositions 'of style and subject, of form and content, of what and how, of intrinsic and extrinsic', each in turn leading us to underplay other basic elements and none able to determine 'what in general distinguishes stylistic features from others'.[4] Every time we look for style we find content, and every time we focus on content we find ourselves forced to notice its dependency on some construction of stylistic features.

Faced with these contradictions, Goodman proposes his own extensionalist concept of style. Style is simply 'signature'.

A property – whether of statement made, structure displayed, or feeling conveyed – counts as stylistic only when it associates a work with one rather than another artist, period, region, school etc. A style is a complex characteristic that serves somewhat as an individual or group signature – . . . in general stylist properties help answer the questions: who? when? where? . . . No fixed catalogue of the elementary properties of style can be compiled; and we normally come to grasp a style without being able to analyze it into component features. The test of our grasp lies in the sureness and sensitivity of our sorting of works.[5]

By settling for so general a model, Goodman can honour the apparent open-endedness of what counts as style in different cases yet still provide a stable role for the discussion of stylistic features. What signature is depends on the comparative discourses that can be generated about it as we try to isolate the distinguishing features of a work and as we develop a complex network of possible relations which will demonstrate the stakes involved in those differences.

Goodman's solution is not an easy one to assess since so much of its force consists in displacing questions about style into more particular historically based discourses. I suspect, however, that this project can do little more than cover up old problems while allowing other versions of the fissures he reveals to emerge under the guise of those historical discourses. Signature is not style. For style need not be motivated by the desire to distinguish an individual hand, and the ways that it does individualize may have very little to do with the aspects of identity that signatures attest to. One does need the historical frameworks Goodman stresses, but they will be as subject to the confusing range of effects he describes as any other framework. It is interesting in this regard to notice how questions of motive, recurrence and foregrounded emphasis sneak back into his discussions. Having separated signature from authorial intentions, Goodman must argue that we distinguish what is stylistic from what is not simply by whether or not the features are 'properties of the functioning of the work as a symbol'.[6] But how do we know how the work functions as a symbol unless we return to the questions of saying, expressing etc.? Clearly all our concerns about that symbolic functioning are not exhausted by matters of signature. We want to know which of a person's signatures are operating, and we want to know the degree to which that signature is being manipulated in relation to the subject matter.

Signatures may identify the distinctive traits of a work, but it takes more than that to show how the traits form a whole with properties distinctive to a specific symbolic operation. For that we need the kind of motivating principles that come into play when signature becomes an expressive moving and desiring hand or when we try to understand how certain devices play a role in an account of the work's formal coherence. No comparison of Wordsworth with his peers would suffice to warrant the intense and complex reading of the syntax in 'Tintern Abbey' necessary if we are to appreciate what he makes of discursive poetry; nor would such a frame provide the context for appreciating how his relationship to Dorothy enters the intricate tense and mood play of the poem's concluding section. It is not the work as symbol which defines what counts as style; rather it is what we take as the patterns of motive – formal, semantic or expressive – which dictate what can count as symbolically significant within the range of options that history can be said to allow at any given point.[7] And conversely it is only by acknowledging this grammar of motives that we can retain the continuities that connect what we say about style in art to what we say of it in other social domains where there is no clear symbolic or metaphoric dimension for the concrete stylistic elements.

As we shall see, I share Goodman's interest in freeing the expressive subject from the ideas of expressive agency fostered by the idealist or the psychoanalytic models of authorial presence in the style. But abstracting agency into signature is not the way to provide a sufficiently deep or flexible conjunction between signature and the range of possible motives which we have been considering. In fact, reductive stances like Goodman's tend to have the opposite effect by tempting us to return to nineteenth-century subjectivist models.[8] At least that subjectivist orientation promises a much broader range of motives for style than signatures do, and, as Jenefer M. Robinson points out, it allows the same range of stylistically relevant features that Goodman's stance addresses. However, this position will not adequately handle either the range of expressive stances which those features create, nor will it fully account for the aspects of saying and exemplifying which Goodman showed can establish an iconic immediacy and integrity subordinating all considerations about the subject to the subject matter the style is asked to render. A brief glance at these issues should then make clear when an adequate alternative to Goodman will have to attribute to the expressive agency which styles define.

The best way to illustrate these problems is to concentrate on the devices which subjectivist theorists need in order to locate the relevant expressive predicates. Jenefer Robinson, for example, makes two necessary but highly questionable and revealing moves. She insists on our having to distinguish between actual and implied authors who do the expressing, and she claims that one must handle the range of stylistic effects that come under a single signature by hypothesizing the author's different 'attitudes' towards the various elements: 'In *Emma* . . . Jane Austen portrays Mrs Elton in a quite different way from Jane Fairfax. This is because Jane Austen's attitude to Mrs Elton is quite different from her attitude towards

Jane Fairfax'[9] In each case the strategy constructs a way of locating motives within the work. But that means of assuring a psychologically coherent interpretable subject may require surrendering many of the most interesting deployments of expressive agency which an attention to style might foreground. Robinson's principles leave no room for Barthes's idea of a writerly presence that can only appear as 'textualité' – precisely because it explores distributions of the pysche available only in the strange space language creates; nor do they address experimental writers like Joyce or Rilke or even Shakespeare who treat styles more like states that people enter than like attitudes subjects hold.

Moreover there are several traditional roles for style which do not easily correlate with hypotheses about an implicit author. Berel Lang provides a good example in his distinguishing of a 'reflexive mode' of philosophical style in which the very idea of authorship yields to an 'ambivalence or shifting between an external and internal center'.[10] In much of Plato and Kierkegaard the philosophical drama is based on the philosopher's effort to undo the typical authority of the master so that reader and author can share a process of discovering where it is that the author is learning to speak from.[11] Then there are cases where the authors themselves refuse to allow clear versions of a textually composed implicit author. At one pole this refusal involves the dialectical exploration of tensions between the actual biographical subject and the 'self' (or selves) that the style constructs. For a Yeats or a Hegel both the history rendered and the possible selves made from that history depend on the constant effort to incorporate what style can project and articulate. At the other pole, such tensions become symptomatic – either because the author reveals certain traits which cannot be attributed to the voice that the narrative composes or because writers like Lawrence and perhaps Dostoyevsky feed on the intricate possibilities inherent in generating implicit authors who must deal with fictive situations where the characters are themselves versions of the biographical author.

Finally, Robinson misses what we might call a basic moral role which style is asked to play in a good deal of Modernist art where, as in Pope's line, the triumph of style consists in expunging all traces of the expressive register, at least as it is traditionally understood. Because the style directly exemplifies its point, the medium is perfectly contoured to the objective condition stated by the semantic level of the text. On that basis a Mondrian or Beckett can treat the working of the medium as carrying the entire expressive register – less to erase the subject than to earn for it something like a state of transpersonal subjectivity in which all responsive agents literally share the same imaginative investments and can describe the specific effects the style creates. There is no implicit author apart from the way that the imaginative structure distributes pyschological energies, and no phenomenon so distanced and partial as an 'attitude' towards what is presented. Instead there is a form of self-referential lucidity that leads Michael Fried to speak of such art as achieving a distinctive form of ethical autonomy: all doubling of the self into inner and outer and all theatrical dependency on a staged personal identity give way to stylistic structures which take full responsibility for the investments that they deploy.[12] There is nothing hidden and no appeal for anything more than style literally makes present.

II

It seems that an adequate theory of style would have to combine the two radically opposed poles of subjective and objectivist models of expression – the one best defined by Fichte and Freud, the other exemplified in Heidegger's model of poetic thinking as the pressing out of imaginative sites where we can subsume the pyschological subject into relational processes of dwelling and of belonging. We do not have such a theory, and I shall not propose one here. The most I can do is tease out some of the basic elements such a theory will have to include – so that we at least realize the ways in which questioning the nature of style becomes a speculative instrument for reflecting on ourselves as expressive agents and for clarifying some of the values basic to the arts that are difficult to incorporate in philosophy's story of itself as the pursuit of general truths transparently rendered.

Let me begin with the question of value, then try to explain how we can see style providing the appropriate constituents. To value style is necessarily to value how things are said. But why should we do that, or why should we take the doing of that as anything more than a matter of taste without significant philosophical consequences? A recent essay by Stanley Cavell provides the beginnings of a very good answer.[13] As always, Cavell is in search of alternatives to the philosophical tradition established by Descartes' insistence on confronting and conquering the sceptic. Here he turns to Emerson's resistance to Descartes, which is based on the realization that in accepting the demand for certainty we bind ourselves to a dualistic framework where the very acts of the *cogito* that guarantee the existence of the 'I' separate it from the things of the world. If I exist only when I think, then my mode of existence is at best a way of haunting the world rather than sharing its mode of presence (which does not involve thinking). And conversely if one bases one's certainties on extensionalist criteria derived from that world, one will find self-consciousness banished to those same margins. But once one becomes aware of those traps one is in a position to reformulate the grammar of the 'I am' in terms of saying rather than thinking: 'I am a being who to exist must say I exist, or must acknowledge my existence – claim it, stake it, enact it'.[14] Now the '*sum*' is a matter of qualities, not thinking substance, since the saying defines a particular hold on what otherwise is only an unyielding otherness.

There are substantial risks in this model of value, since the only real existence one can claim for the self takes place in those moments of enactment, and since the problematic relation of such assertions to the securities of 'character' and history virtually invite ironic redescription of the agent's enthusiasms. Yet it is just these risks that make it possible for individuals fully to engage themselves in what Cavell calls the 'contest of inheritance' which measures our claims to become true authors of our-selves.[15] Style then is not primarily a matter of expressing emotional states. Its function is to ground such states, to anchor the self as value creator in a world that otherwise dismisses us as irrelevant or 'de trop'. It is no accident that a philosophical tradition critical of these enactments as lacking the substantial and repeatable presence on which extensional structures are built and tested itself must lack an adequate theory of value. To paraphrase Wittgenstein, that tradition is condemned to collapse style into technique and thus to dwell in a world where 'spirit plays no part'.[16]

I fear, however, that Cavell's version of spirit is severely limited by the Romantic tradition which he uses to exemplify it. Cavell's model of expression postulates agents torn between the effort to assert their authentic subjective claims on the real and the constant melodrama of watching those assertions decompose before the sceptical third-person perspective. Style remains performance, and it thus enters the endless regress of producing states that can never be recuperated except in further performances ad nauseam. What else could be born of such a union between the all too American Emerson, for whom staking is always a matter of asserted individuality, and the all too German Heidegger, for whom the claim to presence always involves a quasi-theological vocabulary about 'being' which serves to displace the specific terms of the expressive activity? There is perhaps no worse philosophical marriage, since Emersonian individualism enables one to borrow Heidegger's language of presence while escaping the theological echoes that trap it in quiescent contemplative states – Heidegger's 'self-blossoming emergence' now applies literally to selves as both subjects and objects of the clearing which the staking creates. Yet this way of escaping theology seems to me to retain its most problematic features because the individual then assumes all the responsibilities once attributed to God, while finding himself so caught in the limitations of time and mediated language that his demands for presence risk appearing little more than a useless passion.

If we are to escape that melodramatic theatre, we need a model of this affirmative saying less bound to the Cartesian antinomies of self and world. That, I think, is what we find in Wittgenstein, the modern thinker whose early work most fully spells out the problems of handling values within Cartesian epistemology and whose *Philosophical Investigations*[17] offers a much more complex and elegantly restrained picture of expressive agency. Saul Kripke neatly captures the relevant transformation of the Cartesian ghost condemned to haunting the world it desires:

Thus the first person pronoun, for Wittgenstein, is to be assimilated neither to a name nor to a definite description referring to any particular person or other entity. In the *Tractatus*, Wittgenstein bases his account of the self on the Hume – Lichtenberg thought experiment, arriving at his conception of the subject as a rather mysterious 'limit of the world,' which 'does not belong to the world' and 'shrinks to an extensionless point' (5.632, 5.64). In the *Investigations*, the special character of the self, as something not to be identified with any entity picked out in any ordinary manner, survives, but it is thought of as deriving from a 'grammatical' peculiarity of the first person pronoun, not from any special metaphysical mystery.[18]

We cannot fix that self in a name because, as is the case with logic itself, every effort to name it presupposes it. So the self can only be shown, not said: we name the world; we reveal the self. And because such revelations have no place within what language allows us to describe, the world and the self are each confined to its own domain – the one of fact, the other of values. The two worlds converge, but only at the extensionless point where 'solipsism coincides with pure realism' (*Tractatos* 5.64). Even there no empirical constraints will determine whether the subject is happy or unhappy (see 6.41; 6.422, 6.43): 'What brings the self [*Ich*] into philosophy is the fact that the world is my world' (5.641), and that possession is precisely what one cannot express within an empiricist model of language.

In this model the world can be my world without the elaborate performative struggle that proves to be irony's pander. For instead of relying on Cavell's specific enactments, the terms for the world being my world can now be found in the far less melodramatic domain of how one manipulates the grammatical relations which bind language and world. In that context individual performance proves only one component of a more complex expressive process for enacting the distinctively human component of existence. Or so one can claim if one can show that Kripke is wrong in reducing the later Wittgenstein's 'I' to a 'grammatical' peculiarity of the first-person pronoun'. I shall argue instead that the relevant grammar involves an intricate set of relations among terms which allow a range of expressive roles.

The result is not a demystifying of the 'I' but a sense of the grammatical connectives that can give it force and significance without requiring the specular theatre invoked by Emersonian performance. For we can capture much of that play of investment if we focus upon the ways in which the grammar of the first person is woven into the equally complex grammar of the 'as' – our culture's fundamental measure of the stakes intentionality brings to the world described by extensional theory. It is this conjunction,

I submit, which provides the context we need for a full accounting of what style involves and the values which it enables. By tracing some of Wittgenstein's most suggestive passages on the subject I think we shall see how the subjective and objective poles of expression theory are compatible aspects of the agency we attribute to style, how a concern for style allows us to recuperate the values which Cavell describes while aligning them with more fluid and less self-consuming models of agency, and how we can locate plausible grounds for explaining the cognitive and effective roles which stylistic performances afford cultural life. We may even be able to show how a demystified sense of mystery may itself be woven into some of our cultural practices.

My first passage from Wittgenstein does not refer explicitly to style. It does, though, make it clear how the marginal self of the *Tractatus* can enact an existence without risking Emersonian melodrama or Heideggerean effusiveness:

> Let us imagine someone doing work that involves comparison, trial, choice. Say he is constructing an appliance out of various bits of stuff with a given set of tools. Every now and then there is the problem 'Should I use this bit?' The bit is rejected, another is tried . . . He looks for one that fits, etc. . . . If the worker can talk – would it be a falsification of what actually goes on if he were to describe that precisely and were to say, e.g. 'Then I thought: no, that won't do, I must try it another way' . . . I want to say: May he not later give his wordless thoughts in words? And in such a fashion that we, who might see the work in progress, could accept this account? – And all the more, if we had often watched the man working, not just once? . . .
>
> Of course we cannot separate his thinking from his activity. For the thinking is not an accompaniment of the work, any more than of thoughtful speech . . .
>
> Concern with what we say has its own specific signs. It also has its own specific consequences and preconditions. Concern is not something experienced; we attribute it to ourselves, not on grounds of observation. It is not an accompaniment of what we say . . .
>
> We might say: in all cases what one means by 'thought' is what is alive in the sentence. That without which it is dead, a mere sequence of sounds or written shapes.[19]

The extended sequence from which I have quoted allows so many Wittgensteinian themes to converge that it is difficult to say quite what he intends as the main point, especially since he continually worries that he has opened up a host of temptations.[20] None the less it seems clear that at the least he wants to call our attention to an aspect of care or concerned engagement which may provide a fundamental sense of what then can take a variety of expressive forms. Concern with what we say provides a concrete measure of thinking, and thinking takes concrete reflexive form in the capacity of the language to assume a purposiveness that cannot be translated back into biographical accounts of the subject. At times such thinking simply merges with the possibility of the object of thinking assuming a certain kind of life. At others it leads back to the how the agent is defining herself, but with a sense that the process itself is crucial to any attributions we might be able to make about what the person expresses. By foregrounding a certain kind of care within the thinking (or, in other cases, by revealing the dominant force of convention), style calls attention to degrees and modes of engagement which are too intimately connected to its context to be attributed to abstractions like self.

For Wittgenstein those biographical stories can at best tell us what purposes might accompany thought. They do not see how style gets woven into the thinking itself, so that 'Writing in the right style is setting the carriage straight on the rails'.[21] There are no criteria for recognizing or judging how style contours itself to go on those rails, there are only judgements about whether or not the specific signs of care define a path of thinking which can engage attention at the time and can suggest to others that the path promises them a distinctive way of either relating to the agent or of adapting themselves to similar materials. By revealing what is alive in the sentence, style – the thinking that takes place within and upon the constructive activity – brings those paths before reflection. Style invites us to see how worlds are made of the world, how a relatively uniform surface becomes infinitely contoured in accord with emotional investments which we trivialize by imposing a subjective psychology upon them.

Wittgenstein thus walks a very narrow line. He wants to call our attention to how the agent can be absorbed within the conditions of thinking that may derive either from traditional practices or from a particular way of engaging a situation while also allowing room for our seeing the subject as defining certain aspects of herself in this process. Establishing those possibilities then requires Wittgenstein to suggest an alternative to those models of subjective expression which too readily rely on standard concepts of emotions or are content with the self-interpretations we give of our psychic lives. There must be careful distinctions between levels of expressive agency:

'Le style c'est l'homme', 'Le'style c'est l'homme même'. The first expression has cheap epigrammatic brevity. The second, correct version opens up quite a different perspective. It says that a man's style is a picture [*Bild*] of him.[22]

That '*même*' becomes a remarkably rich semantic operator. Through it one can tease out the basic differences between style as a deliberate self-presentation and style as central to the structure of internal relations that define a person's basic investments in certain aspects of experience. In the former case it suffices to engage stylistic expression on the level of theatrical presence, the domain where selves project, audiences interpret and standard emotional predicates prevail. But the reflective '*même*' and the use of '*Bild*' rather than '*Vorstellung*' suggest a more intimate and less deliberately controlled dimension of style, as if there the person revealed mental energies as woven into his sense of the world as are his physical actions. Here interpretation will not suffice. We are not dealing with roles or even with 'contests of inheritance'. Such categories are far too public. Here style marks irreducibly concrete differences which no interpretive psychological categories can bridge. The only appropriate response is to register the differences and adjust our own emotional register to accommodate the particular mode of being that they define.

In order to appreciate how this sense of '*l'homme même*' establishes a model of particular expressive energies connecting art to life, we need to turn now to Wittgenstein's longest meditation explicitly on style. The discussion begins by confronting a pressing example of the sense of difference which style can impose – Wittgenstein's own discomfort before Shakespeare and his resulting difficulty in believing the praise others give. While he can accept 'the authority of a Milton', he suspects that most praise of Shakespeare is merely 'the conventional thing to do', even though 'I have to tell myself that is not how it is'. Then as he tries to make sense of his discomfort he begins to see what it would take to adjust himself to everything Shakespeare represents:

Shakespeare's similes are, *in the ordinary sense*, bad. So if they are all the same good – and I don't know whether they are or not – they must be a law to themselves . . .

It may be that the essential thing with Shakespeare is his ease and authority and that you just have to accept him as he is if you are going to be able to admire him properly, in the way that you accept nature, a piece of scenery for example, just as it is.

If I am right about this, that would mean that the style of his whole work, I mean of all his works taken together, is the essential thing and what provides his justification.

My failure to understand him could then be explained by my inability to read him easily. That is, as one views a splendid piece of scenery.

A man can see what he has but not what he is. What he is can be compared to his height above sea-level, which you cannot for the most part judge without more ado. And the greatness or triviality of a piece of work depends on where the man who made it was standing . . .

But you can equally say: a man will never be great if he misjudges himself: if he throws dust in his own eyes. How small a thought it takes to fill someone's whole life!

Just as a man can spend his life travelling around the same little country and think there is nothing outside it . . .

The country that you keep travelling round strikes you as enormously big; the surrounding countries all look like narrow border regions.

If you want to go down deep you do not need to travel far; indeed, you don't have to leave your most immediate and familiar surroundings.[23]

There are few passages about style that are themselves so insistent on the irreducible individuality of the speaking voice while teasing from it insights that make us reconsider familiar subjects.[24] Yet there are also few passages that do as good a job of clarifying the fundamental relationships between the grammar of the first-person elicited by stylistic expression and the grammar of the 'as' enabling us to speak of that first-person experience as making disclosures significant for a larger public. Therefore I shall try to draw out the implicit connectives between what we might call the 'as' of expressive intentionality and the 'as' of possible audience identification, then I shall try to elaborate the theoretical framework which I think is necessary for locating the imaginative forces which constitute those elaborate yet simple operations. Here Wittgenstein is fascinated with Shakespeare because of the challenge posed by his refusal to abide decorously within the shared grammar of period and genre styles. Because the writer's world then relies on a different structure of values, one cannot respond simply to its isolated parts. One must grasp the work as a whole, locating through the internal relations among the parts of his oeuvre something like its constitutive laws (or what Kant called 'purposiveness'). Those laws are not primarily the expression of a psychological being – if they were they would be a lot easier to assimilate since they would participate in a shared grammar. The laws go deeper, providing the conditions which make the work a distinctive entity in a cultural landscape and requiring us to supplement interpretation by the more difficult task of imagining how we might eventually use its differences as familiar and negotiable aspects of that scene.

Wittgenstein's ensuing observations spin out several paths for using his own landscape metaphors. If one must accept a Shakespeare *as* he is, how do we come to understand what he is? The first step is to recognize the difference between what he has and what he is, primarily because that effort will lead us to appreciate the degree to which the relevant identity involves getting beyond psychological predicates to complicated triangulations enabling us to make judgements about 'where the man who made it was standing'. Style involves places more than it does our typical substance terms for persons, for it is only by the active engagement which defines the site of thinking that style comes to our attention. Therefore attributions of personality of self-regarding performance do not so much constitute the content as emerge from repeated experience of how those marks of thinking are manifest. By attributing personal agency we paradoxically frame those modes of thinking as situated practices which we can then attempt to give a role in our own lives. That is why Wittgenstein can close his remarks by shifting to evaluative criteria. The author must not misjudge himself. He must come to terms with the fact that the expressive agent is necessarily a solipsist – he works within his own laws, exploring the parameters of how his own travelling around the same little country contributes to his happiness or unhappiness. Yet that solipsist can also be a realist, precisely because one need not travel far to go down deep. The depth with which one engages one's own familiar surroundings establishes them as part of the landscape which others too inhabit, and it then creates a complex play of defamiliarization and recovering the terms of belonging as others try to accommodate themselves to that altered landscape. The power of style is its capacity to elicit the forms of engagement which make one take a fresh look at one's own little country as it can be related to its surroundings.

III

Wittgenstein's remarks do not propose a theory of style. They are content to characterize its salient features in a manner that renders them at once familiar and uncannily challenging to our models of expression and understanding. Instead of the psychological subject we encounter this irreducible otherness, and instead of subsuming that otherness under some universalizing model of knowledge he leaves us with perplexing processes of adjustment. But what do we do once we have recognized the nature of those phenomena and even reconciled ourselves to the probability that these phenomena are too complex and fluid to allow fixed definitions or causal explanations? Can we then still postulate broader speculative contexts which help clarify how such conjunctions are conceivable, what needs they satisfy and what social practices they complement or foster? I think we can use Wittgenstein for this purpose, provided that we bracket our speculations as merely useful instruments for drawing imaginative links among particular features of experience.

Engaging Wittgenstein for such work requires first setting his thinking in the more general conceptual framework provided by Spinoza, another displaced Jewish philosopher intent on opposing Cartesian categories and the subordination of individuals to universals. Yet for Spinoza individuation is not a matter to be derived in psychological terms. One understands the nature of expressive individuals by imagining the roles they play in the overall scheme of being. For there to be such a scheme there must be God. For God to have existence he must be substance. For there to be only one God there must be only one substance (just as if there is only one notion of truth there must be only an extensional language able to grasp that substance). But that divine unity must encompass difference, so it is necessary to divide substance into an indwelling cause and a set of modes, which become 'the affections of substance'[25] and thus offer God the being. The richest manifestation of this modal being is the one offered by humans expressing those affections which define their individual beings. Each individual has a *conatus* inseparable from the passions that drive it to take in as much of being as it can and bring that being to the perfection possible as the realization of individuality. Such passions do not allow categorical judgements: *conatus* is what *conatus* does. And what *conatus* does is establish modal colourings of substance. These colouring then can be said to express two different types of force. At one pole they reveal what is passive or determined about the individual being that gives its expression a particular historical and psychological content. At the other pole these expressions are 'active' in the sense that they manifest the agent's capacity to pursue its own perfection while reflecting on the specific qualities of its own distinguishing activity. The passive contents cannot be shared, so to the extent that such emotions dominate there can be no stable feelings of sociality. But if the agent reflects on those active emotions, she can see that everyone shares the effort to foster individual states and must therefore base the individual pursuit of freedom on an understanding of 'the life and the good of the community'.[26] Modes must acknowledge the conditions that make their differences intelligible and significant.

Such claims reveal too much history to have much truth value. Yet they do define a picture of certain elements of behaviour and their possible conjunction which can be quite useful for clarifying the stakes in Wittgenstein's very different way of negotiating the familiar. Spinoza's modal conception of expressive agency suggests an important distinction between conceiving individuals as defined by certain contents (like memories or obsessions) and imagining individuation as consisting primarily in 'how' connections are proposed and tested.[27] I am not sure how to make specific proposals elaborating that difference, but at the least one can say that the modal view makes it possible to imagine personal intensities which are expressed by how they engage a public world rather than by how they displace it into repetitive figures which we must then decode. Because the modal presence is a way of being within that social world, one can imagine its expressive energies assuming a wide range of stances – from the imposition of its own laws to the effort to fuse itself within an exemplifying figure like Pope's. And because the modal operations are often open to view, we can imagine other persons not merely interpreting what makes someone different but also managing to treat the mode as part of the speculative instrumentation they adapt to pursuing their own expressive needs.

This is where the grammar of 'as' comes in. There is no more basic way to cast the modalities of 'how' than in terms of the forms of 'asness' that they make available, and there is no better contemporary way to capture the elemental abstractness of Spinoza's ontology than to replace an emphasis on causal explanations for individual actions by Wittgenstein's grammatical concern for the complex psychology embedded in our ways of using language. We have already seen the 'as' central to Wittgenstein's descriptions of style. Now we need to understand how his related meditation on 'seeing as' as the basis for a new approach to the foundations of pyschology[28] provides a basis for understanding the range of motives that style can carry, and thus the modes of agency that it can make visible.

The 'as' clearly fascinates Wittgenstein because it combines a version of transparency with the irreducible presence of a modal force. The phrase 'seeing as', for example, is closely related to the language of perception – it involves an object which is open to public scrutiny – but its terms cannot be reduced to the extensional measures we invoke when we are dealing with direct perceptions. The 'as' creates conditions 'like seeing and again not like' (*Investigations*, p. 197), so we are tempted to questions like this one: 'Is this a case of both seeing and thinking? or an amalgam of the two, as I should like almost to say? The question is: why does one want to say this?' (p. 197). For Wittgenstein there is no one answer; there is only a cataloguing of temptations and their possible implications for our understanding of the relations between seeing and thinking. Let us therefore try a catalogue of our own culled from section IIxi of the *Investigations* with an eye to those passages which are most suggestive about the role style can play as a dimension of our uses of 'as':

1 'Now I am seeing this', I might say (pointing to another picture, for example). This has the form of a report of a new perception.

The expression of a change of aspect is the expression of a *new* perception and at the same time of the perception's being unchanged. (p. 196)

2 'And is it really a different impression?' In order to answer this I should like to ask myself whether there is really something different there in me. But how can I find out? – I describe what I am seeing differently. (p. 202)

3 Here it occurs to me that in conversation on aesthetic matters we use the words: 'You have to see it like *this*, this is how it is meant'; When you see it like *this* you see where it goes wrong . . . (p. 202)

4 I have a theme played to me several times and each time in a slower tempo. In the end I say '*Now* it's right', or '*Now* at last, it's a march, '*Now* at last it's a dance'. The same tone of voice expresses the dawning of an aspect. (p. 206).

5 One might say of someone that he was blind to the *expression* of a face. Would his eyesight on that account be defective? . . . (p. 210)

6 I can imagine some arbitrary cipher . . . And I can see it in various

aspects according to the fiction I surround it with. And here there is
close kinship with 'experiencing the meaning of a word'. (p. 210)

7 The colour of the visual impression corresponds to the colour of the
object (this blotting paper looks pink to me, and is pink) – the shape
of the visual impression to the shape of the object . . . – but what I
perceive in the dawning of an aspect is not a property of the object,
but an internal relation between it and other objects.

It is almost as if 'seeing the sign in this context' were an echo of a
thought. 'The echo of a thought in sight' – one would like to say.
(p. 212)

8 The 'aspect blind' will have an altogether different relation to pictures
from ours . . . Aspect-blindness will be akin to lack of a 'musical ear'.

The importance of this concept lies in the connexion between the
concepts of 'seeing an aspect' and 'experiencing the meaning of a
word'. For we want to ask 'What would you be missing if you did not
experience the meaning of a word?' (p. 214)

9 The language-game 'I mean (or meant) *this*' (subsequent explanation
of a word) is quite different from this one: 'I thought of . . . as I said
it'. The latter is akin to 'It reminded me of . . .'. (p. 217)

10 I can know what someone else is thinking, not what I am thinking. It
is correct to say 'I know what you are thinking', and wrong to say 'I
know what I am thinking'. (A whole cloud of philosophy condensed
into a drop of grammar.) (p. 222)

Perhaps the most striking refrain in this catalogue is the concern for
what 'seeing as' does to our sense of objects. In many respects the object
remains accessible for all to see – for example in the form of a duck or
even in the form of a duck–rabbit, or in the form of a Hamlet-picture and
of a picture of Hamlet (to invoke Goodman's paradigm for the difference
between an art-object and its referent). Yet something changes radically
as we reflect on the ways that our own intentional processes alter contexts
and imports. If one were to condense this philosophical cloud into a drop
of grammar, one would drop all mentalist talk in order to let the burden of
the case rest simply on the distinctive senses Wittgenstein brings out for
the 'now', the 'this' and the implicit 'then'. When we invoke the appropriate sense of 'as' we expect the object of perception to be regarded in
terms of supplementary contexts – both those brought by the agent (the
'now I see this') and those which Wittgenstein suggests involve internal
relations to other objects (which I take to mean relations that we come to
realize are always possible if the object is seen a certain way). This simple
shift in perspective then has the remarkable effect of casting new light on
aesthetic experience as a domain that thrives on the capacity of certain
versions of the 'now' and the 'this' to elicit a complex drama of discovery
and consequences. Seen like this certain musical figures come to play
significant roles in an entire piece, or understood in this context the entire

piece takes on extraordinarily resonant historical or thematic connections to other works. And yet the proliferation of connections can remain anchored in a specific and shareable picture. In fact the most radical efforts of a Monet to treat the 'now' and the 'this' as literal referential forces within art were precisely the experiments that most defined for the culture how the 'now and the 'this' could refer to the stylistic signature within the picture treated as a one place predicate. The way of rendering the here and now defines a highly individual style.

To be compatible with the referential role of a sign, however, is by no means to be exhausted by that effect. Thus Wittgenstein finds himself forced to ask where the supplementary force of that 'now' and that 'this' comes from and what is it that we see people missing when they are blind to the meaning of a word or to the dimension in which nuances of words elicit the sense of sudden discovery. Such questions are the stuff bad philosophy is made on because they tempt one to try to ask whether there is something different there in me. Yet the questions will not go away. And for good reason. They lead us back to the difference that the 'I' of the *Tractatus* made by its rendering the world of the realist a 'happy or an unhappy one': because it manifests the irreducible modal presence of an intentionality our processing of the world involves considerably more than the mechanisms produced by behaviourism or the screens flaunted by Baudrillard.[29]

Noticing the force of that intentionality need not lead us back to Hegelian meditations on 'Geist', but it does elicit at least two important consequences with regard to the forms of expressiveness that style foregrounds. We are led to appreciate how radically the phenomenology of 'I mean . . .' differs from the phenomenology of 'this reminded me of . . .'. Where the latter requires only an associational psychology, the former involves something like internal relations between intentions and expressions. We read persons through the signs of how they present the 'now' and the 'this'. Yet the 'now' and the 'this' have no distinct content and cannot be understood by introspection. Such terms are modal in Spinoza's sense: they provide an individual presence simply in how they arrange what is open to sight. And while that presence cannot itself be located through empiricist methodology, we can recognize its working by the simple gesture of reflecting on how the 'now' and the 'this' would be lost to aspect-blindness. Therefore, even without locating a distinctive entity for the self, we can speak of a specific mode of attending and caring which makes visible persons' investments in their expressive activity. This, one might say, is what leads us to surround an expression with fictional contexts – we postulate selves in terms of what will enable us to provide motives for the expressive modality of an utterance. Yet because the provocation to such contexts remains among the public features of the language, the entire analogical process is in principle recuperable by others *as* constituents for their own particular uses.

IV

Why then is it wrong to say 'I know what I am thinking' but correct to say 'I know what you are thinking'? Is not the major point of our culture's concern with style and expression the possibility of agents coming to know themselves as distinct beings? I have so far ignored this last item of my catalogue. But now we need to take it up at some length because the questions that the passage raises provide the terms we need to speculate on the ontology of style, the basic motives for expressive activity and its possible significance in public life. For the ultimate significance of attending to style is its demonstrating all that we lose when we let our attention to language narrow to the third person functions that are necessary for us to make knowledge claims. And since no one is more useful at clarifying those stakes than Kripke, I shall return to his description of how Wittgenstein's *Investigations* dissolves the mysterious indefinable subject postulated by his *Tractatus* into the complex grammar of first, second and third person terms, in the hope that I can show how they lead in somewhat different directions from those Kripke intends.

Wittgenstein can distinguish knowing what you are thinking from knowing what I am thinking because only the first statement takes part in a cogent set of grammatical practices. I can know what you are thinking because in such cases I have the criteria necessary to speak about knowledge: I have a clear sense of the person as an extensional entity and I can easily pick out the descriptive terms so that they can be checked against some set of intersubjective norms for 'truth'. Referring to the 'I' is a very different matter. As Wittgenstein elaborated in the *Tractatus*, there can be no way to refer to the 'I' as an entity because it always appears as a limit of the world, not as a fact within it. The *Investigations* has very different priorities, but that same difference pervades the uses we can give to the first person pronoun and those that attach to other pronoun positions:

> If one has to imagine someone else's pain on the model of one's own, this is none too easy a thing to do, for I have to imagine pain which I *do not feel* on the model of the pain which I *do feel*. That is, what I have to do is not simply to make a transition in imagination from one place of pain to another. As from pain in the hand to the arm. For I am not to imagine that I feel pain in some region of his body. (para. 302)

This is not to deny that one can know what the other is thinking when the other says 'I am in pain'. It is to deny that one can acquire such knowledge by referring to one's own pain. What we 'know' is that I exhibit pain behaviours which satisfy the same criteria we use when we think 'he is in pain'. There cannot be a private language because any knowledge which we formulate in language cannot be based on either an agent's introspective states or some veridical images that he knows without the mediation of public practices. Knowledge depends on reading manifest signs in accord with those practices.

But criteria for knowledge are not the limits of our experience or our interests – to this degree Wittgenstein remains Kantian. In fact the effort to understand why public criteria are needed elicits marvellous imaginative ways of suggesting what may be involved in those first-person relations to pain. Why is it that a first person sense of the other's pain would take the form of imagining my feeling pain in his body? Kripke's answer to this question proves extremely useful for speculating on what a modal view of style enables us to see, if not to say. If we wish to elaborate what it means to share a first-person sense of pain, Kripke suggests that we follow with the corollary question why it is more difficult to imagine pain which I do not feel on the model of pain which I do feel than to imagine 'ducks which are not in Central Park on the model of the ducks which [I do see there]'.[30] Put crudely, the difference is that in the case of the ducks both sets of objects are treated in third person terms where we can have distinct criteria for our attributions. But when the first person is at stake it is extremely difficult to separate the subject from the object. Because we cannot locate the 'I' within the world of objects, we cannot separate it from the pain which we want to attribute to the other. Similarly, our inability to locate the 'I' creates serious problems in interpreting what 'having' means for an 'I' in pain. Does one have pain as one has a job or two cars? No wonder that I can only know what 'you' are feeling. For so long as we dwell in first-person terms the appropriate sense of pain appears inseparable from the subject who experiences it. As Kripke puts it, for the first person 'there is no distinction between imagining a pain and imagining my having a pain. To imagine that I am in pain, I do not have to imagine that my pain is connected to anything else',[31] just as for Jones to say he was hungry 'does not mean "Jones said that Jones was hungry", for Jones need not realize that he is Jones'.[32] The first person avows hunger or pain. There is no question of criteria that one refers to in order to check on one's attribution, so there is no question of knowledge. Insofar as we do heed the cry of pain we do so because we have a history of interpreting and responding to such expressions. Simply as behavioural traits seen from a third-person perspective they tell us something about persons and allow us to test our interpretations as we do with any other attribution where we can fix the appropriate conditions. The more indefinable the 'I' the more appealing such strategies are for maintaining a public order.

When we respond to the cry as a cry of pain, then, we ignore any qualities specific to the avowal which would not be relevant to the third-person behavioural signs to which we have learned to respond. There is no place in this language-game for the marks of intentionality that the 'now' and the 'this' confer. But suppose that the first person wants to foreground the 'now' and the 'this' of the avowal – either because she is interested in distinctive qualities of her sense of the pain or because the process of crying defines for her some basic psychological investments that mark it as distinctively her pain. (An observer could also decide to foreground those individual traits, whatever the agent's intentions.) Then we cannot go directly to our practices for dealing with pain behaviour (although we might eventually decide that they are appropriate, but perhaps for a different kind of pain). Instead we find ourselves observing a certain modal conjunction taking public form. While we cannot talk about the 'I's pain *per se*, we can treat the conjunction of the how and the what of language as giving the expression a state analogous to the ontology of the relation between the 'I' and its pain. The object is inseparable from its avowal, so that there is an irreducible intimacy between the intentional agency and the object. But now the purpose is to cast that conjunction within language where it has at least a potential for third-person uses. We cannot know how the 'I' has its pain, but we can observe the way in which the language casts its particular 'now' and 'this' because the terms of the intimacy become manifest in a framework that invites complex adjustments within our interpretive framework. Foregrounding the 'how' invites the grammar of 'as'.

The test of such public qualities is the range of third-person uses which one can then give to the modal intentionality which the language establishes. One could turn back to see how this specific expression relates to other avowals or habits of avowal which the agent offers; one can read the avowal within a typology of emotive expressions; and one can concentrate on the ways in which the formulation defines a specific possibility for language to articulate some possible experience for an audience. In the first case one reads the person's engagement as expressing a distinctive affective state, in the second as typifying some possible emotional configuration, and in the third as raising speculative frameworks about how the formulations we can give to our states are capable of affecting changes in the way other people imagine themselves as agents. All those uses are public, but they all depend on taking the expression itself as a distinctive modal rendering of the world. Therefore if we are not to leave in philosophical limbo all those Wittgensteinian observations about the energies that go into certain expressions and the strange laws they fold in as they use public language to compose new landscapes, we must focus on those aspects of our cultural practices which allow us to trace the range of modal colourings which an indefinable 'I' manages to compose.

Where style is concerned there are not selves and worlds, nor even first and third persons, but rather endless modes for weaving the two together *as* certain ways of experiencing states like pain so that these too become features of the grammar which culture propagates. And having arrived conceptually at this possibility, we can begin to let clouds of philosophy

condense into lines of poetry like these from section XII of Wallace
Stevens' 'Ordinary Evening in New Haven':[33]

> The poem is the cry of its occasion
> Part of the res itself and not about it.
> The poet speaks the poem as it is,
>
> Not as it was: part of the reverberation
> Of the windy night as it is, when the marble statues
> are like newspapers blown by the wind . . . He speaks
> By sight and insight as they are. . . .

Here three basic dimensions of the 'as' define the powers style offers for
enacting and staking our existence. First, the 'as' enables one to distinguish the cry of the occasion from whatever 'was' the case. The equational
or modal force of the 'as' allows us to read descriptions as avowals or
direct expressions. Second, the 'as' defines a modal relation to substance
because it sets up a series of equivalents defining what the windy night is.
The night becomes inseparable from the reverberations that flesh out a
scene where statues can be cast as 'newspapers blown by the wind'.
Finally, the 'as' creates a very complex equation between literal and
figurative exemplification enabling us to flesh out what a modal subject
might be. On the level of substance, the poem makes it clear that in the
place of any single abstract notion of evening we must take our evenings in
accord with the modes of existence created for them by the specific con-
figurations of sight and insight that compose them. In this respect our
engagement in the evening has a great deal in common with the ways we
inhabit our pain or our hunger, as they are. Yet in so arranging the scene,
sight and insight also take on a kind of substance in their own right – we
know the qualities of sight and insight only because of the ways that the
thinking pervades the rendering of the occasion. In art and in life, what is
alive in the sentence defines the modes of intentionality which
idiosyncratic occasions make visible in and as human existence.

NOTES

1 Berel Lang, *The Concept of Style*, rev. edn (Ithaca, NY and London, Cornell
University Press, 1987).
2 For de Man see 'Semiology of Rhetoric', and his essays on Nietzsche in his
Allegories of Reading (New Haven, Conn., Yale, 1979). His influence
obviously derives in part from the general interest in deconstructive themes
that pervades even the new historicism in literary studies, but it also derives
from a largely unchallenged Nietzschean sense of human agency which de
Man shares with decidedly non-deconstructionist work on style, such as
Stanley Fish, 'What is Stylistics and Why are They Saying Such Terrible
Things About It?', in his *Is There a Text in This Class?* (Cambridge, Mass.,

Harvard University Press, 1980), pp. 68–96. In other words, notions of agency will enter our discussion of style even if we do not argue them directly – which is all the more reason to produce the necessary speculative discussions. Moreover, the question of agency makes it important that even if we cannot have one theoretical account of what in general counts as stylistic features, we still indicate the range of motives style can carry. The most promising work I know responsive to this imperative is Ruquaiya Hasan's 'Rime and Reason in Literature', in Seymour Chatman (ed.), *Literary Style: A Symposium* (New York, Oxford University Press, 1971), pp. 229–326 which bases a semantics of style on the understanding of intentions. Unfortunately, deciding what intention is turns out to depend on what we take the basic elements of style to be, since several possible features of style clearly imply choices which authors do not and often cannot bring to consciousness. So I think we do better simply to admit that all this circularity and indeterminacy are themselves significant for what they indicate about the complexities of expressive behaviour: different emphases will be required for different versions of that behaviour.

3   Nelson Goodman, 'The Status of Style', in *Ways of Worldmaking* (Indianapolis, Hackett Publishing, 1978).

4   Ibid., pp. 24–33.

5   Ibid., p. 34.

6   Ibid., p. 35.

7   All these problems have their clearest manifestation in the concluding sentences of Goodman's essay: 'The less accessible a style is to our approach and the more adjustment we are forced to make, the more insight we gain and the more our powers of discovery are developed. The discernment of style is an integral aspect of the understanding of works of art and the worlds they present.' (p. 40). I think it is no accident that these closing remarks are so uncharacteristically pious and sloppy, especially when compared to the concise and elegant passage I quoted earlier. For as he tries to summarize the values at stake in his discussion, Goodman must pay the price of having forbidden himself any direct cognitive or emotional claims for the power of style. Thus he has little choice but to rely on an extensional standard like the practical measure of the effort style forces us to expend. Unfortunately that is a vapid standard unless it is connected to the quality of the effort: Euphues becomes a greater writer than Dante; and the more remote a work is by virtue of either temporal distance or experimental refusals of conventions the richer its cognitive effects on us. This ignores the obvious fact that most critical claims about art concern themselves with much more semantically resonant features, and it leaves no room for the crucial concern, often exemplified by Goodman, that the artist develop a style whose force is its directness and theatricalized lucidity.

For a more general treatment of the limitations in Goodman's extensionalist views of art and the need for a concept of what I call 'expressive implicature' see my *Act and Quality* (Amherst, University of Massachusetts Press, 1981), where I wish I had the benefit of Arthur Danto's *The Transfiguration of the Commonplace* (Cambridge, Mass., Harvard University Press, 1981), with its subtle and compelling demonstrations of the roles the intensional must play in our appreciation of art and of life. (Yet Danto,

p. 163, makes a similar error in assuming that style is always 'invisible' to those who actually rely on the way of seeing that it encodes, for this is certainly not the case with artists like Joyce or Wilde or even Parmigianino and Sidney.) I also want to express my indebtedness to Miles Rind's fine unpublished critique of Goodman on style and Leonard Meyer's eloquent page on the need to supplement the recognition of style with explanatory terms in his 'Towards a Theory of Style' in Lang (ed.), *The Concept of Style*, p. 27.

8   Three good examples of the new expressivist approach are the last chapter in Danto's book, Richard Wollheim, 'Pictorial Style:' Two Views', in Lang (ed.), *The Concept of Style*, pp. 183–202, and the Jenefer M. Robinson essay, 'Style and Personality in the Literary Work', *The Philosophical Review*, 94 (1985), 227–47, which I shall discuss. I should also mention again Ruquaiya Hasan, 'Rime and Reason in Literature', because this essay offers a good linguistic case equating style with rhetorical rather than expressive intention. However her approach cannot handle the presence of stylistic features which are not under the author's reflexive rhetorical control.

9   Robinson, 'Style and Personality', p. 231.

10 Berel Lang, 'Space, Time and Philosophical Style', in *The Concept of Style*, p. 160.

11 For related work on the rhetorical aspects of philosophical style and the difficulty of deciding quite whether these are psychologically expressive, see John Richetti, *Philosophical Writing: Locke, Berkeley, Hume*. (Cambridge, Mass., Harvard University Press, 1983).

12 Michael Fried, 'Art and Objecthood', *Art Forum* (summer, 1967), pp. 12–23.

13 Stanley Cavell, 'Being Odd, Getting Even', in Thomas Heller et al. (eds), *Reconstructing Individualism: Autonomy, Individuality and the Self*, (Palo Alto, Ca, Stanford University Press, 1986).

14 Ibid., p. 282.

15 Ibid., p. 307.

16 Ludwig Wittgenstein, *Culture and Value*, Trans. Peter Winch (Chicago, University of Chicago Press, 1980), p. 3.

17 Ludwig Wittgenstein, *Philosophical Investigations*, trans. G. E. M. Anscombe (Oxford, Basil Blackwell, 1958). See also his *Tractatus Logico-Philosophicus*, trans D. F. Pears and B. F. McGuinness (London, Routledge and Kegan Paul, 1961) discussed below.

18 Saul Kripke, *Wittgenstein on Rules and Private Language* (Cambridge, Mass., Harvard University Press, 1982), pp. 144–5.

19 Ludwig Wittgenstein, *Zettel* (Oxford, Basil Blackwell, 1967) pp. 19–26.

20 This scrupulous sense of possible temptations is intended to dispel the desire to see oneself as winning from the secular certain continuing possibilities for spiritual edification. Yet in that process Wittgenstein remains obsessed with an interest in something very close to 'metaphysical mystery'. The penultimate passage quoted above leads into a speculation on 'Why should something impalpable be more mysterious than something palpable? Unless it is because we want to catch hold of it.' This could be either a realization that the desire elicited by thinking itself becomes a force within empirical existence or another effort of the philosopher to ward off the metaphysician by reducing mystery to the terms of a method of inquiry. But I find it hard not to be drawn

toward the first alternative when the last quoted passage modulates into the reflection that 'How words are understood is not told by words alone. (Theology)'. The intensity of thinking and the demands it places on us to explore the fullness of our interpretive grammars seem to warrant a minimalist version of Heideggerean resistance to the claims of empirical understanding.

21 Wittgenstein, *Culture and Value*, p. 39.

22 Ibid., p. 78.

23 Ibid., pp. 49–50.

24 That Wittgenstein is excruciatingly aware of himself as creating stylistic exemplifications of his claims becomes apparent at the end of this meditation where he remarks. 'My achievement is very much like that of a mathematician who invents a calculus.' This calculus requires the careful distribution of voices and attitudes.

25 Baruch Spinoza, *The Ethics and Selected Letters*, trans. Samuel Shirley (Indianapolis, Hackett Publishing, 1982), p. 31.

26 Ibid., p. 196.

27 I need to distinguish my use of Spinoza from two related concepts of style. The first is the best speculative essay on style we have, even though it too reveals too much history to be very useful in its own terms. I refer to Albert Hofstader, 'On the Interpretation of Works of Art,' in Lang (ed.), *The Concept of Style*, pp. 105–33. While Hofstader is superb on the role Spinozan will must play in a theory of style, his version of the *conatus* is decidedly Hegelian in its emphasis on the 'ought' rather than on the more elemental forces of desire that I emphasize (see pp. 116–17, 121) and he makes the decidedly unSpinozan move of trying to connect that stylistic will to the history of forms *à la* Wölfflin. Secondly, by insisting on a more modal and elemental sense of *conatus*, my argument approaches Norman Holland's speculations on what he calls 'identity themes' in 'Unity Identity Text Self', *PMLA*, 90 (1975), 813–22. However, since Holland's themes are posited from a psychoanalytic context they quickly turn into rather simple repetitive patterns that can easily be absorbed into a developmental story. Holland then becomes a prime example of the dangers in speaking about personal identity without a richer sense of what style indicates are the constituents of personal expressions. For how the 'how' is measured within such expressions see my 'From Expressivist Aesthetics to Expressivist Ethics' in A. J. Cascardi (ed.), *Literature and the Question of Philosophy* (Baltimore, Johns Hopkins University Press, 1987), and the discussion of expressive implicature in my *Act and Quality*.

28 *Philosophical Investigations* II, p. 232. In the following discussion all citations from this volume are referred to in the text by page number only.

29 From the remarks I made in note 20 one could argue that the second part of the *Investigations* takes a somewhat different stance towards the voice whose cautions about philosophical temptation lead it to insist that one must trust quasi-behaviourist criteria. Suppose that this voice is a defensive one attempting to make an older Wittgensteinian pose suffice in the face of reflections which challenge it. Then while all the sentences still make the same overt claims, the text as a whole would have very different force. And any reader could try to 'see it like this' so that this struggle becomes a model for philosophical reflection.

30 Kripke, Wittgenstein on Rules, p. 116. I cannot in this essay do justice to the

ways in which Kripke interprets the private language discussion as preparing for the more inclusive sceptical challenge that he sees shaping the *Investigations* – namely, how can one guarantee any knowledge in the future on the basis of any facts about the past? For a summary of Kripke's specific discussion of the 'I', I offer the following passage:

> We are supposed to imagine another entity, similar to 'me' – another 'soul', 'mind' or 'self' – that has a toothache *just like this* toothache, except that it (he? she?) 'has' it, just as I 'have' this one. All this makes little sense, given the Humean critique of the notion of the self that Wittgenstein accepts. I have no idea of a 'self' in my own case, let alone a generic concept of a 'self' that in addition to 'me' includes 'others'. Nor do I have any idea of 'having' as a relation between such a 'self' and the toothache . . . I have no concept of a 'self' nor of 'having' to enable me to make the appropriate abstraction from the original paradigm. The formulation 'it toothaches' makes this quite clear: consider the total situation, and ask what I am to abstract if I wish to remove 'myself'. (p. 125)

Those critiques of Kripke's book with which I am familiar, preeminently that by G. P. Baker and P. M. S. Hacker, do not take up the 'Other Minds' section on which I rely.

31   Ibid., p. 131.
32   Ibid., p. 144.
33   Wallace Stevens, 'Ordinary Evening in New Haven', *The Collected Poems of Wallace Stevens* (New York, Alfred A. Knopf, 1964) p. 473.

5
Analytic Philosophy and the Meaning of Music

Roger Scruton

Analytic philosophy has made meaning into its principal study: at least, a certain kind of meaning (or, as analytic philosophers used to say, a certain sense of 'meaning') – the meaning of words, sentences and arguments. Through individual analysis, and through theories which show how words are involved in communication, analytic philosophy has removed some of the mystery of linguistic meaning, and stolen a march on the foggy deliberations of phenomenology.

But there are other kinds of meaning, or other senses of the word: the meaning of a face or gesture, for example, the meaning of a landscape, of a friendship, of a religious service or a life. The analytic method stops at the threshold of matters so elusive, and addresses them, if at all, only from a safe and incapacitating distance. Such meanings lie immanent in experience, and an awareness of them is a necessary part of a life wholly lived, and lived for the sake of virtue. Philosophies that promise to explore them have an appeal which cannot be matched by philosophical analysis, and even if they are as abstruse as phenomenology and hermeneutics, cultivated readers will ponder them with more attention than they will ever willingly give to the works of Davidson, Dummett or Quine.

My topic in this essay is musical meaning – the meaning that is given to us in the experience of music. And my method at the outset will be analytic, since there are, I believe, established results in analytic philosophy, and even if we have to pursue musical meaning beyond the limits of that philosophy, we ignore its results at our peril.

The first result – which has all the devastating simplicity of a truism, but which is so far short of being a truism as to have required extensive commentary on the work of Frege to persuade us of its value – is that meaning is the object of understanding. The meaning of a piece of music is what you understand when you understand it. No fact or interpretation that is irrelevant to musical understanding can be part of the meaning of music. And musical understanding is a form of hearing. The content of music is a heard content, and it is heard *in* the tones. The fact that I can decode a piece of music, by following some symbolic scheme or 'semantic' analysis, and so give a complete rendering in English of its alleged semantic force, such a fact tells me no more about meaning than would a similar analysis of a cloud, a tree, a heap of pebbles or a carpet. Only if my theory is also a theory of musical understanding will it be a theory of musical meaning. (And the same goes for all the other cases of 'immanent meaning' which I listed above: I clearly do not give the meaning of a life by engaging in a piece of semantic analysis.)

There are many reasons for thinking that semantic theories (whether of the kind proposed for artificial languages by Tarski, or the kind proposed for natural languages by such writers as Richard Montague) might be genuine theories of meaning. Semantic theories try to explain our understanding of language, and to show how language can be used as an instrument of communication. Both Tarskian truth theory and Montaguvian model theory try to show how a person who understands the words of a language, and the rules for combining them, will be able automatically to understand indefinitely many sentences, and to know, in general, how to ascertain which of those sentences are true and which are false. Such theories capture two of the most important features of language: its iterative creativity and its ability to convey information to one who did not previously possess it.

As I have already suggested, however, there are kinds of meaning which cannot be explained by normal semantic theories. Consider figurative pictures: they are meaningful totalities, but they are not composed of discrete meaningful parts, nor is their meaning derived from the meaning of their parts by rules of semantic composition. Generally speaking, a figurative picture has indefinitely many meaningful parts: the meaning of the whole emerges from the meaning of the parts not by the operations of a rule, but through a comprehensive perception of a single and united totality. Figurative pictures seem to have the same density as the visual field itself. In the analysis of language we always reach a point beyond which further division will not produce separately meaningful components. There is no such stopping point in figurative painting. (Consider a painting of a rope, each part of which represents a part of the rope.) This difference may not, at first, seem of the greatest importance. Nelson Goodman, for example, regards sentences and pictures as members of disparate 'symbol systems'. The fact that the symbols in one system are, as he puts its, 'syntactically dense', while those in the other are syntactically differentiated, is not sufficient to imply that the two kinds of meaning are entirely distinct.[1] On the contrary: it *is* sufficient. For it is the crucial fact which forbids the extension into the realm of figurative painting of the only theories of semantic understanding that have ever got off the ground.

My present concern, however, is with music, and the more general phenomenon of 'aesthetic meaning' (meaning understood in and through an aesthetic experience), of which musical meaning is an instance. If there is musical meaning, it is because there is musical understanding. Current theories of music tend to go wrong either because they neglect this simple thought, or because they describe musical understanding in terms of some theory whose primary application is in a field (such as linguistics) that has nothing to do with music.

Musical understanding is a special case of 'intentional understanding'. A scientific understanding seeks for the causal connections which underlie and explain appearances. Scientific explanation does not destroy or discredit appearance: it merely dispenses with it. An intentional understanding considers the world as 'intentional object' (as *Lebenswelt*, to use Husserl's idiom). It therefore makes use of the concepts through which we perceive and act on the world, and makes no connections that are not already, as it were, implicit in those concepts. Although there is a sense in which we always know how things appear to us, the study of an appearance is appropriate when the concepts which inform it are not fully within the perceiver's grasp. (I may see something as a snake, but have an imperfect grasp of snakehood: here there is something I could learn, which would change the appearance of what I see. Music criticism has just such a 'change of appearance' as its goal.)

Our experience of music depends upon our intellectual capacities and education, upon concepts, analogies and expectations that we have inherited from a culture steeped in musical expression. The understanding that we derive from this culture is manifest in our way of hearing, and not just in our way of thinking about, music. If it were not so, then it would be of no aesthetic significance. It is a general rule, indeed, and one fundamental to music criticism, that no account of a piece of music is of aesthetic significance, unless it is also an account of what we can hear.[2] This stricture applies as much to the most basic elements of musical structure as to the complex paragraphs, and as much to content as to form. Someone who described the first chord of Wagner's *Tristan* as an inversion of a G# minor triad with an added major sixth would be *wrong*, even though that description correctly identifies all the pitches of all the tones. He would be wrong because what we hear lies outside the musical possibilities of such a chord – outside what is implied in the idea of a minor triad. And someone who described the last movement of Mozart's Jupiter Symphony as morose and life-negating would also be wrong, however clearly his judgement was founded in theory. For this description is of something that cannot be heard in the music by a musically cultivated person.

No more than any other art has music escaped the fraudulent attentions of semiologists, for whom significance is both *encoded* in music, and decoded by the receptive listener. But no *sémiologue* seems to be in agreement with any other as to precisely what any particular piece of music means, or how its meaning is 'determined' by the structural relations among its parts. (See, for example, the discussion of the prelude to *Pélleas et Mélisande* in J. J. Nattiez's *Fondements d'une sémiologie de la musique*.[3]) The reason is because no attention is paid to the important question, which is whether the 'encoded' meaning can be, not merely decoded, but also heard – and heard, moreover, in the very same act of attention that engenders the aesthetic experience. Is the meaning part of *the way it sounds*, as the 'smiling through tears' is part of the sound of Beethoven's cavatina? And is it also part of what we attend to, enjoy and value in the sound, when it captures our aesthetic interest? If not, then it is no part of what we understand, when we understand the piece as music. And what is not part of what is understood, by the listener who hears with understanding, is not part of the meaning.

The problem is not, of course, peculiar to semiology. It bedevils many of the 'formal' modes of criticism, such as Schenkerian analysis, in which the question of an extra-musical 'meaning' need never be considered. Schenkerian analysis endeavours to account for the perceived form of a piece of music by showing its derivation from a basic musical idea, or *Ursatz*.[4] (The *Ursatz* may be a harmonic progression, a melodic sequence, or simply an interval, such as the fifth which plays so important a part in the first movement of Beethoven's Ninth Symphony, or the third which governs melody and harmony in Wagner's *Ring*.) Again the problem is, how much of what is said is an account of what we can *hear*? It is not enough that the analysis be ingenious, interesting or fertile. The question is whether we can hear the music as growing (in the manner described) from the suggested *Ursatz*.

The problem is also illustrated by the theories which have influenced the composition (as opposed to the analysis) of modern music – in particular the theory of the tone row, as this was expounded by Schoenberg. In much of the music of the Vienna school there seems to be a peculiar and at times disturbing gap, between the musical experience and the composer's self-analysis, which renders the analysis impotent as an instrument of criticism. The score of Alban Berg's *Lulu* – one of the great masterpieces of modern music – shows vividly what I mean. Each section of music is introduced by a title, in gothic script, which presents it as an instance of some classical archetype – canon, passacaglia and so on. And yet there seems to be no way in which the music can be heard as exemplifying those classical forms. To discover the justification for the titles, is to discover details of the music that escape the educated ear. (To hear something as a canon it is not sufficient to notice, as a result of hearing, that one line of music is following another. It is necessary to *hear their pursuit*, and that means also to hear each line as a thematic unity.) At crucial moments Berg uses the concepts of the Schoenbergian system not in order to create something that can be heard in the music, but in order to provide intellectual justification for the written notes. Consider the music which accompanies the film (showing the typhoid episode, Lulu's imprisonment and the Countess's self-sacrifice). This whole passage is constructed on the mirror principle, with the notes running backwards from the half-way point to the conclusion. And although the listener can hear *that* this is occurring, he cannot, so to speak, *hear it occurring*, when he hears with a musical understanding. The intellectual system, which determines every note and chord in the second half of the passage, is also a musical arbitrariness, and if the passage is powerful it is not *because* of its structure, but in spite of it. This is but one instance of the intellectualism that has bedevilled the music of the 'avant-garde' – the attempt to justify the musically arbitrary by making it intellectually inevitable, and to impose conceptual form on what is tonally formless.

If a work of music means something, then, this is a fact about the way it sounds. The false sciences and cabalisms of musicology are of no significance – not because they are badly argued, nor because they misrepresent what they describe, but because they describe the wrong thing. They offer to explain how the notes are *in themselves*, and not how they are *in the ear of the listener*. The search for the real structure of a musical work (the structure that it has *in itself*) ends by presenting us with something that is not a musical work at all, but an inscription on the page, or a mathematical ordering.

Thus far we have been led by the analytic method – not indeed so far as to understand what musical meaning *is*, but so far as to understand what it is *not*. What is the next step? Analytic philosophy has another useful instrument at its disposal – although this time it is an instrument borrowed from the late idealism of Croce and Collingwood, and often used in clumsy and destructive ways. I refer to the distinction between representation and expression. This distinction is purely theoretical, and has no meaning or justification apart from the theory to which it is attached. Since I do not accept the theories of aesthetic interest advanced by Croce, Collingwood, Gombrich and Goodman (who are the four most important exponents of the distinction), it follows that I do not mean by 'expression' precisely what they do, even though – in the last analysis – I am trying to answer the very same questions that troubled Croce in his *Aesthetic*.

Representation, as I understand it, is characterized by a propositional content (a Fregean 'thought', which might be true or false). Music is not, in any full sense, a representational art. It is beset by a narrative incompetence which derives directly from the way in which we understand it. Music can *imitate* things – but imitation is not representation. You do not misunderstand an ornament when you fail to see that it is derived from the forms of a plant; nor do you misunderstand someone's tone of voice, just because you fail to see that he is imitating his sister. Representation involves the telling of a story, and while music may (as in opera) *follow* a story, it is not necessary to understand the story in order to understand the music. (Bruckner, who understood Wagner's music as well as anyone, never had the faintest idea of what was going on in the drama.)[5]

Musical meaning belongs to the vast (and vague) category of expression. This is the category into which we place those meaningful gestures which are understood not by adducing a propositional *content*, but by a spontaneous movement of sympathy. Music is full of movement. However, nothing in music *really* moves: musical movement is only an appearance of movement.[6] The capacity to hear movement in successive sounds is nevertheless fundamental to our understanding of expression. It is what enables us to hear the musical line as startled, shocked, tender, caressing or melancholy. If the basis of musical expression (the movement) is merely intentional (in Brentano's sense), then so too is expression. It is something that we hear in music, but not something that is independently there.

Analytic philosophers have a tendency to believe that, if music has expression, there must be something that it expresses. They argue that music has meaning for us because it expresses emotion, and that to understand it is in some way to grasp (in thought, feeling or imagination) the emotion that it contains. On this account music is the middle term in an act of communication, which has feeling, rather than thought, as its content.[7]

Perhaps the most serious objection to such a view is the one made by Hanslick, 130 years ago.[8] Hanslick's argument may be expressed (in modern idiom) as follows: Most forms of art which are said to express emotion are also representational. They describe, refer to, or depict the world. Moreover, it is difficult to see how emotions can be expressed in the absence of representation. Every emotion requires an object: fear is fear *of* something, anger is anger *about* something. We can distinguish emotions and classify them only because we can distinguish and classify their (intentional) objects; and we can do *this* only because we can identify the thoughts through which those objects are defined. In which case, it is difficult to see how a non-representational art like music can really have a genuine expressive content. It would be impossible to describe that content – since its object could never be identified. Hence it is impossible to give substance to the claim (which might indeed be plausible in the case of poetry or painting) that music serves as a means for communicating emotion.

Discussions of Hanslick's argument are mostly unsatisfactory. Those writers who have defended some theory of music as the 'language of the emotions' have tended to ignore it.[9] Recently, however, Malcolm Budd has argued explicitly against Hanslick, that each emotion, in addition to its propositional content, has an inner dynamic, a character which is identifiable separately from the thoughts which engender it, and which can be conveyed by music without reference to the content or the object of a propositional attitude.[10] Budd himself does not advance any positive theory as to how this is possible – how it is possible to embody in musical outline the dynamic properties of an intentional state, without touching on its intentionality. But even if it were possible, it would be extremely puzzling that we should be so very interested in the exercise. Why should we wish music to do so strange a thing, and why should we take pleasure in its being done? Why should we enjoy hearing an emotion prized free from its defining context, and presented to us as a mere pattern of tension and release? Are we sure that what we enjoy, when we enjoy such a pattern, is really the *emotion* to which it distantly refers? Why then should the emotion be offered as the meaning of music – as the thing that we understand when we hear with understanding?

But perhaps we should question the assumption which underlies both Hanslick's objection and Budd's reply: the assumption that, if there is to be expression in music, then it must be understood so to speak, transitively – as the expression *of* some state of mind. For we do not always understand expression in such a way. A face, for instance, may sometimes be understood as an expression of anguish, grief, puzzlement or fear; it may also be understood as a 'particular expression', for which we may have no words. (We might call this the 'intransitive' sense of expression, in deference to Wittgenstein's discussion of the words 'particular' and 'peculiar'.[11]) Two faces with an expression of anger could, in the transitive sense, have the same expression, since they might express the same thing. But in the intransitive sense they might have quite different expressions. Indeed, in this intransitive sense, an expression is so little detachable from the thing which wears it, that it is hard to give a clear sense to the idea that two objects might wear the same expression.

'Identity of expression' is then a problematic idea – and the problem bears on the root problem of aesthetics, the question of the relation between content and form (between what we understand, and what we understand it *in*). We resist the idea that there could be rules of expression in art; and this fact indicates that we have to do, in the artistic case, with an intransitive concept of expression. Using that concept, we find ourselves unable to say which physical features of a face (for example) are responsible for its expression – which features might be reproduced so as to guarantee the 'same expression' in whatever possesses them. If any feature is responsible, then so are they all. Expression is a character of the whole appearance – the whole *Gestalt* – and to understand it is not to decode it in accordance with some rule of reference, but rather to situate it in the world of human interest and communication.

We might describe an expression in mental terms, without implying that it is an expression *of* the state to which we refer. A face may have a melancholy expression, without being an expression of melancholy. Similarly, our description of certain passages of music as tense, sad, joyful or grieving does not commit us to the view that these emotions are being expressed in what we hear.

How then should we respond to Hanslick's objection? Imagine a painting of a crowd. One of the people is staring out of the picture with startled gestures, and our attention is drawn to him. His face, hands and posture impress us. Observing them, we feel an instinctive movement of sympathy, even a truncated impulse to imitate. Yet we do not find, anywhere in the picture, the object of this man's attention, nor any narrative of his thoughts. He presents us with a picture of attention seized, of inner life engaged by an outer world. We can neither complete nor begin the narrative of his mental content. Even so, the man comes before us as an object of spontaneous sympathy.

The example shows us that expression may be not only described, but also understood, intransitively – and understood, moreover, in and through an appearance. And this appearance becomes the focus of those imaginative emotions which lie at the heart of aesthetic interest. Is not the example, then, a paradigm case of artistic meaning? The problem is to proceed further; to say something more about *what* we understand in responding sympathetically to the expressive gesture, and what we gain – cognitively, emotionally, morally – from doing so. We might also reasonably ask whether musical meaning is really analogous to the meaning that we discern in a painted gesture. For a painted gesture is not a real gesture: it is something imagined, towards which we can feel the freeest sympathy, precisely because we know that it is not real. (That which is imagined is no *trouble* to us, even when it troubles us. In imagination we 'play', in Schiller's sense, and when we play our sympathy, which costs us nothing, can be entire.) It is the representational nature of painting which liberates our sympathies, by presenting us with imagined objects to which we need have no practical concern. In what way, then, is an abstract art like music analogous to representational painting? What is it that enables the one to serve as an object of the same sympathetic responses that are directed towards and fulfilled through the other?

If we are to answer such questions then we must, I believe, cast the net more widely than it has been cast by analytic philosophers. We need to say something about matters which have been relegated to literary criticism and cultural history, and which have seldom interested the practitioners of semantic analysis. In particular, we need to understand the relation between musical experience and musical culture, and to describe the context in which sounds come to us imbued with a meaning that is neither subjective nor objective, but commonly created and genuinely shared.

Musical communication is possible only because certain sounds are heard as music – are heard as exhibiting the 'intentional order' of rhythm, melody and harmony. This order is not a material property of the physical world; it resides in the perceptual experience of those who hear with understanding.[12] Unless such people exist, or can be brought into existence, the act of composition is incoherent. Moreover if their response is to have the depth and seriousness that will give cogency to the artist's labour, their musical understanding must connect, in some way, with their social and critical faculties. The audience must distinguish, among the sounds which they hear, the varied aspects of their own spiritual existence; they must be able to hear sounds as tragic or comic, as solemn and graceful, as passionate and disheartened. They must be able to hear musical relations and musical development in terms of values and interests that govern their life as a whole. They must be familiar with such musical experiences as the following: hearing a rhythm as a dance, as a march, as a call to arms; hearing a stretch of counterpoint as a unity of concurrent movements advancing towards a common stasis; hearing energy, languor, hesitation and resolution; hearing a chord as a question, an answer, a quiescence; hearing a melody as a character, a declaration, a common resolve; hearing a passage as song-like, hymn-like, recitative-like. And so on. What holds that bewildering class together? The only answer that I find persuasive is this: in each of those experiences we discern a peculiar operation of the imagination (which I have referred to by the words 'hearing as', and which parallels the act of imagination – 'seeing as' or 'seeing in' – involved in understanding paintings). By virtue of the auditory imagination, the excitement of music can become, in an immediate and intuitive way, the excitement of life itself.

The facts that I have referred to are obvious, even if the theory of them is not. It is also obvious that a composer who does not envisage an audience with those capacities (whose music is not essentially 'to be appreciated' in the terms that I have laid down) has fallen out of communication not only with other people, but also with his art, and – ultimately – with himself. For music is not sound: it is sound understood in response. To aim to produce music is to aim to produce a musical response. And only in the context of a musical culture is such an aim coherent. It is custom, habit, the intertwining of music with everyday life, which generate the basic discriminations to which I referred, and which therefore permit the more refined and adventurous musical enterprises that are the prerogative of high art.

To understand musical meaning, therefore, is to understand how the cultivated ear can discern, in what it hears, the occasions for sympathy. I do not know *how* this happens: but *that* it happens is one of the given facts of musical culture. And once we accept that fact, we have no problem in seeing the analogy between musical expression and painted gestures. Let us consider an example. In the slow movement of Schubert's G major quartet D. 887, there is a tremolando passage of the kind that you would describe as foreboding. Suddenly there shoots up from the murmuring sea of anxiety a single terrified gesture – a gesture of utter hopelessness and horror, like the outstretched hand of a drowning man. No one can listen to this passage without instantly sensing the object of this terror; without knowing, in some way, that death itself has risen on that unseen horizon. What you hear, however, contains no reference to death. It is a gesture only. But it is the gesture of an intentional being, a sign of an observing consciousness. It pulls you into awe-filled regions, and leaves you captivated by sympathetic feeling.

In the song or the opera, these gestures which point to something
unseen are returned to their context. Here their 'world of reference' is
revealed to us. What then is happening in the orchestra pit? I should like
to say that the pit contains another observer, one who sometimes lends his
voice to the protagonists and who is sometimes content to comment or
sympathize. As Wagner argued in *Opera and Drama*, the orchestra is the
chorus of the play, and in recognizing its expressive character we are
hearing expression in the gestures of an imagined onlooker. The music
does not 'express the emotions' of Tristan, Manon or Leporello. It
sympathizes with them, mocks them, derides them. To the cultivated
listener the role of the orchestra is no more puzzling than are the gestures
of an observing chorus. The expression worn by the music matches our
own, as we inwardly move under its influence.

If we accept that (and I realize that I have let the matter rest, so far, on
an unexplored idea of musical culture), then we can say something about
the beneficial results of musical experience. Musical development can also
involve a kind of moral development, and musical understanding can
thereby lead us into a greater understanding of the human world which is
intimated through it. Again, I can do no better than to offer an example,
this time from opera (the *Ring*), in the hope that the facts will speak for
themselves. When Alberich first takes the Tarnhelm from Mime and
places it on his head, the music stands as it were with its mouth open in
amazement. Its gesture, as it hovers about G# minor and E minor, and
finally staggers on to the open fifth of B, wears a quite peculiar expression. Responding to it, we share in the music's intentionality, and perceive
the world of the *Ring* as *it* perceives:

(1)

The Tarnhelm music thereafter undergoes a gradual development, culmi-
nating at last in the terrifying conclusion to *Götterdämmerung* Act 1, when
the evil of transformation is manifest in the heroic soul of Siegfried:

(2)

The leitmotive serves not as a 'sign of the Tarnhelm', but as the record of an original experience. The music remembers its own past, embellishes and interprets it, just as we ourselves add to and reinterpret our critical experiences. (This is precisely analogous to those passages in Greek tragedy, when the chorus recalls, through its words, some previous reaction, but in circumstances which are irremediably changed.)

To understand the music is to recognize the gesture which it enacts. When Siegfried compels Brünnhilde to prostitute herself, and all unknowingly violates the thing he loves, the music throws up its hands. 'I have felt this before,' it says, 'in another place and another time.' Looking at the stage, we can complete the thought. Something happened, when Alberich first placed the Tarnhelm on his head, which happens now. But it happens differently; awe becomes terror, and in the place of wonder there is the knowledge that I am *not at home* in the world which I am now observing. In the music of the Tarnhelm we remember; and, remembering, we feel Siegfried's transformation as *unheimlich*.

In such instances we are being led by the ears towards a knowledge of the human heart. A musical development can synthesize two separate moments of emotional reaction, and bring to bear on a new scene the sympathy that was first awakened by the old. In the very act of responding to Alberich's bitterness:

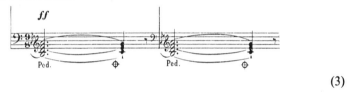

(3)

we are re-enacting our wonder at the gold of the Rhine:

(4)

In the very hearing of the two chords in (3), therefore, is a kind of emotional history. The musical experience rehearses a moral truth: that worship of nature, which is the end of life, stands next to the idolatory of power, which is the means. The holy is the neighbour of the corrupt, and that which is loved is adjacent to that which is bought and sold. Such is the *way the music sounds*, however strange it may be to say so.

I have given examples, only, of what I mean. Analytic philosophy tells us what we cannot say in trying to explain them. But it offers, so far as I can see, no explanation of its own. The question is, whether some other method exists – if 'method' is the word – which will guide us forward into these obscure regions. I end on a note of scepticism, recognizing only that the problem of musical meaning has an answer – for if it did not, then my description of the *Ring* would be not merely false, but meaningless. It seems to me, however, that it is both meaningful and true.

NOTES

1 Nelson Goodman, *Languages of Art* (London, Oxford University Press, 1969) p. 136.

2 I have argued this point at length in 'Understanding Music', in *The Aesthetic Understanding* (London, Methuen and Manchester, Carcanet, 1983).

3 J. J. Nattiez, *Fondements d'une sémiologie de la musique* (Paris, Union Géneral d'editions, 1976). See also R. Scruton, 'The Semiology of Music' in *The Politics of Culture* (Manchester, Carcanet, 1981) (a review of Nattiez).

4 H. Schenker, *Neue musikalische Theorien und Phantasien*, (Vienna and Leipzig, Universal Edition, 1906–35).

5 For a proof that music is not a representational art, see 'Representation in Music', in Scruton, *The Aesthetic Understanding*.

6 See again my 'Understanding Music'.

7 Among analytic philosophers subscribing to the view that expression is always expression *of* some state or property (whether or not a state of mind) are S. K. Langer (*Philosophy in a New Key*, Cambridge, Mass., Harvard University Press, 1942), Goodman (*Languages of Art*), and Peter Kivy (in *The Corded Shell*, Princeton NJ, Princeton University Press, 1980).

8 E. Hanslick, *Vom musikalisch-Schönen* (Leipzig, Bratkopf and Hartel, 1910, first published 1854).

9 See for example Deryck Cooke, *The Language of Music* (Oxford, Oxford University Press, 1959).

10 M. J. Budd, *Music and the Emotions* (London, Routledge, 1986).

11 See Ludwig Wittgenstein, *The Blue and Brown Books* (Oxford, Basil Blackwell, 1958), pp. 158ff, and the discussion of this in Richard Wollheim, *Art and its Objects*, 2nd edn (Cambridge, Cambridge University Press, 1980), ss 41 and 48.

12 See again the argument in my 'Understanding Music'.

6

Reading Donald Davidson: Truth, Meaning and Right Interpretation

Christopher Norris

I

The writings of Donald Davidson have generated widespread discussion among Anglo-American analytic philosophers and, more recently, literary theorists.[1] The reasons for this interest are by no means uniform, but they tend to divide along fairly predictable lines. Of the two possible readings of Davidson, one seems to me a very definite *mis*reading that goes clean against the logic and significance of his work. The other (I shall argue) is the more authentically Davidsonian reading, though it does not fit at all with currently fashionable ideas about language, meaning and representation. That the work of one thinker should support – or at least appear to support – two such diametrically opposed understandings is indeed a curious phenomenon, and all the more so in view of Davidson's commitment to a truth-conditional theory of interpretative reason. In fact it might be argued by proponents of the rival (poststructuralist or pragmatist) view that the very existence of uncertainties like this lends weight to their case for regarding Davidson's talk of truth as holding good only relative to a certain culture-specific set of ideas and assumptions. His work would then serve as a nice illustration of the fact that even 'mainstream' analytic philosophy has at last come round to their way of thinking, i.e. the view of 'truth' as an essentially contested concept, produced by the various discourses of power/knowledge that compete for cultural hegemony.

It will help if we adopt a simplifying shorthand to distinguish these two viewpoints. 'Davidson I' is the philosopher who asserts that some notion of truth – or what it means to make a truthful statement – is simply indispensable to all our thinking about language, logic and the nature of human understanding. Otherwise, he argues, we would lack any basis for deciding between rival interpretive claims, or indeed for making sense of language at the level of day-to-day communicative grasp. That is to say, the attitude of holding-true is a kind of logical primitive, a notion presupposed by every form of linguistic inference, even in cases (like fictional language or metaphor) where this standard has no very obvious relevance. For without it we would be forced back upon an attitude of wholesale cultural relativism, the idea that languages or texts only signify according to their own inbuilt codes and conventions, so that meaning must ultimately lie beyond the grasp of any speaker not trained up in the same culture-specific habits of thought. And this conclusion is insupportable, Davidson argues, both in principle and as a matter of empirical fact. For we can and do very often make a tolerable job of interpreting unfamiliar forms of utterance, whether in cases like that of the anthropologist faced with a puzzling new piece of ethnographic data, or – nearer home – as native speakers given to interpret some strange or puzzling metaphor. And we do so by a mixture of inspired guesswork and basic assumptions about the truth, intelligibility and semantic structure of human language in general. Understanding simply could not get off the ground unless there existed this general willingness to assume, first, that other people make sense of experience in ways not radically unlike our own, and secondly, that the attitude of holding-true – of attaching a particular significance to sentences that get things right – is as important for them as it is for us.

These beliefs are not optional, Davidson thinks, or merely a product of our own ethnocentric values and assumptions. Rather, they are the necessary *precondition* for any hope we may have of getting to understand other people's language and behaviour. That is to say: unless we operate what Davidson calls this basic 'principle of charity' – the principle that holds it more likely than not that their ascriptions of truth-value to statements will correspond pretty much to our own – we will have no way of comparing the various possible accounts of what their words or actions signify, and thus of deciding which come closest to fulfilling the requirements of rational accountability. The hypothetical test-case here is that of the anthropologist confronted with a language and culture whose conventions are maximally remote from his or her own. A native informant might point to some object and utter a word, apparently by way of straightforward ostensive definition. But according to some philosophers – among them W. V. Quine – this situation is nowhere near as simple as it seems, since the native informant might be offering all kinds of information as regards the object concerned.[2] It could be a matter of the object's desirability, of its threatening character, its tribal-totemic role, some bit of it or aspect of its past history, the unlikelihood of coming across it *here*, or any number of alternative hypotheses. From this Quine moves to his general thesis: that we cannot translate between cultures, language-games or different 'forms of life' without at some point coming up against the problem of deciding just which interpretive gambit will best make sense of the informant's words or behaviour. And this problem cannot be resolved, he argues, by appealing to supposedly invariant features of language, like the gesture of naming an object by simply pointing straight at it. For ostensive definition is itself a language-game, one that only makes sense – as Wittgenstein remarked – in the context of a cultural form of life which might always turn out to be peculiar to us, or to speakers trained up on our particular set of naturalized responses and expectations.[3]

Thus Quine denies the very possibility of 'radical translation', if by this is meant a kind of rock-bottom assurance that people can indeed communicate effectively across cultures by first getting down to the basics and then building up a more complex set of definitional equivalents. Any putative 'translation manual' compiled on these principles would still have to face the disturbing possibility that the native informants were in fact trying to communicate something quite different, and that therefore its entire system of semantic links, collocations and associative networks was based on a systematic misconstruction of everything that had passed between the communicating parties. For Quine, therefore, 'radical translation' is a strictly impossible undertaking. And this predicament extends far beyond the somewhat exotic instance of an anthropologist working from scratch within a totally alien culture. Similar problems can arise, he argues, with any attempt to assign meanings to statements in our own language, especially where these involve some unfamiliar or problematic terms of description, but even where there seems to be no obstacle in the way of straightforward comprehension. For it is always the case that those terms just *might* have been used in a sense either markedly or subtly at odds with our normal ways of understanding.

Davidson I comes out strongly against what he sees as the disabling relativist assumptions bound up with Quine's way of posing these questions. He does so by denying that truth must always be a product of the codes, conventions and language-games that determine what shall normally *count* as true in any given cultural context. On the contrary, Davidson argues: we can make no sense of such assertions unless we acknowledge some basic level of communicative grasp that allows us to recognize these local instances of cultural difference. Hence his objection to the so-called 'Sapir-Whorf hypothesis', namely, the idea that since experience is always mediated by language – since language provides the very concepts and categories by which we interpret experience – *therefore* it is impossible to translate from one language (or cultural context) to another without inescapably imposing our own habits of thought and perception. But such arguments fail, according to Davidson, as soon as they claim to offer some account of the cultural differences involved.[4] Thus 'Whorf, wanting to demonstrate that Hopi incorporates a metaphysics so alien to ours that Hopi and English cannot, as he puts it, "be callibrated", uses English to convey the contents of sample Hopi sentences' (*Inquiries*, p. 184). Davidson's argument here amounts to a form of transcendental-deductive riposte, showing that Whorf – and others of the same persuasion – cannot for a moment accept the consequences of their own relativist position. Where they fall into error, he suggests, is in thinking that every language must impose some ultimate 'conceptual scheme', some network of signifying codes and conventions peculiar to itself, such that any standards of validity and truth will be internal to that one language and hence beyond the grasp of speakers or translators belonging to a different language-group. But this is to get the whole matter upside down, Davidson argues. The very idea of a 'conceptual scheme' must logically depend on our possessing the means to interpret and compare what evidence we have, deciding where the salient differences occur on the basis of at least some measure of reciprocal grasp. Such agreement 'may take the form of a widespread sharing of sentences held to be true by speakers of "the same language", or agreement in the large mediated by a theory of truth contrived by an interpeter for speakers of another language' (*Inquiries*, p. 197). For otherwise – and this is Davidson's central point – it simply would not make sense to talk about alternative conceptual schemes, since we would have no way of knowing or describing just where and how they differed from our own.

This is one of the ways in which Davidson arrives at his anti-relativist conclusion. Another is more technical and has to do with a form of canonical notation for truth-functional semantics developed by the logician Alfred Tarski. On this account, as Davidson describes it,

> a satisfactory theory of truth for a language L must entail, for every sentence *s* of L, a theorem of the form '*s* is true if and only if *p*' where '*s*' is replaced by a description of *s* and '*p*' by *s* itself if L is English, and by a translation of *s* into English if L is not English. (*Inquiries*, p. 194)

But this way of stating the matter amounts, as Davidson admits, to a form of elaborate tautology, and is in any case not much use when dealing with the complexities of natural language. What his argument comes down to in practical terms is the point that we could not make a start in understanding *any* kind of language without the two basic assumptions, (1) that some statements must indeed be veridical, and (2) that its speakers must at least have a grasp of the conditions that have to be satisfied in order for this or that statement to count as true. Thus 'the methodological problem of interpretation is to see how, given the sentences a man accepts as true under given conditions, to work out what his beliefs are and what his words mean' (*Inquiries*, p. 162). From this point one can go on to interpret those other, problematical instances where it may be that some deep-seated difference of assumptions is getting in the way of an adequate grasp. But there is no reason (so Davidson argues) to follow those thinkers, like Whorf and Quine, who would persuade us that such instances are paradigmatic, or that all translation must involve such ultimate problems. For it is precisely on account of their exceptional nature – our knowledge that they are *not*, in fact, typical cases – that these problems can be recognized as such and referred to other, more perspicuous contexts where meaning is not in doubt. And what enables us to do just that is the general conviction that language makes sense, that truth-conditions hold across the boundaries of cultural difference, and therefore that translation is not the impossible enterprise that sceptics would have it.

Thus 'we compensate for the paucity of evidence concerning the meaning of individual sentences not by trying to produce evidence for the meanings of words but by considering the evidence of a theory of the language to which the sentence belongs' (*Inquiries*, p. 225). The main task of this holistic approach is to make explicit the various presuppositions that speakers of a language must bring to bear in producing and interpreting statements held to be true. And the same applies to those forms of utterance where truth is not directly in question, where meaning comes about through fictive, metaphorical or other such devices which cannot be accounted for in truth-conditional terms. For here also the condition of intelligibility is that we recognize such cases for what they are and then make sense of them by looking to the context in which they occur. This would be impossible, Davidson argues, if convention went all the way down; if meaning were entirely a product of the cultural codes or signifying structures that determine the limits of intelligible sense. 'Philosophers who make convention a necessary element in language have the matter backward. The truth is rather that language is a condition for having conventions' (*Inquiries*, p. 280). And furthermore, the condition for having language at all – or for knowing what to make of it in any given context – is that we grasp what is involved in the paradigm case of sentences that do possess the character of truthful statements.

II

If Davidson is right – 'Davidson I', the philosopher whose arguments I have so far attempted to summarize – then clearly this poses a considerable challenge to current poststructuralist theory. For it is a basic premise of all such thinking that language is indeed conventional through and through; that meaning consists in the 'arbitrary' link between signifier and signified, a link sustained only by the system of culture-specific relations and distinctions that makes up any given language. On this view, questions of truth and reference simply do not arise, at least within the terms of a general linguistics or semiotic theory whose aim is to account for the structural economy of language as a self-contained signifying system, and *not* to explain how this or that sentence achieves the condition of truthful utterance. Thus Saussure takes it as axiomatic that the sign is a localized point of intersection between two distinct planes: on the one hand the system of *phonological* contrasts that enables us to register meaningful differences of sound, on the other the network of *semantic* relations that comprise all our operative concepts and categories.[5] For Saussure, as for Whorf, this entails the further point that we cannot raise questions of reference or truth except in relation to some signifying practice (or 'conceptual scheme') which alone makes sense of such questions. And it is this way of thinking that induces us, in Davidson's view, to invert the real order of priorities, to treat convention as the basis of all language, or the source of what counts as valid or true within any given language. But the problem disappears, he would argue, as soon as we switch these priorities around and see that the appeal to conventions in fact explains nothing; that the very idea of a conceptual scheme is logically dependent on our prior grasp of the truth-conditions that must presumably operate across all languages. For unless we accept this fact – namely, that 'whether we like it or not, if we want to understand others, we must count them right on most matters' (*Inquiries*, p. 197) – we shall simply have no grounds for comparison when it comes to assessing the finer points of cultural difference.

So the following might be Davidson I's critique of poststructuralism, consonant with what he has to say about Whorf and the logical shortcomings of relativist doctrine. Poststructuralism goes wrong when it takes Saussure's notion of the arbitrary sign – a notion adopted strictly for the purposes of structural-linguistic description – and extrapolates from it a wholesale theory of language, meaning and interpretation. More specifically, it errs by ignoring the fact that *sentences*, not individual words or signs, are the units of intelligible meaning, and that any attempt to assign meaning to sentences must involve the appeal to some form of truth-conditional logic before we can begin to grasp how they function in larger contexts of discourse. And from this basic error poststructuralism goes on to assert (like Foucault) that 'truth' is nothing more than a localized effect of power/knowledge, of the will-to-truth that gives certain hegemonic discourses the power to impose their perspective on other, more marginal languages.[6] Thus from Foucault's avowedly Nietzschean standpoint, truth is nothing more than a species of persistent rhetorical illusion, a pretence that we can get outside this arena of competing discursive strategies to some detached high ground of critical reason whence to adjudicate the issue between them. Then again there are those, like Roland Barthes, who celebrate the advent of a new kind of writing, a practice that breaks altogether with mimetic constraints or the myth of authorial presence, and which thus opens itself up to a utopian play of plural signification.[7] This writing would constitute an implicit critique of those repressive ideologies – like the discourse of high classic realism –

which have hitherto worked to enforce what amounts to a restricted economy of language, meaning, and representation.

Davidson's counter-argument to all such claims can be stated briefly enough. What they fail to remark is the elementary fact that language – even fictional language – can only make sense on condition that *some* sentences be taken to refer successfully, or to possess the basic attributes of validity and truth. Otherwise our response when confronted with one of Barthes's hypothetical limit-texts would be something like that of the Whorfian ethno-linguist exposed to a radically alien form of life and convinced that, since meaning is entirely a matter of cultural convention, therefore no means could possibly exist for translating observation-sentences from one language to another. And the same would apply to Foucault's idea that truth is nothing more than a reflex product of discursive power-relationships, a value attached to certain forms of utterance that currently enjoy that status. For if this were indeed the case – if we possessed absolutely no means of distinguishing truthful from false, fictitious or merely indeterminate statements – then the relativist would be in the untenable position of asserting it as a generalized truth about language that language could assert no truths. What Davidson says about Whorf would then apply equally to Foucault, with the difference that Whorf's hypothesis at least captures something of the genuine puzzlement that must sometimes result from the encounter of radically alien cultural life-forms. Even so, Davidson writes, 'there does not seem to be much hope for a test that a conceptual scheme is radically different from our own if that test depends on the assumption that we can divorce the notion of truth from that of translation' (*Inquiries*, p. 195). And for Foucault, this puzzlement would have to extend to every single act of interpretation, even where the language or the text in question belonged squarely within our own cultural heritage. For it is, Davidson argues, an unavoidable consequence of relativist thinking – or of any such appeal to linguistic conventions as a bottom-line of accountability – that we are left with no reason to suppose that understanding can *ever* take place on a footing of reciprocal intelligibility. Hence the need for an alternative paradigm, one based on the reasonable premise that 'from the moment someone unknown to us opens his mouth, we know an enormous amount about the sort of theory that will work for him – or we know we know no such theory' (*Inquiries*, p. 278). And in the latter case the fact of our perceiving the problem will itself provide a starting-point for the process of reinterpretation.

So it might seem that Davidson's arguments come out clean against the kind of radical conventionalism that unites thinkers like Whorf, Saussure, Foucault and Barthes. But this is to assume that Davidson I is demonstrably right on all the basics; that any workable theory of interpretation will have to start out from the conditions that hold in the case of truthful utterances; and that therefore the only right reading of

Davidson's work is one that applies exactly this set of assumptions to his own texts. But there is, as I have mentioned, another way of construing those texts that has proved more adaptable to the purposes of poststructuralism, and more attractive to commentators – notably Richard Rorty – who would wish to have done with all such talk of truth, epistemology and right reading. This is not the place for a detailed exposition of Rorty's neo-pragmatist outlook. Very briefly, he argues that philosophy went wrong when it took (with Descartes and Kant) a turn toward epistemological questions as its area of chief concern.[8] Truth became a matter of accurate *representation*, of achieving a proper correspondence between ideas, propositions or a priori concepts on the one hand, and experience, perception or sensuous intuitions on the other. Henceforth the various schools would divide not so much on the question of whether such knowledge was available, but on how best to attain it. Thus rationalists started out from transcendental assumptions about the nature, the constitutive powers and limits of human reason in general, while empiricists largely rejected such claims and sought a grounding for knowledge in the supposed self-evidence of straightforward sensory perception. Kant sought to reconcile these two conflicting creeds by demonstrating first, in the transcendental mode, that we could only make sense of experience in so far as its forms were given a priori through concepts of pure understanding, and secondly that these forms must necessarily match up with our sensuous intuitions, since otherwise there was nothing to prevent reason from becoming lost in metaphysical abstractions of its own giddy devising. Hence Kant's claim to have effected nothing less than a 'Copernican revolution' in the history of thought. It would now be the task of a truly critical philosophy to examine its own truth-claims and establish more precisely the powers and the limits of human cognitive inquiry.

But on Rorty's view this was just one more attempt to 'solve' problems which only existed because philosophers had dreamed them up in the first place. And it is here that Davidson enters the picture as one of those modern 'post-analytic' thinkers who can help us out of this conceptual fix by showing how it rests on mistaken notions about language, meaning and truth. For the main source of all such delusions, according to Rorty, is the idea that thought and language depend on 'conceptual schemes', or systems of representation, whereby reality is somehow construed in accordance with our sense-making concepts and categories. For Kant, these had the character of strictly a priori truths, intrinsic to the nature of human thought and perception, and therefore invariant across all languages, thought-systems or cultures. To others (like Quine) this claim has seemed implausible, since different languages may impose different ways of conceiving the distinction between analytic or a priori truths on the one hand, and contingent or empirical facts on the other. At most there may be sentences which the observer can label 'stimulus-analytic', i.e. sentences in our own and some other language which are uttered in the same context, and with apparently similar objects in view, and which therefore it is reasonably safe to pair off in any basic translation-manual. But this only gives grounds for a kind of ad hoc inductive guesswork, and would certainly not justify any larger claims of a generalized a priori character. For such claims could be warranted only if we had some means of knowing for sure that we had grasped the operative truth-conditions for at least some sentences of the language in question. And this cannot be the case if, as Quine argues, our very notions of truth, meaning and analyticity are bound up with the language we speak and the structure of beliefs embedded in that language. Thus Quine serves Rorty as a prime example of the way that philosophy has at last given up on the quest for knowledge, as opposed to presently valid or workable belief.

Davidson I offers various reasons for rejecting this kind of argument. They involve (as we have seen) his denial that anything useful is achieved by appealing to 'conceptual schemes', and his assertion that some form of truth-conditional theory is simply indispensable to coherent thinking about issues in the province of language and translation. But Rorty sees no great problems in assimilating Davidson to his own neo-pragmatist view of what is best for philosophy in its current, 'post-analytic' situation. And he does so by pointing to those elements in Davidson's theory which appear to weaken the idea of 'truth' to a point where – as Rorty would argue – it serves no real argumentative purpose and might just as well be dispensed with. In *Philosophy and the Mirror of Nature* (1980) Rorty suggests that Davidson's work 'can best be seen as carrying through Quine's dissolution of the distinction between questions of value and questions of fact – his attack on the linguistic interpretation of Kant's distinction between the receptivity of sense and the a priori concepts given by spontaneity'.[9] That is to say, Davidson has helped along the process of belated self-deconstruction by which philosophy has come round to the view that those distinctions are simply redundant, that they are the product of a certain (now obsolete) line of metaphysical talk which contributed nothing to our knowledge of the world except a whole series of insoluble 'problems' which will surely disappear as soon as we find some alternative, preferable idiom.

Quine's essay 'Two Dogmas of Empiricism' is Rorty's chief model for this way of shedding unwanted epistemological baggage. But he finds Davidson a useful ally in the same campaign, or at least that side of Davidson's thinking which apparently lends itself to the purpose. For the upshot of rejecting all talk of 'conceptual schemes' is surely (as Rorty would have it) that we must give up thinking of *truth* as some ultimate correspondence between knowledge on the one hand and objects of knowledge on the other. This only made sense so long as the main problems of philosophy presented themselves in epistemological terms, that is to say, through metaphors of the mind as a 'mirror of nature', or of concepts as more or less accurately picturing the world through a kind of internal representation. Once this picture loses its hold, we can simply dispense with such misleading notions and accept that truth is nothing more than an honorific title, a name attached to those ideas and beliefs that count as true for all current practical purposes. Any theory that claimed to do more – whether in Kantian terms, by matching up concepts with sensuous intuitions through some form of transcendental deduction, or by analysing language into its logical or truth-conditional components – would then appear simply unworkable or beside the point. Such ideas went along with the notion of philosophy as a quest for epistemological grounds, an enterprise whose ultimate purpose was to give us better, more cogent reasons for believing what commonsense had always in any case led us to believe. But it has now turned out, after so much misdirected effort, that belief (so to speak) goes all the way down; that there is no difference between holding-true on the basis of shared values and assumptions and *knowing* what is true on grounds of purported rational self-evidence. ' "Truth" in the sense of "truth taken apart from any theory" and "world" taken as "what determines such truth" are notions that were (like the terms "subject" and "object", "given" and "consciousness") made for each other. Neither can survive apart from the other.'[10] These terms are all involved – so Rorty argues – in a play of specular representations which has held philosophy captive at least since Descartes and Kant, and which continues to exert a seductive and mystifying power over many thinkers in the modern analytic tradition.

So truth-claims are fallacious in so far as they take this strong Kantian form, starting out from the idea of a 'conceptual scheme' and then trying to *prove* that this particular scheme is the one that demonstrably gets things right. And they are merely redundant in so far as they appear (as with most modern versions) in a weaker form, translating Kant's epistemological arguments into a linguistic register, and claiming that the project can best be carried through by examining the truth-conditional structure of language or the difference between analytic and contingent propositions. For this way of thinking is equally vulnerable to Quine's argument: that we can make sense of such distinctions only in terms that derive in the end from our own, culture-specific concepts and categories. So we might as well admit, Rorty urges, that truth is indeed as the pragmatist would have it: 'what's good in the way of belief'. Any desire to think otherwise – any residual craving for grounds, first principles, clear and distinct ideas, concepts of pure understanding or whatever – is nothing more than the old metaphysical yearning for a knowledge ideally exempt from the vagaries of mere consensus belief. It can best be cured, Rorty thinks, by remarking first how this project has collapsed under the pressure of argument from 'post-analytic' thinkers like Quine, and secondly (by a less technical route) that we just cannot be in a position to know anything other or anything more than those things we actually believe. For there is no difference between believing this or that to be the case, and claiming to *know* – on whatever grounds – that our belief corresponds to the truth of the matter. Belief just is the condition of thinking that one has good warrant or adequate grounds for believing whatever one does. Saying 'I believe X' is just the same as saying 'I hold it to be true that X is the case', or 'I know for a fact that X'. Nothing is added to the belief-statement except perhaps a measure of rhetorical emphasis or subjective commitment. And this is indeed, as Rorty would argue, the end-point of all epistemological or truth-based theories: that they answer to our need for something more to believe in than consensus, 'warranted assertability', or simply 'what's good in the way of belief'. But the mere fact of our having this need – this desire to distinguish opinion from knowledge, *doxa* from *episteme*, that which we (perhaps wrongly) hold true from that which we genuinely know to be the case – gives no grounds at all for thinking such distinctions valid in epistemological terms. On the contrary, Rorty asserts: it just goes to show, once again, that what counts as true for us and like-minded individuals will always be decided in the last instance by appeal to some consensus of shared values and beliefs.[11]

Thus Rorty offers an approving summary of William James's view that ' "true" resembles "good" or "rational" in being a normative notion, a compliment paid to sentences that seem to be paying their way and that fit in with other sentences which are doing so'.[12] It has no work to perform – certainly no conceptual or epistemological work – apart from this purely honorific function. And he thinks that Davidson can be read as providing further good arguments for the same pragmatist position. On Rorty's account, what is valuable in Davidson is the doing away with 'conceptual schemes' and with all those other kinds of surplus metaphysical baggage that philosophers produce in the effort to justify such talk. What is less helpful from this point of view is Davidson's insistence on adopting a truth-conditional theory of meaning as a hedge against the threat of linguistic or cultural relativism. But in fact there is no great problem here, Rorty thinks, since we can always point to those passages where Davidson concedes that such truth-conditions must be taken as holding between all the sentences that count as true in any given language, and thus (in the end) as being culture-specific in pretty much the way that pragmatists would have them. This is where Davidson II parts company with the far stronger truth-claims apparently advanced by Davidson I. For if the argument comes down to this weak version of the thesis – that meaning is fixed by truth-conditions, but that these must in turn be relativized to the whole set of sentences believed true by speakers in a certain cultural community – then it might seem that nothing much is gained by continuing to talk in these terms.

Truth then becomes a piece of redundant technical equipment, an obsolete notion brought in just to save appearances, or to give some semblance of epistemological rigour to a theory that would work perfectly well without it. Thus, according to Rorty,

[t]he point of constructing a 'truth theory of English' is not to enable philosophical problems to be put in a formal mode of speech, nor to explain the relationship between words and the world, but simply to lay out perspicuously the relation between parts of a social practice (the use of certain sentences) and other parts (the use of other sentences).[13]

On this account there is nothing more to Davidson's talk of truth than a sense that there *ought* to be some way of hooking up sentences with the real-world objects or states of affairs that enable us to pick out truthful from other kinds of utterance. But there is no need to carry on thinking in this way if one chooses instead to follow out the holistic implications of Davidson's theory, his point that we can assign truth-conditions to sentences only on the basis of a generalized grasp of the relations holding between all sentences of the language concerned. And from here it is no great step to the pragmatist conclusion that truth comes down to what is warranted as such by our current beliefs, language-games, cultural forms of life or whatever. One can then treat Davidson in much the same fashion that Rorty recommends with Hegel and others; that is, by discounting their talk about reason, truth, ontology or other such delusive metaphysical absolutes, and picking out those passages that happen to fall square with the general pragmatist view.[14] In Davidson's case this amounts to a claim that we can lop off the truth-conditional apparatus, along with its realist premises, and then simply keep what is left: a coherence-theory in which 'truth' functions as an intra-linguistic (and to this extent a more or less redundant) term.

III

In a recent essay Davidson sets out to clarify his differences with Rorty. He agrees that (in Rorty's words) 'nothing counts as justification unless by reference to what we already accept', and that therefore, in this ultimate sense, 'there is no way to get outside our beliefs and our language so as to find some test other than coherence'. But he differs in thinking that there is still a real question as to how, given all this, 'we nevertheless can have knowledge of, and talk about, an objective public world which is not of our making'.[15] Rorty considers this world well lost, since it was never (on his view) anything more than a construction out of various philosophical pseudo-problems, notably those post-Cartesian metaphors of mind as the 'mirror of nature', and knowledge as an accurate matching-up of inward with outward representations. And if Davidson I had only taken the point of the arguments advanced by Davidson II, then he would have seen that coherence – or the way that our beliefs hang together at any given stage of the ongoing cultural conversation – is all that is required to put an end to such otiose metaphysical talk. But Davidson clearly rejects this reading of his own work, and does so moreover on grounds of rational self-evidence which – according to Rorty – just cannot be had, since all truth-claims in the end come down to the question of whether or not they happen to fit with our current pattern of values and beliefs. So if Rorty is right about Davidson then Davidson must himself be wrong about at least one part (and it would seem a major part) of his own philosophical enterprise. That is to say, Davidson II has provided the necessary arguments for regarding 'truth' as a dispensable term, for accepting a coherence-theory (a holistic account of meaning and context) as the best available alternative, and thus for denying Davidson I any privileged voice as to how we should interpret his work.

Rorty meanwhile manages to occupy a position where no counter-argument could possibly prove him wrong. For whatever may be Davidson's intentions, his truth-claims, reasonings, ontological commitments or whatever, the pragmatist can always set them aside as so much redundant conceptual baggage, incapable of resolving the issue one way or the other. So it is simply *beside the point* for Davidson to argue – in what amounts to a kind of transcendental deduction – that we could not make sense of language at all unless we took it for granted that most sentences (in our own or some other tongue) were either true or at any rate intelligible in terms of some truth-conditional schema. For Rorty, this just goes to show once again that 'true' is synonymous with 'good in the way of belief', that it is the label we standardly apply to what works for present argumentative purposes (in Davidson's case, the purpose of 'proving' pragmatism in some sense wrong), and that nothing more is to be had in the way of ultimate justification. It is therefore no embarrassment to Rorty's position that this means discounting a great deal of what Davidson I has to say on the topic. For the pragmatist need not claim to get anything right, or to interpret Davidson in a manner that he (Davidson) would acknowledge as capturing the essential points of his argument. There is no ultimate truth of the case, whether as regards our knowledge of objects and events in the world, our ways of construing utterances about them, or our reading of texts (like Davidson's essays) that take some particular stand on such matters. It is enough that any reading should fulfil the main conditions of (1) playing its role in an ongoing cultural 'conversation', (2) hanging together in an interesting way with other contributions to the same broad enterprise and (3) making sense – acceptable sense – on whatever terms are provided by the present-day consensual rules of the game. And it so happens, as Rorty reads the signs, that pragmatism is currently the best option for fitting everything together in a large, historically satisfying picture.

This viewpoint is expressed most concisely in a passage from *Consequences of Pragmatism* where Rorty sketches in some background detail for the current neo-pragmatist turn.

The history [of recent analytic philosophy] has been marked by a gradual 'pragmaticization' of the original tenets of logical positivism . . . I think that analytic philosophy culminates in Quine, the later Wittgenstein, Sellars, and Davidson – which is to say that it transcends and cancels itself. These thinkers successfully, and rightly, blur the positivist distinctions between the semantic and the pragmatic, the analytic and the synthetic, the linguistic and the empirical, theory and observation . . . Davidson's holism and coherentism shows how language looks once we get rid of the central presupposition of Philosophy: that true sentences divide into an upper and a lower division – the sentences which correspond to something and those which are 'true' only by courtesy or convention.[16]

So there is no point sticking with 'technical' programmes in philosophy – whether Kantian, logical-positivist, truth-conditional or whatever – which have not yet come up with the goods and (for reasons attributable to Davidson II) are unlikely to do so. In this case there would be no compelling reason for the commentator to get Davidson 'right', or give due weight to his arguments about meaning and truth. Rather, the aim would be to make sense of Davidson's writings from a post-philosophical, post-analytic or generally 'postmodern' viewpoint. And so it would not matter – or at least would not count as a decisive objection – that much of what Davidson writes goes clean against the pragmatist drift of Rorty's understanding. Any arguments brought up by Davidson I in defence of a stronger truth-conditional theory – one that held out for the logical primacy of sentences that do 'correspond' or refer to factual states of affairs – would of course fail to carry conviction with anyone persuaded by Rorty's account of how philosophy has developed in recent times. And they would fail *not* because they did not give reasons (logically adequate reasons) for conceiving of language in this way, but because the conversation has now moved on and left such reasonings pretty much devoid of interest, appeal or consensus-viability.

Davidson's response to Rorty (cited above) makes it clear that he does not think his work gives warrant for settling the question on pragmatist terms. While certainly espousing no form of metaphysical realism, he still wants to argue that there *is* a genuine difference – and not just a choice of alternative vocabularies – between Rorty's and his own way of posing the issue. Rorty has confused matters, according to Davidson, by assuming that any talk of 'truth' must involve some version of the scheme/content dualism, the idea that sentences are made true by their matching up with real-world objects or events through some kind of inward mirroring process. Certainly this is just the sort of notion that Davidson wants to do away with by discouraging talk of 'conceptual schemes' and other such phantom entities. But there is no reason to suppose that this error infects all strong versions of the truth-conditional claim, or indeed all forms of correspondence-theory. For it is facts, situations or states of affairs that determine the relevant truth-conditions, and not – as Rorty's metaphor suggests – objects, realia or discrete events. Thus (in Davidson's words) '*that* experience takes a certain course, that our skin is warm or punctured, that the universe is finite . . . makes sentences and theories true' (*Inquiries*, p. 194). The plausibility of Rorty's deconstructive move comes from his lumping all realist philosophies into the same metaphysical basket, treating them as mere technical variations on a common (deluded) theme. But this involves a determinate misreading of Davidson, one that takes him not to have pursued the logic of his own best insights. What Davidson is saying is *not* that sentences are true because they have a meaning that somehow corresponds (through a covert appeal to the old metaphor) with the way things are in reality. In fact Davidson has no use for such ill-defined appeals to 'meaning', regarding them as just another place-filler for talk of 'conceptual schemes'. The relation between paradigm sentences and factual states of affairs is one that avoids such question-begging terms by taking truth (not meaning, convention or other intermediary concepts) as its logical point of departure.

So Rorty is getting the matter backwards when he suggests that Davidson (Davidson I) has failed to follow out the consequences of his own pragmatist position. What makes a sentence true is not that its 'meaning' corresponds to some pre-given, ultimate reality whose nature in this case could never be determined outside the language (or conceptual scheme) in question. Rather, it is the fact that we always start out – as Davidson says – in the position of knowing a great deal about the kinds of evidence, justification, reasonable inference and so forth that will work for any conceivable language, no matter how remote from our own. Hence his objection to those, like Whorf, who are over-impressed by the sheer variety of languages and cultures on display, and who thus fall into the relativist trap of assuming that translation must be in some sense a radically impossible enterprise. Their mistake is to suppose that these localized problems of linguistic and cultural grasp cannot in principle be sorted out by reference to the much wider areas of agreement that must exist between all communities of language use. This agreement, says Davidson, 'may take the form of a widespread sharing of sentences held true by speakers of "the same language" ', or it may be a matter of 'agreement in the large mediated by a theory of truth contrived by an interpreter for speakers of another language' (*Inquiries*, p. 192). This latter would count against the kind of ethno-linguistic relativism espoused by thinkers like Whorf, or those obstacles to the project of 'radical translation' that are often taken to follow from Quine's brand of ontological scepticism. The first line of argument – having to do with problems of grasp between speakers of 'the same language' – would serve as a rejoinder to the pragmatists, poststructuralists, Kuhnian philosophers of science and others who raise the idea of conceptual schemes (alternatively, 'paradigms' or 'discourses') into a doctrine that denies the commensurability of different orders of knowledge. In each case Davidson asserts just the opposite: that we do, when required, manage to get a grip on languages or discourses outside our immediate cultural domain, and that our starting-point for any such attempt will be the truth-conditions, rational constraints, procedures of logical inference and so forth which we *must* take as holding for the language in question if it is to make sense at all for us or for anyone else. In short, translation is a feasible project – whatever the distance of cultural horizons – because there exists this large central core of necessary presuppositions.

This is why the pragmatist version of Davidson cannot (or should not) claim to be a right reading, one that respects either the logic or the intended force of his argument. For it is a reading which chooses to pass clean over a crucial point in Davidson's argument: namely, that any workable account of language, meaning and interpretation will have to be grounded in something more than a coherence or consensus model of truth. This is not to say that Davidson is committed to one or other of the classical alternatives, whether a naive correspondence-theory or a version of foundationalist epistemology which would leave him open to all the well-worn objections rehearsed by (among them) Quine, Rorty and Davidson himself.[17] Rather, it is to claim that these alternatives do not exhaust the field, and that there is a way of addressing the issue that can satisfy the twin conditions of (1) taking truth as something more than 'truth relative to this or that language, culture or system of beliefs', while (2) not going along with ideas of correspondence or privileged epistemic access that would beg the whole question from a relativist viewpoint. This position has been argued by thinkers like Jürgen Habermas and Karl-Otto Apel, theorists who take their bearings partly from the Frankfurt tradition of post-Kantian critical thought, and partly from developments in Anglo-American philosophy of mind and language.[18] For the rest of this paper I shall be looking at one essay in particular, Apel's 'The Problem of Philosophical Foundations in Light of a Transcendental Pragmatics of Language'.[19] And I shall argue that this offers not only some useful points of comparison with Davidson's thinking, but a means of defending his central propositions against the generalized pragmatist drift that Rorty finds everywhere in current 'post-analytic' philosophy.

Apel starts out by distinguishing different kinds of foundationalist truth-claim. 'From the point of view of transcendental pragmatics, the logical process by which sentences are deduced from sentences – indeed, all "axiomatics' – can only be considered as an objectifiable means within the context of the argumentative grounding of statements through epistemic evidence' (Apel, p. 271). That is to say, there is no question of simply rejecting the pragmatist argument, adopting a straightforward neo-Kantian approach and asserting that truth can be arrived at through critical reflection on the a priori powers and limits of human cognitive grasp. One could only maintain this position by ignoring the problems that arise as soon as one considers the extent to which truth-claims are in fact argued out, refined and developed through an ongoing dialogue whose rules are set by some existing community of shared interests and assumptions. In this sense at least the anti-foundationalist will always have knock-down arguments in plenty against anyone who seeks to put philosophy back on an epistemological footing, or to rehabiliate truth-as-correspondence in any of its classical forms. But we can take the full force of these objections – so Apel argues – without giving up on the idea of truth as something more than 'what's good in the way of belief'. For there is still the choice between Rorty's kind of pragmatism – one that in the end has no use for truth, reducing it to the way that beliefs hang together in some given cultural context – and Apel's 'transcendental pragmatics', a theory which seeks to conserve the truth not just as an honorific term but as simply indispensable to any form of reasoned philosophical or scientific thought.

This is why Apel denies that we can separate the 'argumentative grounding of statements' from the question of 'epistemic evidence'. Certainly it is the case, he acknowledges, that agreement within some existing consensus is the precondition for a statement's possessing any warrantable claim to truth. But equally, such claims must always be subject to agreed-upon procedures of verification, procedures that involve (among other things) the effort to match up hypotheses with experimental data, or the selection between rival theories in light of continuing research. And this principle extends beyond the specialized domain of scientific method to the practices of everyday language use and intersubjective understanding. For here also we must start from the knowledge that statements can be more or less truthful, informative or relevant to the matter in hand; that there will (at least in the majority of cases) be better reasons for accepting or rejecting such claims than the mere appeal to consensus belief; and that ultimately what counts as a good reason is the fact that some statements do correspond to the way things are in reality. So we are *not* confronted with an ultimate choice between, on the one hand, some version of metaphysical realism (or foundationalist epistemology) which ignores the role of discursive constraints in the social production of truth, and on the other a wholesale pragmatist creed which rejects all talk of truth as so much obsolete conceptual baggage. Rather, it is a question of seeing how these viewpoints cannot (or need not) get into conflict; how the 'argumentative grounding' of statements is always bound up with the presupposition that such statements can be checked against the facts in some not merely circular, trivial or self-confirming way.

So we should not be misled into thinking that Apel's choice of the term 'transcendental pragmatics' signifies a broad measure of agreement with Rorty's pragmatist position. On the contrary: what Apel sets out to defend is a strong truth-conditional theory of interpretive reason whose grounds are 'transcendental' in a sense much akin to the Kantian use of this term. Thus he argues (1) that sentences can indeed be assessed in terms of their ultimate truth-value, (2) that this process of assessment is carried on by a community of rational inquirers, and (3) that what qualifies a proposition as true is not just the present state of consensus belief within that community but also the community's readiness to make trial of it against evidence that may overthrow the consensus. To this way of thinking, Apel writes,

> it makes no sense to speak of 'appeal to epistemic evidence' without presupposing linguistic discourse as a context for interpretation and logical coherence. Likewise, it makes no sense to speak of substantial argumentative discourse without presupposing certain epistemic evidence, which the particular participants of discourse apply as their criteria of truth in the argumentative procedure of building a discourse. (Apel, p. 262)

In support of this contention Apel cites the example of modern theoretical physics, where successive 'crises' have been brought about by a perceived mismatch between the different orders of evidential reasoning. On the one hand experiments may fail to confirm some particularly powerful or elegant hypothesis. In this case the upshot may be *either* that the theory is eventually abandoned as problematic evidence keeps coming in, *or* that it is borne out in the long run when science develops the technical means (maybe a microscope with higher powers of resolution) to validate what had been, up to then, an attractive but epistemically ungrounded hypothesis. On the other hand, there may exist situations where a certain hypothesis continues to appear both counter-intuitive and devoid of experimental warrant, but where its sheer argumentative cogency and rigour compels widespread assent. Such was at one time the case, Apel argues, with those alternative geometries or time-space dimensions presupposed by the General Theory of Relativity.

From this it might seem that the Rortyan pragmatist must have the last word; that 'truth' is indeed what counts as such within a given community of knowledge, and therefore cannot be defined in terms of correspondence or epistemic access. But Apel rejects this conclusion, arguing instead that the business of sustaining an apparently counter-evidential hypothesis must always be justified *at some point* by the appeal to an available means of verification. Thus the testing of such theories 'is carried out by means of measuring instruments which for their part, in both their function and their manufacture, presuppose evidence in the sense of the perception of ideal space, which is paradigmatic in the "protophysical" language-game of Euclidean geometry' (Apel, p. 270). That is to say, any hypothesis will have to make sense not only in terms of its role within some specialized discourse of speculative knowledge, but also in the context of those checks and procedures that count elsewhere as providing well-founded scientific evidence. 'This example', says Apel, 'elucidates the a priori necessary connection between argumentation related to discourse and (sufficient justification by means of) appeal to epistemic evidence' (p. 270). And his point also holds for those non-scientific uses of language where truth is not a matter of stringent verification but of knowing, in a general way, that some kinds of utterance have a genuine claim to be more accurate, more reliable or closer to the facts than others.

IV

There are two main points that Apel seeks to establish by taking this example from modern theoretical physics. One is the insufficiency of any Cartesian or Husserlian appeal to intuitive self-evidence, apodictic certainty, a priori concepts of pure understanding or the like. For such arguments cannot account for the fact that their truth-claims are validated only within a certain discourse of knowledge, a discourse whose terms must at least make sense and carry some degree of logical conviction with users of the same language.[20] 'Like Descartes, Husserl could not even bring to his own consciousness the indubitability of his ego-consciousness, in a form both intelligible and valid for him, unless he could formulate this insight as an argument in the framework of a transcendental language-game of an ideal communication community' (Apel, p. 280). So it is impossible to set aside the arguments of those (like Wittgenstein in his remarks on the 'private language' fallacy) who point to the radical incoherence of foundationalist thinking, at least in so far as such thinking is tied to notions of privileged epistemic access.[21] And the analogy from physics supports this case by offering evidence that there are forms of knowledge that presently lack any kind of epistemic self-evidence, but for which it suffices that their claims hold good within a given, albeit highly specialized community of language use. This is why it was possible for proponents of relativity theory 'to question the inter-subjective validity of classical physics on the basis of a reinterpretation of experience through explanatorily more powerful theories', even though the older model still accorded not only with commonsense perception but with 'certain a priori evident connections between representations, as subjective conditions of the possibility of primary experience (for instance, conceptual connections in the sense of Kant's "forms of intuition" and "schematized categories")' (Apel, p. 269). So there can always develop situations like this where the constraints of a language, discourse or set of intra-theoretical assumptions count for more than the appeal to any kind of epistemic self-evidence. But – and this is Apel's second main point – science would scarcely exist as such if the truth-claims arrived at through this process of purely argumentative enquiry were not ultimately subject to procedures of empirical verification. And the same applies to 'ordinary', non-scientific discourse in so far as interpretation depends on our grasping the structures of logical inference, the truth-conditions and semantic implications, that we just could not grasp were it not for the fact that language *paradigmatically* refers to objects of real-world experience. In short, the very notion of argumentative validity – of 'truth' as the product of general agreement within some currently existing paradigm – can only make sense on the prior assumption that statements may success-fully refer to the world and thus lay claim to a stronger (epistemic) order of truth.

So where the pragmatists go wrong, from this point of view, is in assuming that the two kinds of theory cannot possibly be reconciled. That is, they equate all epistemic truth-claims with the sort of rock-bottom foundationalist argument that denies to language (or to discourse in its knowledge-constitutive aspect) any role in the social production of truth. And since clearly this position must be untenable – since we cannot con-ceive of any knowledge that could ever be arrived at outside some context of validating argument – they conclude that truth is *purely and simply* a product of consensual discourse. But, according to Apel, this line of argument leaves them open to a form of transcendental *tu quoque*: namely, that the pragmatist reduction of truth to what is good in the way of belief can offer no means of distinguishing valid from invalid forms of consensus knowledge. For if, as Rorty argues, the purported 'founda-tions' of rational discourse come down to nothing more than some par-ticular language-game or choice of 'final vocabulary', then there is no possibility of criticizing false claims-to-truth on the basis of better, more cogent or adequate arguments. That such arguments will never be founda-tional in the absolute, Kantian sense – that they will always seek validation according to a set of currently-prevailing discursive rules and constraints – is therefore no reason for espousing the wholesale pragmatist position and rejecting all talk of truth. 'From the point of view of a transcendental pragmatics of language, the fact that evidential consciousness achieves intersubjective validity only as publicly acknowledged language-game paradigms shows that giving reasons in arguments necessarily leads back to appeals to epistemic evidence' (Apel, p. 271). For if this were not the case then the activity of giving reasons could be nothing more than a species of circular argument that would always confirm its own inbuilt logic of assumptions. What therefore distinguishes Apel's 'transcendental pragmatics' from the anti-transcendental version propounded by Rorty is precisely his insistence that rational debate cannot be conducted in the absence of epistemic truth-claims.

At this stage Rorty would doubtless respond by arguing first that any such claims must involve some appeal to foundationalist criteria – thus running into all the familiar problems – and secondly, that Apel has already undermined these delusive foundations by conceding that 'truth' can only be arrived at through the process of intersubjective debate. So one might just as well (indeed must, for consistency's sake) abandon all forms of transcendental argument and accept the pragmatist point without further ado. But it is precisely this way of posing the issue that Apel seeks to avoid by way of his appeal to the 'transcendental pragmatics' of discourse involved in every kind of rational, truth-seeking inquiry. The pragmatist fallacy rests on the argument that *since* all reasoning is conducted in the context of particular languages, paradigms or communities of discourse, *therefore* reasons can only hold good in so far as they cohere with certain culture-specific values and assumptions. In the end this involves a covert appeal to conventions or 'conceptual schemes', despite Rorty's agreement with Davidson that such talk just obscures the issue. For if truth is indeed defined (for all practical purposes) by the way that statements fit in with some prevailing consensus, then it is hard to envisage just how such a fit could come about unless on the basis of a matching-up between shared structures of meaning or belief. And one could argue further that Rorty gets into this awkward position by the same route that leads him to misconstrue Davidson; namely, his refusal to countenance any stronger form of truth-claim than the pragmatist reduction of all such issues to the level of consensus belief.

This is why Apel rejects the wholesale pragmatist argument and proposes instead a 'transcendental pragmatics' that would not lead on to such circular reasoning.

By virtue of the propositional acts (the identifying acts of reference and predication) upon which the formation of judgments depends, epistemic evidence is interwoven from the outset with language use and the capacities of knowing subjects . . . Justification, as giving reasons for the validity of knowledge, must always rest on the possible evidential consciousness of the particular knowing subjects (as autonomous representatives of the transcendental knowing subject as such) and on the a priori intersubjective rules of an argumentative discourse in the context of which the epistemic evidence, as subjective proof or objective validity, has to be brought to the level of intersubjective validity. (Apel, pp. 261–2)

This is a Kantian form of argument in so far as it locates the possibility of truth in the achievement of a state of rational (enlightened) consensus, a knowledge brought about by critical reflection on its own claims to validity. It is distinguished from the Rortyan pragmatist position partly on account of the role played within it by the knowing, self-critical subject; partly by the link that it maintains between knowledge and questions of epistemic evidence; and partly by the fact that it holds out for an informed or rational consensus – for truth at the end of inquiry – and thus maintains the necessity of criticizing false ideas and beliefs, no matter how widely accepted these may be in some given cultural context. It is Kantian also in the sense that it argues from the 'conditions of possibility' for human understanding in general; that is to say, from the fact that we would be in no position to argue, criticize, give reasons or engage in purposeful debate unless we acknowledged the truth of its premisses. But it does not involve the kind of foundationalist truth-claim that would render it vulnerable to those arguments so deftly rehearsed by Rorty in his deconstructive reading of the mainstream tradition. And this for the reason, as Apel makes clear, that 'the Kantian claim of the definitive completeness of the "system of pure reason" can no longer be maintained; our task is rather that of progressively opening up new transcendental horizons, which grow wider with the expansion of the human knowledge that we are questioning as to its conditions of possibility' (Apel, p. 273).

Davidson can best be read in light of these qualified but none the less powerful Kantian arguments. That is to say, we should accept his holistic approach (the idea of truth-conditions as holding between all sentences of a given language) along with the stronger theory in which truth figures as a matter of epistemic warrant. The alternative (pragmatist or poststructuralist) reading is one that must finally reject such claims and regard truth as wholly relative to the language, discourse or cultural paradigm in question. On this account (as argued by S. Pradhan in a recent article on Davidson and Derrida) one can indeed embrace the holistic implications while discounting any version of the strong truth-conditional or epistemic theory.[22] Thus Davidson may be taken to agree with Derrida on the following points: (1) that the appeal to linguistic 'conventions' in fact explains nothing, since signs, sentences and speech-acts can always be 'grafted' into novel or unlikely contexts where they continue to function despite the absence of normative constraints; (2) that such appeals would in any case involve a kind of infinite regress, since a rule would be required to determine just how, when and where the relevant convention came into force, and this rule would be dependent in turn upon some third-order level of linguistic convention; and (3) that we should therefore dispense with such question-begging talk and make do with what Pradhan calls a 'minimalist semantics', one that allows speech-acts to function across the widest possible range of contexts without always asking how their 'meaning' allows them so to function. This is why Davidson and Derrida both have an interest in anomalous cases, speech-acts that would count (on conventionalist terms) as deviant, non-standard or somehow 'parasitical' in relation to other, authentic or normative uses of the same verbal formula.[23]

Such is Derrida's response to John Searle, pointing out that *all* speech-acts are iterable, i.e., capable of being cited, parodied, taken 'out of context' etc., so that Searle runs up against insuperable problems in attempting to distinguish genuine from non-genuine varieties. And

Davidson is arguing to similar effect when he denies that 'deviant' uses of language (e.g. metaphor or malapropism) have to be referred back to our grasp of the proper, literal meaning before we can begin to make sense of them.[24] For there is nothing that could serve as an adequate 'scheme', or set of agreed-upon interpretive conventions, for effecting this shift from the level of deviant to non-deviant usage. Quite simply, 'the same declarative sentence may have the same meaning when used to make an assertion, to tell a joke, to annoy a bore, to complete a rhyme, or to ask a question' (*Inquiries*, p. 269). And this is so *not* because (as Searle would argue) the normal case provides guidance enough for interpreting deviant instances, but because no semantic conditions determine the possible range of meaning that attaches to any given speech-act in context. Hence the need for a 'minimalist semantics', one that can account for this capacity of signs to function across a vast (potentially infinite) range of contexts without falling back on redundant talk of conventions, conceptual schemes and so forth. In Pradhan's words:

If a sentence can be put to any use, and if its meaning does not restrict its use in any way and it retains the same meaning in the context of those multiple uses; or if a sign can always be removed from its context and grafted into another context and its identity as a sign does not hamper its functioning as that sign in those new contexts; then we had better posit only the minimum required semantically to constitute that sentence or that sign as that unit of language.[25]

And from this it follows – according to Pradhan – that truth on the Davidsonian model must somehow be relativized to the entire language or set of logico-semantic relations which determines what shall count as a proper understanding of each particular utterance. 'Even though a theorem which states the truth conditions of a sentence explicitly refers only to that sentence and no other linguistic element, nevertheless to understand what is stated in stating the truth conditions of a sentence we must bring in its relation to other linguistic elements.'[26] Thus Davidson can be seen as concurring with Derrida in the argument that meaning cannot be fixed by any appeal to convention, to normative ideas of context, or to theories of the sign (or individual speech-act) as possessing a semantic identity that would make it possible to distinguish proper from improper uses. In which case truth more or less drops out of the picture, except in the largely redundant guise of 'truth relative to some particular language as a whole'.

But this comes down to yet another version of that same linguistic-conventionalist idea that Davidson is so anxious to avoid. And the reason is that Pradhan, like Rorty, chooses to stress certain elements in Davidson's thinking – those that can be used to make the link between his broadly holistic approach to language and poststructuralist notions of the arbitrary sign – while ignoring his insistence that any such theory must also take account of epistemic constraints upon the class of sentences held true. Thus, in Davidson's words, '[a] sentence or theory fits our sensory promptings, successfully faces the tribunal of experience, predicts future experience, or copes with the pattern of our surface irritations, provided it is borne out by the evidence' (*Inquiries*, p. 193). And this despite the fact that any such theory or sentence will always be construed, and its truth-claims assessed, in some broader context that may extend from the idiom of a specialized sub-group, research-programme, 'interpretive community' or whatever to the whole linguistic and cultural tradition within which that idiom arose. For it is Davidson's chief point that these two requirements do not necessarily get into conflict; that truth can be *both* a matter of epistemic warrant and a matter of the way propositions hang together with others in the same language.

Thus it is wrong to suppose that there must be some ultimate choice between, on the one hand, foundationalist theories that isolate truth from the context of discursive or linguistic justification, and on the other the wholesale pragmatist view that truth is simply what counts as such according to our present, culture-specific aims and purposes. On this point Davidson would surely go along with the line of 'transcendental-pragmatic' argument advanced by thinkers like Habermas and Apel. That is to say, he accepts that truth-claims must indeed be subject to a process of validation in and through language, a process whereby they come to be accepted by members of the relevant community. But it is also prerequisite to any workable theory of truth and interpretation that an appeal should be open from language – or the realm of intra-discursive concepts and meanings – to the conditions under which statements are tested against various kinds of epistemic evidence. For otherwise, as Davidson argues, we could never make a start in that process of assigning determinable truth-conditions which is always presupposed in attempts to clarify the meaning of any given utterance. 'Of course truth of sentences remains relative to language, but that is as objective as can be. In giving up the dualism of scheme and world, we do not give up the world, but re-establish unmediated touch with the familiar objects whose antics make our sentences and opinions true or false' (*Inquiries*, p. 198).

There is no doubt that Davidson's writings – or selected passages from them – can be so construed as to offer support for the pragmatist/poststructuralist standpoint in matters of language, truth and representation. Furthermore, this approach has the dubious advantage of placing itself effectively beyond criticism by denying that there can be, when all is said and done, any right reading or demonstrable truth of the Davidsonian text. But in doing so it has to ignore not only some crucial aspects of his argument but also – more importantly – the entire logical structure of assumptions upon which that argument rests.

NOTES

1 See especially Ernest Le Pore (ed.), *Truth and Interpretation: Essays on the Philosophy of Donald Davidson* (Oxford, Basil Blackwell, 1986).

2 See W. V. Quine, *From a Logical Point of View* (Cambridge, Mass., Harvard University Press, 1953), and *Ontological Relativity and Other Essays* (New York, Columbia University Press, 1989).

3 Wittgenstein, *Philosophical Investigations* trans. G. E. M. Anscombe (Oxford, Basil Blackwell, 1953), pp. 89ff.

4 Donald Davidson, 'On the Very Idea of a Conceptual Scheme', in *Inquiries into Truth and Interpretation* (London, Oxford University Press, 1984), pp. 183–98. Hereafter cited in the text as *Inquiries*.

5 Ferdinand de Saussure, *Course in General Linguistics*, trans. Wade Baskin (London, Fontana, 1974).

6 See for instance Michel Foucault, *Language, Counter-Memory, Practice*, trans. Donald F. Bouchard and Sherry Simon (Oxford, Basil Blackwell, 1977) and *Power/Knowledge: Selected Interviews and Other Writings* (Brighton, Harvester, 1980).

7 See particularly Roland Barthes, *S/Z*, trans. Richard Miller (London, Jonathan Cape, 1975) and the essays collected in *Image-Music-Text*, trans. Stephen Heath (London, Fontana, 1977).

8 Richard Rorty, *Philosophy and the Mirror of Nature* (Princeton, NJ, Princeton University Press, 1980).

9 Ibid, p. 261.

10 Richard Rorty, *Consequences Of Pragmatism* (Minneapolis, University of Minnesota Press, 1982), p. 15.

11 This line of argument has been taken up by neo-pragmatist literary critics who seek to demonstrate that 'theory' is a pointless, misguided or redundant activity. See especially Stanley Fish, *Is There a Text in This Class?* (Cambridge, Mass., Harvard University Press, 1980); Steven Knapp and Walter Benn Michaels, 'Against Theory', *Critical Inquiry*, 8 (1982), 723–42; Knapp and Michaels, 'Against Theory 2: Hermeneutics and Deconstruction', *Critical Inquiry*, 14 (1987), 49–68. In this second piece they cite Davidson's work in support of their case against theories that rest on the idea of meaning as a product of conventions or conceptual schemes. However, their version of Davidson is similar to Rorty's (and yet more extreme) in its acceptance of a thoroughgoing pragmatist approach to questions of meaning and interpretation. For Knapp and Michaels, meaning is synonymous with authorial intention, but only because it does not make sense to raise 'theoretical' issues of validity, truth etc.

12 Rorty, *Consequences of Pragmatism*, p. xxv.

13 Rorty, *Philosophy and the Mirror of Nature*, pp. 261–2.

14 See especially Rorty, 'The World Well Lost' and 'Dewey's Metaphysics', in *Consequences of Pragmatism*, pp. 3–18 and 72–89.

15 Davidson, 'A Coherence Theory of Truth and Knowledge', in Le Pore (ed.), *Truth and Interpretation*, p. 310.

16 Rorty, *Consequences of Pragmatism*, p. xviii.

17 Rorty rehearses these arguments succinctly in his Introduction to *Consequences of Pragmatism*, pp. ix–xlvii.

18 See for instance Jürgen Habermas, *Knowledge and Human Interests*, trans. Jeremy Shapiro (London, Heinemann, 1972); *Communication and the Evolution of Society*, trans. Thomas McCarthy (London, Heinemann, 1979); Karl-Otto Apel, *Towards a Transformation of Philosophy* (London, Routledge and Kegan Paul, 1980).

19 K.-O. Apel, 'The Problem of Philosophical Foundations in Light of a Transcendental Pragmatics of Language', in Kenneth Baynes, James Bohman and Thomas McCarthy (eds), *After Philosophy: End or Transformation?* (Cambridge, Mass., MIT Press, 1987), pp. 250–90. Hereafter cited in the text as Apel.

20 Jacques Derrida pursues a similar line of argument in his early work on Husserl. See Derrida, *Edmund Husserl's 'Origin of Geometry'*, trans. John P. Leavey (Stony Brook, NY, Nicolas Hays, 1978).

21 On this topic see for instance Saul Kripke, *Wittgenstein on Rules and Private Language* (Oxford, Basil Blackwell, 1982).

22. S. Pradhan, 'Minimalist Semantics: Davidson and Derrida on meaning, use, and convention', *Diacritics*, 16 (Spring, 1986), 66–77.

23 See J. Derrida, 'Signature Event Context', *Glyph*, vol. 1 (Baltimore, Md, Johns Hopkins University Press, 1977), pp. 172–97; also John R. Searle, 'Reiterating the Differences', *Glyph*, vol. I, pp. 198–208; and Derrida's response to Searle, 'Limited Inc abc', *Glyph*, vol. 2 (1977), pp. 162–254.

24 See D. Davidson, 'What Metaphors Mean', in *Inquiries*, pp. 245–64) and 'A Nice Derangement of Epitaphs', in Richard E. Grandy (ed.), *Grounds of Rationality* (Oxford, Basil Blackwell, 1986), pp. 157–74.

25 Pradhan, 'Minimalist Semantics', p. 75.

26 Ibid, p. 74.

7

Beauty and Truth: the Apotheosis of an Idea

Anthony Savile

I

In the arts, as in the sciences and practical life one sometimes comes across what might, without too much exaggeration, be called the apotheosis of an idea. The mechanism is easy enough to describe and will be familiar to anyone sensitive to this sort of thing. Initially the theorist-cum-philosopher puts an idea into play; it quickly comes to exert appeal beyond the confines of the schoolroom or the scholarly journal and wins its seal of approval from those who enjoy a limited but nonetheless powerful public voice; that voice soon reaches the ears and hearts of those whose doings and makings are widely seen and admired. Their deeds, fashioned now according to the new idea, come through their snowballing effect to be taken as verifying or authenticating the idea to which they conform. So the once novel idea becomes established commonplace. Thus is the first phase in the process complete.

The next stage protects the now established commonplace against rejection or refutation. So convincing and pervasive may be the manifestations that are taken to verify it that deeds or makings not conforming to that same intellectual mould are judged as defective *by the very standards that are themselves implicit in it* and which we have now become accustomed to seeing around us. The idea has become unassailable just because in its instances it exerts a power that prevents non-conforming action from challenging it. The non-conform can only be thought of as failing to come up to the standard, newly legitimized, that it seeks to contest and displace. Successes against challenge naturally strengthen the idea, and as success is repeated a carapace forms around the idea that grows increasingly difficult to penetrate. So what starts out as a tentative nursery hypothesis may finally assume the status of hallowed doctrine; the once puny mortal is decked in the mantle of divinity. Not that such doctrine cannot be undone. It can; only slowly, and only when the right strategy is adopted. Just as successful scientific theory is not to be refuted by any single negative experiment – auxiliary hypotheses stand ready to man the breach – but only by a developed and powerful competing theory, so too a dominant artistic, aesthetic or practical idea will not be unseated by examples of alternative possible practice however appealing, but only by the laborious demonstration at the working bench of the weakness of the original hypothesis together with the introduction of appealing alternatives. Only when the original foundations are sapped in this twofold fashion does it become possible in the wider world to judge newcomers on the artistic or the practical stage by canons other than those that they reject and to see them clearly for what they truly are. Only then can the stifling weight of established practice be thrown off.

This schematic picture of intellectual and practical change is one that finds a place for the theorist at two separate points. First, he bears an initial responsibility for elaborating the original position that gains empire; later on, and very likely in a different person, his role is critical, to subject the now powerful theory or idea to more testing scrutiny than may originally have been possible to give it. And while in the erection of the original theory the thinker or theorist may hail from any background at all, depending largely on the nature of the idea in point, there may be a special and fairly obvious virtue at the second, more testing, stage in his work being conducted from a professionally scrutinizing stance. At its best, analytic thought and the style of philosophy associated with it promises tangible practical outcomes; then it emerges from what is often, often wrongly, thought of as its ivory tower and can claim a rightful place in the public world.

Unsurprisingly, this reminder of a familiar pattern of events is prompted by a particular example. At the London Hayward Gallery's 1987 exhibition of work by the fêted figures Gilbert and George, I was struck to see the handout given to visitors epigraphically embellished by a quotation from R. D. Laing's 1967 *Introduction to the Politics of Experience*. 'Our social realities', it ran, 'are so ugly if seen in the light of exiled truth, and beauty is almost no longer possible if it is not to lie. What is to be done? We who are still half alive, living in the often fibrillating heartland of a senescent capitalism – can we do more than reflect the decay around and within us? Can we do more than sing our sad and bitter songs of disillusion and defeat?'

Now certainly the montages of the two artists on display do express some of the bleaker realities of contemporary British urban life and make little concession to those who more traditionally seek lightness or beauty in the images with which they surround themselves. But it seems to me that so dominant has the thought become that 'beauty is . . . no longer possible if it is not to lie' that the traditionalist is, as it were, bullied into fearing that his unsatisfied yearning is merely self-indulgent, and the artist contemplating his next work into thinking that the old avenues are firmly closed and could tempt only those whose emotions are sentimental and whose minds superficial. The truths of our day, both parties are inclined to reason, must be told, and they lead in quite the opposite direction. The message that Laing was proclaiming, powerful still twenty years on, is not originally his. We can trace the theme through the Frankfurt school of social criticism and at least in some of its elements back to the writings of Lukács and Marx, but perhaps we find the fullest elaboration of it in Theodor Adorno's posthumous and widely disseminated *Äesthetische Theorie* (1970), recently made available in English,[1] and which brings together in a somewhat tangled skein the scattered elements that have made up his aesthetic thinking since the early 1930s. It is on his particular version of the deified idea that I want to concentrate.

Adorno's central theme is that beauty and truth are distinct, logically independent, fulcra around which the concept of art is organized. Ideally we look for art to achieve both. However, at certain moments in cultural history, most notably in our own century, the two inevitably strain against each other, and when they do, it will be to the immediate detriment of the first, junior, member of the pair, and subsequently to the existence of art itself. Fundamentally art is aimed at truth, and where the truth that has to be conveyed is that society is rotten to the core, for the artist to offer his public beautiful images could only be to connive in this corruption. But since art also, importantly, aims at beauty, Adorno thinks we may well eventually have to say either just that it achieves its beauty through renouncing beauty or, more honestly, that the prospect looms that for the sake of art itself the artist must be silent (p. 85).

II

This position of Adorno's is itself clearly heir to a certain history in pre-Marxist aesthetic theory, and before turning to a detailed discussion of his own radical line of thought we should remind ourselves of the largely eighteenth-century background from which it springs. A natural enough starting place is Hume's essay *Of the Standard of Taste* (1757). There we see developed for the first time the now familiar non-reductive idea that in view of the essential subjective response-based nature of beauty and of the wide variety of response that greets the individual object, it will only be possible to evaluate aesthetic judgements as true or false if some uniform natural human response to it is to be found among those of us in whom our nature finds free and authentic expression.[2] Such, roughly, are people who are unprejudiced, not blinkered by passion, and who possess (sound moral understanding[3] and) a delicacy of taste arrived at through practised discrimination.

Hume's suggestion is itself a development of the main idea of Shaftesbury's *Characteristics* (1711) 'that in the very nature of things there must of necessity be the foundation of a wrong and a right *Taste, Relish* or *Choice* as well in respect of inward Characters and Features, as of outward Persons'.[4] However, it was apparent to later thinkers than Hume that even if we do think of human nature under liberating training as capable of setting a standard for proper aesthetic delight, not everything of importance about the concept *beauty* and its congeners can hope to be conveyed by an elucidation cast in such terms. In particular, no such formulation just by itself does anything to explain why the beautiful should be thought of a priori as a worthy object of pursuit, or why we regard it as of its essence that beauty should demand the attention of people whose sharpest pleasures are found elsewhere. A rewarding way of understanding much post-Humean thought on the subject, in particular the thought of Kant, Schiller and Hegel, is to see it as struggling to provide an answer to those pressing questions, so notably passed over by the empiricist tradition.[5]

Kant's response in the *Critique of Judgement* comes in two alternatives. Along one, ultimately fruitless, line[6] he argues that there cannot at bottom be people who fail to share a uniform natural pleasure ('a common sense', in his parlance), because to do so is a necessary condition of our having experience at all (cf. Introduction VI, §9, §22.2). Alternatively, and nearer to the point, he reasons that we are to think of the beautiful as that in which, when viewed in the appropriate way, we ought all to take delight (§19, §22.2). He then goes on (§§41, 42, 49) to speculate on what compelling, *ought*-generating reasons we may all have to take pleasure in the disinterested contemplation of nature and of art, and eventually comes up with the idea that their subjugation to the discipline of form, be it imposed by the lover of nature in perception or by the artist in the works he fashions, enables us to think enrichingly of the objects of our gaze or the themes of which his works treat. This ability, Kant supposes, is an indefeasible requirement for a fulfilled human life.

Schiller and Hegel in their turn undoubtedly took themselves to be improving on what they saw as the deficiencies in Kant's brand of formalism, but to a later eye it is evident that neither of them fully understood his thought and each went on to make suggestions about the importance of aesthetic experience that were certainly continuous, if not strictly identical, with Kant's own. So, in his letters *On the Aesthetic Education of Man* Schiller proposes that we elucidate the beautiful in terms of images which when internalized bring us closer to an a priori human life-ideal that insists on breadth of experience fully informed with depth and meaning. Significantly, here the beautiful and the true are for the first time implicitly brought together in that the image of the world that the artist presents to us in his outstandingly successful offerings is one which in our ideal state we could not but endorse. They are tressed together in a vision of the world that, at the end of the day, must accurately reflect what our world, through our construction, has become. Beauty and truth coincide when 'semblance overcomes reality and art, nature' (Letter IX,7).[7]

Twenty years or so later on, in the Introduction to his *Lectures on Aesthetics* (delivered between 1818 and 1828/9), Hegel is full of praise for Schiller and wants only that his thought be clad in proper system, system that Hegel is only too happy to provide. For him, beauty, which is now definitionally what art aims at[8] is explicitly characterized in terms of truth: art's aim is to reveal truth in pleasing sensible form, and the particular truths Hegel has in mind are those that make for active self-understanding. 'The absolute and universal need from which art springs has its origin in the fact that man is thinking consciousness, that he constructs himself, and indeed everything that there is, from within himself and for himself'.[9] As the unification of form and matter (and a number of other resonant contrasts as well) beauty will, as in Schiller's version, articulate ways of understanding ourselves and our surroundings that cohere with all pertinent considerations that we can bring to bear and which can be given expression in sensible form. Hegel notoriously thought that in time further developed understanding would take us beyond these sense-bound confines and that there we would be in a domain in which art and beauty had little place to play, the domain of religion and of philosophy itself. However before that moment has come we are to look to the arts for truth, and it is in their beautiful products that we will find it.

Notice how the internal connection between the beautiful and the true that in the late eighteenth and early nineteenth century comes more and more explicitly to the fore is in each case well suited to answer the problem that Hume's self-standing conception of the beautiful gives rise to but to which he and like-minded thinkers in the empiricist stamp had no adequate solution. In the idealist tradition, once Kant's first, transcendental, avenue of exploration is set aside, definition of beauty by reference to truth looks well suited to supplying that problem with an answer. If someone does not find themselves appreciative of the beauties that the arts offer them – and for Kant the beauties of nature too – they will be turning their backs on something which they genuinely need and should rightly value, to wit self-understanding mediated through sustainably constructed sensuous attachment to images of the world of which they are a part.

III

In Adorno's *Ästhetische Theorie* we see the closer and closer association of the two values that marked the earlier epoch coming to a halt, being reversed even. While they may not be exhaustive of our aesthetic interests, in the domain of art beauty and truth continue to exercise a central function, only now they are thought of as independent of one another and even as potentially conflicting. As in earlier periods beauty itself remains an ineliminable value. 'Beauty reminds us of something essential to art, even if not immediately expressive of it.[10] If we did not judge artefacts as beautiful – no matter how distorting of reality [*modifiziert*] they may be – the interest we take in them would be incomprehensible and blind, and no one, neither artist, nor spectator, would have cause to take that step away from the practical realm, from the domain of self-preservation and the pleasure principle, that is constitutive of art' (p. 82).

However, by contrast with earlier assumptions, beauty, conceived of still in Kantian style very largely as a formal matter (pp. 82/3), a balancing of contending forces (*Homöostase von Spannung*) (p. 85) and functioning to affirm or reconcile us to a reality whose images are so handled (p. 10), no longer makes up the heart of the matter. That is the business of truth. Thus Adorno repeatedly claims: 'Art stands in quest of truth' (p. 419); 'Nothing in art is understood whose truth or falsity is not understood' (p. 194); 'Great art cannot lie' (p. 196); 'The heart of a work of art is not what it means or what it aims at, but its truth-content' (p. 423) and so on.

What encourages the divorce of the two values is the perception that either one can find expression without the other. The beautiful, which promises reconciliation, may offer it in despite of truth – Adorno readily speaks of much widely admired art as lying – and much harsh and bitter truth that has come to find so prominent a place in modern art makes no concession to pleasing form. But the novelty of Adorno's position does not simply consist in the return to an earlier view of these two values as essentially independent of one another; it is that in opposition to the thought of an earlier age, truth is now acknowledged outright as the senior member of the pair. It is not hard to see why.

Given that the function of beauty is to reconcile us to the world of which it presents pleasing images, many of its manifestations are liable to lend themselves to the charge of sentimentality or self-delusion. The world to which we wish to be reconciled is our world, yet the only way to achieve the desired integration may be through a wilful cognitive distortion of it. Since 'reconciliation' is itself in part achieved under the goal of self-understanding, where this honest integrating aspiration turns out to be impossible of fulfilment on account of the nature of the world itself, concern for understanding furnished by non-reconciling, astringent truth will rightfully claim priority.

So one might say in summary that for Adorno the beautiful is what appeals and affirms; only it is truth that lends that affirmation intellectual tenability. Perhaps beautiful images may still appeal, but they will no longer be images that we can unreservedly embrace, because we can no longer be certain they will be true ones. Conversely, true images of our times are all too likely to repel; and while they cannot be counted on to exert any of the self-standing pleasurable pull that their predecessors once did, we may nevertheless think them images which in our quest for understanding we have to come to terms with.

Anyone encountering these ideas for the first time may sensibly enough want to protest that there are after all truths and truths, and that it is anything but apparent why, if it is fundamentally truth that matters, the artist should not devote himself to such deep truths that his public will find more easily digestible, more congenial to contemplative taste. Seriously to raise such a query though would be profoundly to misunderstand Adorno's thought. In the first place, it would assume that the truths that the great artist's work discloses are the focus of his intention in the construction of his art; and secondly it supposes that as far as the value of truth goes, one commanding truth is as available to the artist as another. Neither supposition is correct to Adorno's way of thinking, and it is his denial of the first of these naive suppositions that conditions his response to the second.

'Pictures', Adorno tells us, 'become art by articulating processes that have developed in them to the point of objectivity. The images of art proper tend to be confused by the bourgeois conception of it . . . with their very opposite, the private stock of images that is the psychological property of the artist' (p. 133). A while later he elaborates:

> How little the truth content of art coincides with the subjective idea, with the intention of the artist, that is, is shown by the simplest of considerations. There are works of art in which the artist achieved what he wanted, through and through and without any snags, but whose end result is no more than an index of what he had in mind, impoverished to the level of impenetrable allegory. They wilt away the moment that academic critics [*Philologen*] have pumped out of them what the artist once pumped in . . . (pp. 194/5)

Once he has allowed himself to be persuaded by this reflection and to say that the truth of a work of art has little to do with what the artist meant or wanted to achieve (cf. also p. 47), it is not surprising that the answer to our initial query should strike Adorno as obvious. It is that 'the latent [not-intentional] processes in works of art, occasionally breaking through into the open, are their inner historicity, they are the sedimentation of external history' (p. 133). That is, 'the configuration of elements of the work of art in a whole obeys immanent laws, which are related to those governing society beyond it. Both social productive forces and relationships of production recur in works of art, shorn of their facticity, just because artistic work is social work . . . Scarcely anything can be achieved or produced in art that does not, however latently, have its model in social production' (pp. 350/1). The work of art is then, like a Leibnizian monad, a reflection of these forces. Thereby, we must suppose, it possesses its essential truth.

To paraphrase: once we set aside the private intentions of the artist as determining which truths his work shall disclose we are bound to turn to such truths about our society as are deterministically reflected in his choice of autonomous aesthetic problems and in the material he is presented by his past and his present to resolve them. Since the artist's work itself is the product of his society and of the forces that dominate it, it can come as no surprise that the truths that will be revealed in the art he creates are truths concerning those same productive forces and the very relationships of production that generate it.

There is none the less something slightly misleading about this crude way of putting it. For it certainly cannot be that in this domain the intentions of the artist are bound to misfire, and that there has to be a realm of truth which is both what fundamentally legitimates our interest in art and which necessarily escapes the artist's reflective activity. That would be too implausible a view to take. Rather it must be that here we light on a realm of truth that is difficult to discern, hence not one that the artist can be relied on intentionally to bring to life in his work, and which also happens to be one that has the deepest call on us. It is this, above all, that we need to be apprised of in our search for self-knowledge. And that is something that we can easily understand: for the image that the arts offer us is an image of our own lived world, and only with a vivid perception of its underlying realities, distasteful though they may be, can we hope to achieve anything like reasonably reflective self-understanding.

The final purely expository remark I want to make bearing on this issue touches Adorno's often recurring thought that the work of art is akin to the Leibnizian monad, a permanent living mirror of the universe. Here, because art is the product of those very social forces that prevail at any moment, we are liable to see our social world microcosmically reflected in it. To understand it, with philosophical and interpretative critical assistance (pp. 193/4), is to be able to understand the social macrocosm and to take a step to the understanding of ourselves as elements in it. Just as the monad reflects its surrounding universe directly, by expressing in its own substance truths about it, so in Adorno's sociological account of art, truths about the social world and its power relations are directly written into the works of art, however the artist may think of them. He is, so to speak, the passive conduit of a reality that he may not fully comprehend, but which in his finest works he can faultlessly show forth. In Adorno's own words:

> That works of art, like windowless monads, 'represent' what they themselves are not, can hardly be understood except through the fact that their own dynamics, their inner historicity as a dialectic between nature and mastery of nature, is not simply of the same essence as that of the outer world, but also has an internal resemblance to it, without however imitating it. (p. 15)

Adorno's strategy then, one that he must evidently take to be empirically underwritten if it is to have any suasive force, is to identify a class of truths that it is rationally incumbent on us to appreciate and to validate the importance for us of art through its peculiar liability to convey them, even though they may not reliably engage the artist himself. The artist's special skill lies in resolving autonomous aesthetic problems of his own, but since those artistic problems are posed precisely in material that presents itself to him as an outcome of social pressures, the reflecting mirror-like powers of his activity give his products a particular interest for us.

If I have understood it aright, it is within this overall framework that Adorno wants to insist on the likely incompatibility of beauty and truth. Not, of course, as I have already observed, that the two may never coexist. Some social truths in times gone by have evidently been particularly well suited to presentation in beautiful art; but this is no longer so, or only so at the margins. 'Even for the sake of beauty, there can no longer be beauty because it is no longer beautiful' (p. 85); and again, 'we must look forward to a time in which for the sake of art itself the artist must keep silent' (p. 85). I take it that what Adorno has in mind is that the absence of stable harmony in our social relations is enough to forbid its presence in art. There the dire nature of the social truths that hold the institution and the practice of art in place could not be disclosed through the balanced forms of beauty. Truth must out, and once out will smash such fragile delicacies.

So at least I envisage Adorno saying. And since it is this opposition of truth and beauty that has become such notably powerful doctrine, it is worth going slowly here and asking whether the response is as evident as it is represented to be. As far as possible it will be advisable to do this without disturbing more than need be the fundamental assumption, that truth has to be taken as the leading value for us of the artist's activity and of his works.

IV

One puzzle will strike almost everybody at this point. If the work of art is a monad-like reflection of the society in which it originates and thereby has its truth-content, since any art-producing society is, by Adorno's own implicit admission, likely to generate some works of beauty,[11] there seems to be no evident reason to think that revealed artistic truth and artistic beauty are ever bound to live at odds. We know that Adorno will resist this thrust, since for him much beautiful art is downright mendacious. What he really thinks is that only *some* art has truth-content, great art, that is, 'the only art that really merits the name'; the rest is not so happily placed. And this brings home how misleading in one way the metaphor of the monad is, since in Leibniz's view all monads are equipollent in their reflective power, whereas for Adorno only this privileged art is endowed with socially reflective truth-content.

Still, one wants to persist, why should great contemporary art of our day not aspire to beauty? Within the edifice I have described, what

Adorno is bound to say is, first, that the deepest truths of a given society are best revealed – most perspicuously, most penetratingly, most accurately – by art of its avant-garde, and secondly, that there is some special reason why in its progressive art those truths cannot be beautifully disclosed. The progressive artist, Adorno holds, confronts autonomous (i.e. independently of considerations of truth) aesthetic problems that are set in advance by the particular material at his disposal, by the immediate history of his art and by the concerns that his medium best lends itself to, and in our times these are such as not to allow of beautiful handling.[12] So given that beauty is excluded from the satisfactory resolution of contemporary artistic problems, since their resolution is the place where the deepest truths of our time are to be located, they could not be combined with beauty. Beautiful treatment of the given material would be regressive from the avant-garde; or, if within the ambit of some Other Worldly avant-garde, would not be one whose given materials were the products of, or sufficiently analogous to, our world's pressing realities. Doubtless it is a merit of putting this like this that we can avoid (for a while, though maybe not for ever) claiming something so apparently empty or unpersuasive as that the beautiful and the true cannot consist just because today's truths are not themselves beautiful – a thought I came perilously close to relying on in my initial exposition of Adorno's position, and which I then fudged over by saying that our social realities were not 'stably harmonious'.[13] Even so, there is something smacking of wishful thinking about the device. In the first place, if the aesthetic problems that the artist faces are genuinely autonomous it needs a good deal of explaining why they cannot be beautifully resolved. It cannot just be a bald datum. The suspicion lurks of course that what Adorno is willing to identify as progressively avant-garde is already heavily determined by whether it promises to be suitably revealing of truth, and that then puts unacceptably heavy strain on the idea of aesthetic autonomy that is meant to do work of its own, and takes us very quickly back to the idea I said we should be glad to avoid.[14]

However, in the hope of circumventing it a little later on, I want to set this particular problem aside and raise a number of other difficulties that confront Adorno's scheme. The principal of these is one that will affect his position no matter what resolution he might eventually propose of this last matter and it demands urgent attention. I put it thus: once all non-fortuitous connection is severed between the truth that the finer class of work of art allegedly manifests and the intention of the artist in producing it, the truth of the favoured work is one that is better described as revealed *by* the work than *in* it. That is, the information about the social world that is transmitted is information that these art objects carry with them, even though it is not information that bears closely upon their critical understanding and appreciation *as the particular works of art they are*. That they have been produced in such and such circumstances, in such and such social conditions and so on, is a fact that we can, it is supposed, elicit from them, but this is fundamentally information of no different an order than, say, that a work is made of this material or that and as a consequence will weigh so many pounds or will have been made in such and such an atelier. Neither fact by itself is liable to be essential to the appreciation of the work (though of course either fact might well help us to understand it, give us proper access to it, by getting us to see what it was that the artist envisaged it as having by way of its own aesthetic properties). The truth that Adorno thinks of as so important might thus well be called *archaeological truth*, and however salient it might strike us as being, however fascinating, however important to us, that by itself will not give it any particular aesthetic force; it will not on that account genuinely be an aesthetic property belonging to the work, just something ancillary to it.

The bearing of this reflection comes out clearly when we remember that the greatness of individual works of art for Adorno is a matter of their having a notable truth-content. Now the assessment of them as of great stature *is* an assessment that has to bear on them as the works of art that they are, not just on an image of them that we form from their material base. Yet if the truth that they transmit is merely archaeological this demand cannot be met. For that it needs to be closer to them, more intimate than merely retrievable from them.[15]

Someone may want to protest that my reasoning here simply assumes the centrality of the place of intention to our understanding of art that Adorno wants to deny, and that therefore it cannot be used against him. That would not be correct. It should be common ground between his supporters and myself that there is a difference between those properties of a work of art that are relevant to its appreciation as the work it is and those that are not. My thought about the archaeological nature of Adornoesque truth is simply that it is liable to belong to those properties which are not relevant – there is no reason to regard it otherwise on the simple basis of the fact that it is a property that we can see transmitted by certain productions of art, whether their makers desire it to be so or not. Whether it is ultimately intention that does delimit these properties is a further issue. What cannot be denied is that the assessment of the work's stature, its greatness, is certainly an assessment that bears on the character the felicitous work has in its own right, and to the extent that greatness is a function of truth, that too needs to be a feature that the work possesss in its own right; to be apparent *in* the work, as I put it, and not merely be revealed *by* it.

A worry immediately consequent on this is that archaeological truth cannot have the motivating or valorizing power that Adorno wants it to. For him, I said, truth is the prime value of art in that it is what we are rationally bound to find worthy of pursuit and to appeal to to underwrite art's significance for us. Now there is something unsatisfactorily under-described about this claim. First, and obviously, truth is only interesting if it is noticed. Secondly, and no less obviously, it needs to be noticed as being true. But what is it that is so important about noticing and recognizing truth? In all consistency Adorno must say that revealed and recognized truth conveys knowledge to us, but it must be a fair response to say that there risks being something not very stirring about this. One might feel that just such truths as Adorno has in mind as revealed by great art are very likely to be in our possession all along. We *know*, don't we, what forces govern our world; are *aware*, aren't we, of its metaphysically evil character; and surely we do not make genuine discoveries about these things as we confront and internalize the works of art that are particularly suitable for transmitting them. In these circumstances, what is the point of interesting ourselves in art on account of its truth? What, one wonders, is so great about great art?

A hint of the right way to go is given in the thought I mentioned before, and which I heavily relied on in my earlier exposition, that Adorno sees the beautiful as serving to affirm what it represents. What that suggests is that through the microcosmic reflection of the truth in art we *understand* the truths, understand them in ways that take us beyond mere objective knowledge, involving us as it does in adequate, 'correct' (p. 134), or critically sustainable consciousness of it. Following up this idea, let me suggest now that truth in art is interesting only in so far as it provides understanding, and that understanding depends on our forging sustainable response to the truth that we recognize as revealed by the artist's work. In that case it will follow that to say that truth is the leading value is art is misleading. By itself truth does not have the rational motivating capacity that Adorno supposes it to, but this is serious because as long as truth is taken *archaeologically* it cannot furnish understanding of a kind that does have this power either. Let me elaborate.

Understanding, I say, involves coming to find an adequate intellectual and affective response that relates me, the thinking subject, to a certain subject matter or to a truth of a certain subject matter. In this respect it is quite different from knowledge, though like knowledge must also involve us with truths about the topic in hand. That is why talk of truth is not entirely beside the point. If it is understanding though, as opposed to cognitive discovery, that is to be conveyed by art, then what we need to say at the very least is that understanding will depend on how the truth that is involved in it is presented. It needs, that is, to be shown *in a certain light*, and we have in consequence to be able to talk about the way in which it is handled. This is of course not to say anything much about what understanding consists in, but it does pick out a necessary ingredient that no one should want to dispute. Now, I contend, if we think of truth as merely archaeologically conveyed by art, as Adorno's model has us suppose, we shall not be able to say that the truth is handled in any particular way at all, it is merely monadically reflected in the artist's attack on those aesthetically autonomous problems that he sets himself to resolve. Truth is at most a byproduct of that, so to speak, and no attitudes to it are reflected in the artist's work because what makes for truth is merely the fact that the productive forces under which he labours are, at the frontier of progressive art, the same as those that deeply determine the structure of his society (pp. 350/1). Since what the artist's handling impinges on is his immanent, autonomous problem, there is no reason at all to expect that the happy solution to that will even suggest to us an understanding of the truth that is disclosed by his work. So as long as truth remains archaeological, we shall not be able to appeal to it to explain why we should care about art. Truth is not then explicable as its leading value, and it must be doubtful whether stripped down like this it could in all consistency long be thought of as an artistic value at all.

There is one further thing to notice specific to the argument of this essay. As long as truth is conceived of in this fashion we shall find it even more difficult than I may already have made it seem to insist, even at the frontier of art, that there is a likely opposition between revealed truth and beauty. The reason is that beauty is allowed on all hands to be a proper aesthetic feature of the work, bearing on its assessment as successful or not. Consequently it is best deployed in discussing the outcome of the artist's (intentional) struggle with his immanent problem. Now, it may well be the case that on occasion archaeologically revealed truth is not in fact associated with beauty in the resolution of aesthetic problems, but Adorno wants to be able to say this is a matter of some theoretical generality. What is needed for that, under his conception of beauty, would be the thought that in socially corrupt times there just *could not be* artistic problems whose successful resolution would require some formal balancing of contending aesthetic forces. It is of course problematic whether this description really captures very much at all, but on the assumption that it, or some improvement on it, does delineate what we mean by beauty, as far as I can see there is absolutely no reason to believe it.

Nor would there be any reason to believe a weaker, less problematic and moralized formulation of the idea – namely that in the beautiful work of art we can at times be irresponsibly encouraged to affirm or be reconciled to the unreconcilable truth (p. 202). For to be encouraged to affirm or to reject a truth is itself to be brought to adopt an attitude to it by the work of art, and we have already seen that that is something that belongs to what is manifest in the work rather than merely revealed by it. The encouragement stems from the work proper that is, and from the artist's attitude to what he handles as expressed in the work. Once more, if the truth escapes him and bypasses the agency of his mind then in his engagement with the beautiful he could hardly be encouraging, irresponsibly or not, any reconciliation with that.

V

The criticisms of the last section – the absence of truth from the work; the incapacity of disclosed truth to function as art's prime value; the impossibility of establishing any even limited conceptual or moral opposition between truth and beauty – all flow from the archaeological conception of truth Adorno obliges himself to work with. In turn, that conception is forced on him because of the way in which appeal to the artist's mind, fundamentally to his intentions, is believed to be unavailable. Rather than conclude directly that the main body of *Äesthetische Theorie* must just be dismissed, it is more fruitful to ask whether when, contrary to its author's theoretical convictions, intention is encouraged to play a major role in the matter, a route round these various obstacles cannot be found.

The argument against intention that I mentioned before, the only one we find in the text, is after all singularly weak. What Adorno says, you recall, is that the artist may have achieved what he wanted to in a pure and faultless fashion, while only in fact having brought off a faint shadow of his aim (pp. 194/5, 226). Obviously there is something here that borders on contradiction; how can the artist possibly have achieved what he wanted, yet only have brought off a shadow of that? When taken *au pied de la lettre* the idea is nonsense, but once the nonsense is straightened out, it becomes clearer what is going on.

What Adorno is getting at must be this: often the artist will say that he has achieved what he wanted, yet have failed. He does not in fact bring off what he intends even though he asserts and believes himself to have done so. That is true enough and quite uncontentious, and it brings to our attention the distinction between fulfilled intention and the assertion of intention fulfilled. Now, clearly, if we take what the artist claims as criterial of what he intended and of what he achieves, there is no good reason to think that that will regularly match up with what we and other sensitive critics find in his work. Since it is rightly obvious to Adorno that the work has to reveal itself to the perceptive critic, it is natural for him, assuming that intention and assertion of intention are one and the same, to feel the need to detach himself from it. However, once we see that ready assertion is not infallibly criterial of what is intended nor of the fulfilment of an intention that someone owns himself to have, this detachment need not recommend itself to us. The assumed underpinning of the archaeological conception of truth thus collapses.[16] This is entirely to the good; for by seizing the opportunity the collapse affords, we can set about putting back in place the major themes of Adorno's thought in a way that makes them worthy of closer attention than they would otherwise merit. So let me reconstruct as best I can the position to be defended.

The difference between truth revealed in the work and truth revealed by it is an instance of the distinction between those properties that are genuine

properties of the work in its own right, critically relevant to its appreciation, that is, and those that are not. This distinction needs to be drawn by
reference to the artist's mind, primarily, I suggest, to his intentions; and
once we consent to lift the self-denying ordinance Adorno imposes, this
crucial distinction becomes available. With it to hand we retrieve too the
desired notion of truths that belong to the work other than as critical
irrelevances no matter how curious, interesting or significant to us they
may be.

The perceptive artist may consequently see the disclosure of truth as
something well worth aiming for. It need not be the sole or even necessarily
the leading value with which he may hope to invest his art, but there is no
reason to think that it is not a deep-going one. Furthermore, he can say
now, as he could not say before, that the reason why truth is as important
as it is, is because of the way in which it is involved in the procuring of
understanding of this subject matter or that. Of these truths one may
indeed be the effective power relationships and relations of production in
the society in which his works are created, but it is now quite unnecessary
to think of them as monadically reflected in his work or to think that, if his
work is any good, they are deterministically imposed upon it. Some of his
art may concentrate on these matters, some may not, and which of his
works reveal truth of Adorno's favoured brand and bring understanding
with it will be a matter of the artist's fulfilled intentions, not of spurious
metaphysics.

There are moments in *Äesthetische Theorie* at which the metaphysical
determination of social truth in progressive art is backed up by a kind of
supplementary moralism. So, for instance, Adorno cites with favour
(p. 66) lines from Brecht's 'An die Nachgeborenen':

Was sind das für Zeiten, wo
Ein Gespräch über Bäume fast ein Verbrechen ist
Weil es ein Schweigen über so viele Untaten einschließt![17]

suggesting that not only will the artist working at the aesthetic cutting edge
inevitably reflect the truths of his times, but that any attempt on his part to
do otherwise would have to be judged a paltry evasion of such reality.
Perhaps the target of attack here is not so much the artist – how after all
could he be guilty of not doing what he is willy nilly causally obliged to
do? – but the spectator or reader, who does have a choice of confronting
the grubby truths of the avant-garde (pp. 196/7) or of switching on the
television or radio instead. But neither version of this strong-arming tactic
survives the emergence of intention into the argument.

Under my reconstruction, the artist can well allow that the truths of our
times are a fit subject for his attention. Not only do we need to know them
and remember them; we also need to understand them. But for him to say
this is not itself to make engagement with other themes a refusal to engage

with these. Matters other than the social relations of production and their consequences can claim attention, and enrichingly receive it, and when they do it is a mistake to suppose that that could only involve denial of something else. *Pace* Brecht, talk about trees does not have to be a silence about the horrors of war or famine or the exploitation of the proletariat by multinational monopoly capitalism or whatever; it can be talk about trees, and none the worse for that. Similarly, the reader can well be enlarged to find that trees are given honour by the contemporary poet without thereby turning his back on other matters. Of course if it were true that great art could *only* treat these topics, then there might indeed be something to be said about an equivalence of denial between the television and the trees, but appeal to the poet's choice and the importance of his perceptions of value that I am insisting on excuses us from any such excess.

When we reflect on the artist who tackles what Adorno thinks of as autonomous aesthetic problems imposed by the very nature of his material and supposedly linked by the mysterious power of sedimentation with the furthest-reaching truths of the society that generates them, we make more progress by saying instead that the artist who makes the truths of his own time the central themes of his art will tend to identify the challenging *aesthetic* problem in terms of just such artistic material that can assist him to achieve that. His problems no longer have to be thought of as *autonomously* given. Then at least there is no particular mystery about why at the frontier of art we may find a close liaison between artistic production and the truths of our times. The desire to achieve understanding of them itself plays a crucial part in fixing the challenging artistic problem, and the resolution of that problem in turn brings understanding with it.

Understanding is brought along with truth now because associating the aesthetic problematic with content in this way makes crucial consideration of how the content of the work is handled. Handling escaped consideration before because having its place fixed by artistic perception, intention and desire it could not, except fortuitously, stretch as far as was needed. But handling brings with it intentional modes of perceiving that engage the reader or the spectator's responses to the material before him or her and fashions reflection upon how he or she stands to it. That in brief is the core of the understanding which previously was forced to sell itself short.

With these desiderata in hand it is at last possible to say what the truth is about that opposition between the beautiful and the true in our own day's art that Adorno so insistently proclaims. First, it cannot be a general truth that in certain epochs, notably our own, great art has to eschew beauty. There is no ground for that thought because there is no reason left for claiming that the only proper material worthy of the artist's attention is something that excludes handling with beauty. Once the monadic metaphysic – Leibnizian, Hegelian or Marxian – is abandoned, no basis for that claim is left beyond mere stipulation. However there may still well seem to be room for something closely reminiscent of it when we confront art that intentionally embraces those themes that convey the sort of truth-content that Adorno favours.

In earlier discussion of this topic we came to grief because at root there seemed to be no readily discernible conceptual incompatibility between the beauty of a work that reveals a certain class of painful truths and the truths that such work discloses. Nor was there sufficient richness in the tools at our disposal to treat the combination of beauty and truth at such a delicate juncture as morally rather than conceptually unthinkable. Now certainly the latter strategy is not denied us, but much more interestingly something far closer to logical incompatibility emerges that makes the moralizing quite redundant.

This comes from putting together the insistence on the importance of understanding (rather than bare truth) with that element in Adorno's conception of beauty that sees its essence as lying in reconciliation (*Versöhnung* or sometimes *Trost*). Reconciliation, Adorno sees, involves at the very least a lack of resistance to what one is reconciled to; opposition is abandoned, and affective response to it as something to be valued or even welcomed colours the ways in which one experiences it. From the artist's point of view, in a beautiful representation of his subject he will handle it in such a way that what is on view is so on view that it is, in the work, correctly perceived as welcome or valuable. Certainly, harsh and bitter truths can be represented in such a way – indeed, it is precisely because they can that we were able to find no genuine opposition between bare truth and beauty even when the truth in question is the truth of the sombrest matter. Now, however, we can say that reconciliation cannot be accommodated with understanding, for reconciliation to the harsher truths as conveyed in art will precisely inhibit or prevent perception of them as harsh, terrible or morally unacceptable. It is here if anywhere that the inconsistency lies: the artist aims at 'correct' understanding, and this involves him in revealing the truths that he concentrates on for what they are, not just bare objectively cognitive truths, but truths which we can only properly perceive as having particular subjective implications for us quite at odds with anything that reconciliation would provide. Failure to achieve that perception is not to achieve understanding. Achieved under-standing forbids reconciliation.

So I submit that by abandoning the archaeological conception of truth we make it possible for Adorno to argue coherently for some slightly retrenched version of the claim he wants without giving up anything essential to our concept of art. In particular by doing so we achieve a sharp understanding of the supposed tension between beauty and truth in art of our own day, which at the start I have said seems so often to have achieved the standing of unchallengeable doctrine. This, however, is not to endorse the doctrine; it is, more modestly, merely to find a formulation of it that makes it worth discussion.

VI

I have said that the value of truth can only underpin the idea of art if we take it as coinciding with the idea of understanding, in which of course the notion of truth *stricto sensu* itself is central. I have also said that understanding a subject matter involves the appreciation and indeed formation of adequate affective sensitivity to the matter on the subject's part. I now want to leave Adorno aside for a moment and briefly to digress in developing, if only minimally, this idea of understanding, which has come firmly to take up its position centre stage.

The observation I have to make bears on the idea of adequate response on the part of the subject to his matter. It is that, fundamentally, this involves a judgement that can be formed only in the light of an appreciation of what alternatives lie before us. That such and such a sort of action or situation is terrible, that certain truths are intolerable, is a thought that is in part conditioned by what we recognize – or should recognize – to be alternatives available to us. The idea is very familiar. To know what to make of your generosity in giving me a mite, I have to know that you are a widow who disposes of very little more. A mite from Arnold Hammer should not properly elicit the same response as a mite from Mother Teresa. One may be an insult; the other a sacrifice. How terrible certain truths may properly be seen as being may be a function of what alternatives stood open to us at the time.[18]

A direct application of this truism to my theme is that our understanding of a subject matter or a topic may be enhanced by an exploration of the nature of some alternative to it; we may need a sharp view of the nature of what we are lacking to know what to make of the actuality that is ours. By being brought to awareness of the attractions and virtues of the absent possibility we come to see in better relation to ourselves the nature of our actual reality. It may even be that the information we take away from reflection on one thing is most significantly how we stand to another. The ultimate intended subject matter of an artistic rendering of the former may thus be the true nature of the latter.

In the history of the subject it is Schiller who most sharply draws on these perceptions in his prescription for the artist fashioning our understanding of ourselves and our surrounding world. He encourages the tyro to surround his contemporaries with images of the worthy and noble, so that in their hours of liberty they turn from preoccupation and contentment with a fundamentally rotten present and play instead with pleasure around the image of an ideal. As we come to appreciate the virtues of what we do not have, so he believes we cast off attachment to what we are habituated to. We shall then come to understand that present through engagement with the absent ideal. Understanding it better, taking a 'correct' attitude, as Adorno would say, toward it, we shall be better placed than we now are to change it. Thus the artist provides understanding without didacticism: he avoids preaching, but forms sustainable understanding through the critical development of taste.[19]

The relevance of these reflections to the topic in hand is straightforward. At the start I said that we needed two things to unseat an entrenched theory; a competing alternative and convincing counterexamples to the established model. Perhaps the first of these requirements has now been met, but the second is still outstanding. The difficulty here is evidently to persuade oneself that any case one lights upon does more than simply reflect one's own personal taste and that it does not draw its apparent force from permitting easy description in terms which comply with that alternative, which we know in advance is going to accommodate it. With these considerations in mind I propose to call in witness the paintings of Mark Rothko; and to ward off suspicions that might arise on either of these two fronts I rely for commentary entirely on a essay by that most perceptive of critics, Michel Butor; an essay whose origin is completely divorced from any theoretical considerations of the sort I have here been engaged with. It should suffice for my purpose to cite a few lines from his 'L'art de Mark Rothko ou les Mosquées de New York' though I cannot praise too highly the whole essay from which I take them.

Rothko's art is a response to an overcrowded city [New York]. All the city's rectangles [preponderantly its buildings and its road-grid so insistently called up for Butor in the work of Mondrian – A. S.] – of which the canvas itself is but one example – are laden with crowds of things and of all sorts of people who have lost all sense of their true bonds with one another. The windows are so stuffed with shoddy goods that even the most authentic of treasures would be unrecognizable. A rind of dirt and superabundance degrades everything. If I go into a drugstore wherever my eyes are turned they meet advertising slogans extolling the most ordinary of objects in the most florid and pretentious terms. Amidst all that how could a truthful line have a place, a nicely chosen word be heard in the surrounding din?

All these objects should be plunged in a caustic bath to strip them down, but without destroying the best of them; into this turbulence an empty space must be inserted, a blank sheet, so that the spirit can find the tranquillity for its work that it needs.

Just as in moslem towns the bustle of the bazaars and the dirt of the alleys are opposed by the blocks of silence and oases of cleanliness that are the mosques, so in the midst of the tumult, the heaving and blockage that makes up New York, Rothko proposes in his paintings to set up a space for breathing, for purification, and for the calm of judgement.[20]

Apply this thought in the light of my argument to one of those structures of halo-like glowing rings superposed upon a uniform background lightly margined within the frame executed for (and subsequently withheld from) The Four Seasons restaurant in the Seagram's Building on Park Avenue, at the end of the fifties the most expensive and fashionable of all New York's expensive and fashionable restaurants. One finds there a needed counterweight to the self-absorbed frenzy and triviality of commercial and social life that the restaurant set itself to serve, where the really taxing business of life is impressing the client from Kansas or Europe or the social talk of the ladies who lunch, activities that Rothko's pictures were commissioned to compliment and flatter. The peace and beauty of those canvases however is only fully appreciated when we see them as reminding us of the real loss of self in the world to which they stand opposed. As Butor puts it 'it is when the invitation to the spectator to respond becomes pressing, a response whose first moment is to avoid places like The Four Seasons as much as possible, that the incompatibility between the series of paintings and the place irrevocably blazes forth. Image par excellence of New York high society, the locale becomes, precisely through the work that is so powerfully missing from it, the images of its own gnawing contradiction. In these so tranquil paintings tolls a funeral bell.'[21]

These works then display what Adorno should acknowledge as a corruscating understanding of our own situation by offering an alternative whose beauty is not in the least diminished by the truth we are obliquely brought to recognize. The conclusion to draw is plain. Once we concentrate on understanding a given subject matter rather than allowing it to disclose itself archaeologically, the critic may point out that that may be achieved as much indirectly and obliquely through the exploration of alternatives to what is actual as overtly and monadically through direct presentation. Under Adorno's own regime this perception is not really available, for social truths as monadically immanent in the art of a period (p. 345) will be directly reflected and not obliquely so. Obliquity comes only with the flexibility provided by the artist's intentions and reflective strategies and his expectation of the spectator's sensitivity to them. But obliquity is the artist's privilege, and it is a privilege that allows him to outface if he cares that possible form of conflict between beauty and truth which I identified in the previous section. We can now say that once the artist opts to concentrate on the provision of understanding of a given subject matter, one that we may take to be as pressing in its demands on him and us as may be, it still remains open to him to decide how best that understanding may be conveyed. A standard route that cannot be ignored is, as Schiller saw, through a contrasting vision that throws our own lived situation into sharp relief. If what I have been saying is anywhere near right, then it may not be unreasonable to suppose that if a direct approach would indeed be one that could not combine truth and beauty, that is all the more reason for thinking that obliquely the two may happily be combined: we achieve adequate understanding of the real through the beautiful image of its counterpart.

I conclude then that once art is thoroughly desociologized, the most that can be honestly said is that there are some ways in which the artist may seek to deploy important truths that will have to eschew beauty. That is a long way away from the doctrine that we started with. There we were encouraged to believe that any engagement with the beautiful was in our own day bound to be a turning away from the truths we need to see, or a deformation of them beneath a contemptible kind of sentimental gloss. No one in his right mind would deny that these are possibilities that lie in wait to trap the unwary, and it is easy enough to find cases of each. But that is an entirely different matter from supposing these to be the logical consequences of a concern for beauty.

Although I have said nothing about it, right at the start of his book Adorno recognizes the importance of the artist's power to conjure up a world that is opposed to our own. One wonders why he does not see that beauty there can be an aid to understanding. The trouble, he suggests is that the alternative world is presented as if it were real (p. 10). Then the beauty with which it is displayed casts a dangerous glow over our own reality – we tend to take the image for the reality and 'affirming' the image, connive in the evil of the given. Only something goes badly wrong here. Of course an image can be an image of reality, and be an image of how things really are, without our being inclined to believe that that is how they are. It is a doctrine that belongs firmly to the seventeenth and eighteenth centuries, to the thought of Fénélon, of Diderot and of Lessing to think that the graphic image is one that we take to be a *true* image of the real, or which we even believe to be reality itself. Their assumptions at this point have no power over us, nor should they have any over Adorno.

VII

If my diagnosis is right, the underlying theory that carries the work of the Gilberts and the Georges or the protagonists of the slightly more recent Artists in Contemporary Britain show at the same gallery[22] is deeply flawed. Seeing this we shall be less impressed with the rhetorical power of Laingian pessimism than were the directors of the Hayward or the authors of the catalogue I mentioned at the beginning of this essay, quite independently of our response to the underlying Marxist ideology from which it springs and which that particular civic institution has for some years openly endorsed. If one reflects on this together with the metaphilosophical question of what service the bookkeeping or underlabouring function of philosophy in the analytic mode can perform, it is a nice conceit to think that it may function as an effective tool in setting the working artist free from the shackles of bad theory. This it does by proving gods have feet of clay.

NOTES

1 Translated as *Aesthetic Theory*, trans C. Lenhard (London, 1986). A helpful review by Raymond Geuss, on which I rely at several points, can be found in the *Journal of Philosophy*, (1986), 732–41. Page references in the text are to the 1974 German edition, Suhrkamp Taschenbuch Wissenshaft 2. English renderings, often fairly loose, are my own.

2 It is worth emphasizing the non-reductive character of Hume's proposal to counter Kant's famous charge against the empiricists' aesthetic thought that it supposes a science of beauty to be possible and wrongly supposes the judgement of taste to be cognitive (viz. objective, as we would now say). The only empiricist of the century I can think of who comes remotely close to this position is Burke, who in part III.xviii of *On the Sublime and the Beautiful* singles out the beautiful as the small, the smooth and the gaily coloured. He does however explicitly say there that these are qualities on which beauty depends, and that non-reductive position is supported by the definition he offers at III.i of beauty as 'that quality or qualities in bodies by which they cause love, or some passion similar to it'.

3 This may be piety on Hume's part, and not too much should be made of it. But it is tempting to see the moral requirement that he lightly gestures at as a forerunner to the more moralizing thought of Kant and Schiller.

4 Shaftesbury, *Complete Works*, standard edn., I.i, (Stuttgart, Frommann-Holzboog, 1981), p. 286.

5 Defining the beautiful in terms of love and not of simple pleasure, Burke might prove an exception but still one can repeat Shaftesbury's question whether there may not be a distinction between those loves that are right and those which are wrong and not find much in Burke by way of answer.

6 For detailed commentary see my *Aesthetic Reconstructions* (Oxford, Basil Blackwell, 1987), ch. 5.

7 I do not say that Schiller ever presents this idea quite so explicitly. But in Letter X.4 there is criticism of an anonymous figure, who must be Kant, for divorcing beauty from truth, and the condensed reading I offer of the text is meant to indicate how Schiller conceives of the unity of the two in his anti-formalist emendation of his revered teacher's ideas.

8 Curiously, a thought that Hume also has. In *Of the Standard of Taste* a thing's goodness is presented as its capacity to fulfil its purpose. Good history, Hume suggests, is therefore instructive history; good art is art that pleases, viz. beautiful art. Since we could explain neither history nor art without reference to purpose, Hume should hold that art essentially aims at beauty.

9 G. W. F. Hegel *Sämtliche Werke*, Jubiläumsausgabe (Stuttgart, Fr. Frommanns, 1937), vol. XII, p. 57.

10 The context suggests that this something is the truth-content that the beautiful form clothes. Other than that Adorno offers no hint here.

11 Implied, that is, by the remarks about beauty from p. 82 which I commented on above.

12 And of course in periods of similar social corruption to our own, since Adorno's claim has to enjoy a broader generality than simply observation of the fact of present-day non-beautiful avant-garde art. That observation alone could not underpin the practical reflections that I noted at the outset.

13 It is, after all, anything but clear just what a beautiful social reality would be, and generosity demands that we do better for Adorno if we can than to suppose him holding the incompatibility he desires to be rooted in the simplistic idea that reality itself is not beautiful and hence a true reflection of it in art could not be beautiful either. That line of argument is not available if only for the reason that Adorno's understanding of beauty relies on our accepting it as a perceptible formal balance of contending forces, which either gets too little or else too much purchase on society itself.

14 Then, also, it will require a good deal of credulity on our part to believe that the genuinely autonomously given artistic problems should be those that are better adapted to reveal deep truths about the artist's period than any others. The great artist, one is inclined to think, is not as surely bound to act as linear continuer of his predecessors' work as Adorno's aesthetic determinism supposes – surely there are as marked paradigm shifts here as in the sciences; 'normal' art is not the only possibility – and when we find notable discontinuities in art's development we have no particular reason for thinking that must reflect some parallel breach of continuity in social reality. Neither is it an a priori truth that we shall; nor have we any empirical reason to regard it as a lawlike truth. On this last point see R. Wollheim 'Sociological Explanation of the Arts: Some Distinctions', *Proceedings of the IIIrd International Congress on Aesthetics*, 1956, pp. 404–10. It is difficult even to think what might reasonably move us to suppose that there was some genuine law to be found here.

15 It is notable that Adorno should say that 'the immanence of society in the work is the fundamental social truth about art, not the immanence of the work in society' (p. 345) (see also pp. 16, 350), suggesting thereby that he does require the truth-content of art to speak from within it and not just to be revealed by it. My point is that he does not allow himself the resources to secure this entirely desirable aim. The monadic image serves to make idle any appeal to a world-spirit, and we are in the end simply left with the insufficient thought that social truth is in the work because the work is social work (p. 351).

16 In his brief discussion of Adalbert Stifter (p. 346) we are again given the contrast between what the writer intends and what he achieves against his intention (viz. truth). Here the option is now open to say that within the conventions at his disposal he was not able to achieve what he wanted, and was at points forced uncomfortably to break those conventions for the sake of that. Certainly there is no reason to think that the power of Stifter's writing bypasses his discernment of a desirable end he attempts to reach.

17 "What sort of times are these when a conversation about trees is almost a crime because it involves a silence about so many monstrous deeds" (B. Brecht, *Gesammelte Werke* (Ffm., 1967), vol. 9, p. 723).

18 In *Journey without Maps* (London, Heinemann, 1948) Graham Greene

records: 'Suddenly I felt curiously happy and careless and relieved. One couldn't, I was sure, get lower than Duogobmai. I had been afraid of the primitive, had wanted it broken gently, but here it came on us in a breath, as we stumbled up through the dung and the cramped and stinking huts to our lampless sleepingplace among the rats. It was the worst one need fear, and it was bearable because it was inescapable' (p. 118).

19 This is loosely adapted from Letter IX of *On the Aesthetic Education of Man*, especially its last paragraph.

20. Michel Butor, 'L'art de Mark Rothko ou les Mosquées de New York', in *Répertoire III* (Paris, 1968), pp. 351–69, this quotation p. 355.

21 Ibid., p. 369.

22 For a dismal report here see Bernard Levin's commentary in *The Times* for 16 November 1987.

8

The Historical Genesis of a Pure Aesthetic

Pierre Bourdieu

Let us begin with a paradox. It has occurred to some philosophers to ponder the question of what enables one to distinguish between works of art and simple, ordinary things (I have in mind Arthur Danto), and to suggest with unflinching sociologistic daring (which they would never accept in a sociologist) that the principle of this ontological difference must be sought in an institution. The art object, they say, is an artefact whose foundation can only be found in an *artworld*, that is, in a social universe that confers upon it the status of a candidate for aesthetic appreciation.[1] What has not yet occurred (although one of our postmodernists will surely come to it sooner or later) is for a philosopher – one perfectly 'worthy of the name' – to treat the question of what allows us to distinguish a philosophical discourse from an ordinary one. Such a question becomes particularly pertinent when, as in the case here, the philosopher, designated and recognized as such by a certain *philosophical world*, grants himself a discourse which he would deny (under the label of 'sociologism') to anyone like the sociologist, who is not a part of the philosophical institution.[2]

The radical dissymmetry which philosophy thus establishes in its relationships with the human sciences furnishes it with, among other things, unfailing means for masking what it borrows from them. In fact, it seems to me that the philosophy labelled postmodern (by one of those labelling devices until now reserved for the artworld), merely readopts in a denied form (i.e., in the sense of Freud's *Verneinung*), certain of the findings not only of the social sciences but also of historicist philosophy which is, implicitly or explicitly, inscribed in the practice of these sciences. This masked appropriation, which is legitimized by the denial of borrowing, is one of the most powerful strategies yet to be employed by philosophy against the social sciences and against the threat of relativization that these sciences have held over it. Heidegger's ontologization of historicity is, indisputably, the model for this operation.[3] It is a strategy analogous to the 'double jeu' which allows Derrida to take from social science (against which he is poised) some of its most characteristic instruments of 'deconstruction'. While opposing to structuralism and its notion of 'static' structure a 'postmodernized' variant of the Bergsonian critique of the reductive effects of scientific knowledge, Derrida can give himself the air of radicalism. He does this by using, against traditional literary criticism, a critique of binary oppositions, which, by way of Lévi-Strauss, goes back to the most classical analysis of 'forms of classifications' so dear to Durkheim and Mauss.[4]

But one cannot win at all the tables, and the sociology of the artistic institution which the 'deconstructor' can carry out only in the mode of *Verneinung* is never brought to its logical conclusion: its implied critique of the institution remains half-baked, although well-done enough to arouse delicious shudders of a bogus revolution.[5] Moreover, by claiming a radical break with the ambition of uncovering ahistorical and ontologically founded essences, this critique is likely to discourage the search for the foundation of the aesthetic attitude and of the work of art where it is truly located, namely, in the *history* of the artistic institution.

I THE ANALYSIS OF ESSENCE AND THE ILLUSION OF THE ABSOLUTE

What is striking about the diversity of responses which philosophers have given to the question of the specificity of the work of art is not so much the fact that these divergent answers often concur in emphasizing the absence of function, the impartiality, the gratuitousness, etc.[6] of the work of art, but rather that they all (with the possible exception of Wittgenstein) share the ambition of capturing a transhistoric or an ahistoric essence. The pure thinker, by taking as the subject of his reflection his own experience – the experience of a cultured person from a certain social milieu – but without focusing on the historicity of his reflection and the historicity of the object to which it is applied (and by considering it a pure experience of the work of art), unwittingly establishes this singular experience as a transhistorical norm for every aesthetic perception. Now this experience, with all the aspects of singularity that it appears to possess (and the feeling of uniqueness probably contributes greatly to its worth), is itself an institution which is the product of historical invention and whose *raison d'être* can be reassessed only through an analysis which is itself properly historical. Such an analysis is the only one capable of accounting simultaneously for the nature of the experience and for the appearance of universality which it procures for those who live it, naively, beginning with the philosophers who subject it to their reflections unaware of its *social conditions of possibility*.

The comprehension of this particular form of relationship with the work of art presupposes the analyst's understanding of himself – an understanding which can be submitted neither to simple phenomenological analysis of the lived experience (inasmuch as this experience rests on the active forgetting of the history of which it is a product), nor to the analysis of the language ordinarily used to express this experience (inasmuch as it too is the historical product of a process of dehistoricization). Instead of Durkheim's saying 'the unconscious is history', one could write 'the a priori is history'. Only if one were to mobilize all the resources of the social sciences would one be able to accomplish this kind of historicist actualization of the transcendental project which consists of reappropriating, through historical anamnesis, the product of the entire historical operation of which consciousness too is (at every moment) the product. In the individual case this would include reappropriating the dispositions and classificational schemes which are a necessary part of the aesthetic experience as it is described, naively, by the analysis of essence.

What is forgotten in self-reflective analysis is the fact that although appearing to be a gift from nature, the eye of the twentieth-century art lover is really a product of history. From the angle of phylogenesis, the pure gaze, capable of apprehending the work of art as it demands to be apprehended (i.e., in itself and for itself, as form and not as function) is inseparable from the appearance of producers of art motivated by a pure artistic intention, which is itself inseparable from the emergence of an autonomous artistic field capable of formulating and imposing its own ends against external demands. From the side of ontogenesis the pure gaze is associated with very specific conditions of acquisition, such as the early frequenting of museums and the prolonged exposure to schooling and to the *skhole* that it implies. All of this means that the analysis of essence which overlooks these conditions (thus universalizing the specific case), implicitly establishes as universal to all aesthetic practices the rather particular properties of an experience which is the product of privilege, that is, of exceptional conditions of acquisition.

What the ahistorical analysis of the work of art and of the aesthetic experience captures in reality is an institution which, as such, enjoys a kind of twofold existence, in things and in minds. In things it exists in the form of an artistic field, a relatively autonomous social universe which is the product of a slow process of constitution. In minds, it exists in the form of dispositions which were invented by the same movement through which the field, to which they immediately adjusted themselves, was invented. When things and minds (or consciousness) are immediately in accord – in other words, when the eye is the product of the field to which it relates – then the field, with all the products that it offers, appears to the eye as immediately endowed with meaning and worth. This is so clearly the case that if the extraordinary question of the source of the artwork's value, normally taken for granted, were to arise at all, a special experience would be required, one which would be quite exceptional for a cultured person, even though it would be, on the contrary, quite ordinary for all those who have not had the opportunity to acquire the dispositions which are objectively required by the work of art. This is demonstrated by empirical research and is also suggested by Danto, for example.[7] Following a visit to an exhibit of Warhol's *Brillo Boxes* at the Stable Gallery, Danto discovered the arbitrary character, *ex instituto* as Leibniz would have said, of the imposition of the value created by the field through an exhibit in a place which is both consecrated and consecrating.

The experience of the work of art as being immediately endowed with meaning and value is a result of the accord between the two mutually founded aspects of the same historical institution: the cultured habitus[8] and the artistic field. Given that the work of art exists as such, (namely as a symbolic object endowed with meaning and value) only if it is apprehended by spectators possessing the disposition and the aesthetic competence which are tacitly required, one could then say that it is the aesthete's eye which constitutes the work of art as a work of art. But, one must also remember immediately that this is possible only to the extent that the aesthete himself is the product of a long exposure to artworks.[9] This circle, which is one of belief and the sacred, is shared by every institution which can function only if it is instituted simultaneously within the objectivity of a social game and within the dispositions which induce interest and participation in the game. Museums could bear the inscription: Entry for art lovers only. But there clearly is no need for such a sign, it all goes without saying. The game makes the *illusio*, sustaining itself through the informed player's investment in the game. The player, mindful of the game's meaning and having been created for the game because he was created by it, plays the game and by playing it assures its existence. The artistic field, by its very functioning, creates the aesthetic disposition without which it could not function. Specifically, it is through the competition among the agents with vested interests in the game that the field reproduces endlessly the interest in the game and the faith in the value of the stakes. In order to illustrate the operation of this collective endeavour and give an idea of the numerous acts of delegation of symbolic power and of voluntary or forced recognition through which this reservoir of credit (upon which the creators of fetishes draw) is engendered, it will suffice to recall the relationship among the various avant-garde critics who anoint themselves critics by consecrating works whose sacred value is barely perceived by cultured art lovers or even by the critic's most advanced rivals. In short, the question of the meaning and the value of the work of art, like the question of the specificity of aesthetic judgement, along with all the great problems of philosophical aesthetics, can be resolved only within a social history of the field, a history which is linked to a sociology of the conditions of the establishment of the specific aesthetic disposition (or attitude) that the field calls for in each one of its states.

II THE GENESIS OF THE ARTISTIC FIELD AND THE INVENTION OF THE PURE GAZE

What makes the work of art a work of art and not a mundane thing or a simple utensil? What makes an artist an artist and not a craftsman or a Sunday painter? What makes a urinal or a wine rack that is exhibited in a museum a work of art? Is it the fact that they are signed by Duchamp, a recognized artist (recognized first and foremost as an artist) and not by a wine merchant or a plumber? If the answer is yes, then isn't this simply a matter of replacing the work-of-art-as-fetish with the 'fetish of the name of the master'? Who, in other words, created the 'creator' as a recognized and known producer of fetishes? And what confers its magical or, if one prefers, its ontological effectiveness upon his name, a name whose very celebrity is the measure of his claim to exist as an artist and which, like the signature of the fashion designer, increases the value of the object upon which it is affixed? That is, what constitutes the stakes in quarrels of attribution and the authority of the expert? Where is one to locate the ultimate principle of the effect of labelling, or of naming, or of theory? (Theory is a particularly apt word because we are dealing with seeing – *theorein* – and of making others see.) Where does this ultimate principle, which produces the sacred by introducing difference, division, and separation, reside?

Such questions are quite similar in type to those raised by Mauss when, in his *Theory of Magic*, he pondered the principle of magic's effectiveness, and found that he had to move back from the instruments used by the sorcerer to the sorcerer himself, and from there to the belief held by his followers. He discovered, little by little, that he had to confront the entire social universe in whose midst magic evolves and is practised. Likewise, in the infinite regress in search of the primary cause and ultimate foundation of the artwork's value, one must make a similar stop. And in order to explain this sort of miracle of transubstantiation (which is at the very source of the artwork's existence, and which, although commonly forgotten, is brutally recalled through strokes of genius à la Duchamp), one must replace the ontological question with the historical question of the genesis of the universe, that is, the artistic field, within which, through a veritable continuous creation, the value of the work of art is endlessly produced and reproduced.

The philosopher's analysis of essence only records the product of the real analysis of essence which history itself performs objectively. History does this through the process of autonomization within which and through which the artistic field is gradually instituted and in which the agents (artists, critics, historians, curators, etc.) and the techniques, categories, and concepts (genre, mannerisms, periods, styles, etc.) which are characteristic of this universe are invented. Certain notions which have become as banal and as obvious as the notion of artist or of "creator," as well as the words which designate and constitute them, are the product of a slow and long historical process. Art historians themselves do not completely escape the trap of 'essentialist thought' which is inscribed in the usage – always haunted by anachronism – of historically invented, and therefore dated, words. Unable to question all that is implicitly involved in the modern notion of artist, in particular the professional ideology of the uncreated 'creator' which was developed during the nineteenth century, and unable to make a break with the apparent subject, namely the artist (or elsewhere the writer, the philosopher, the scholar), in order to consider the field of production of which the artist (socially instituted as a 'creator') is the product, art historians are not able to replace the ritualistic inquiry concerning the place and the moment of the appearance of the character of the artist (as opposed to the craftsman) with the question of the economical and social conditions underlying the establishment of an artistic field founded upon the belief in the quasi-magical powers attributed to the modern artist in the most advanced states of the field.

It is not only a matter of exorcizing what Benjamin called the 'fetish of the name of the master' in a simple sacrilegious and slightly childish inversion – and whether one wishes it or not, the name of the master is indeed a fetish. It is a question of describing the gradual emergence of the entire set of social conditions which make possible the character of the artist as a producer of the fetish which is the work of art. In other words it is a matter of constituting the artistic field (which includes art analysts, beginning with art historians, even the most critical among them) as the locus where the faith in the value of art and in the artist's power of valuable creation is continually produced and reproduced. This would yield not only an inventory of the artist's indices of autonomy (such as those revealed through the analysis of contracts, the presence of a signature, or affirmations of the artist's specific competence, or the recourse in case of a dispute to the arbitration by peers, etc.), but also an inventory of the signs of the autonomy of the field itself, such as the emergence of the entire set of the specific institutions which are a necessary condition for the functioning of the economy of cultural goods. These include: places of exhibit (galleries, museums, etc.), institutions of consecration or sanction (academies, salons, etc.), instances of reproduction of producers and consumers (art schools, etc.), and specialized agents (dealers, critics, art historians, collectors, etc.), all of whom are endowed with the dispositions objectively required by the field and the specific categories of perception and of appreciation, which are irreducible to those in common use and which are capable of imposing a specific measure of the value of the artist and of his products. As long as painting is measured by surface units and duration of production, or by the quantity and price of the materials used (gold or ultramarine), the artist-painter is not radically different from a house painter. That is why, among all the inventions which accompany the emergence of the field of production, one of the most significant is probably the elaboration of an artistic language. This involves first establishing a way of naming the painter, of speaking about him and about the nature of his work as well of the mode of remuneration for his work, through which is established an autonomous definition of properly artistic value irreducible to the strictly economical value and also a way of speaking about painting itself, of pictorial techniques, using appropriate words (often pairs of adjectives) which enable one to speak of pictorial art, the *manifattura*, that is, the individual style of the painter whose existence it socially constitutes by naming it. By the same logic, the discourse of celebration, notably the biography, also plays a determining role. This is probably due less to what it says about the painter and his work than to the fact that the biography establishes the artist as a memorable character, worthy of historical account, much like statesmen and poets. (It is known that ennobling comparisons – *ut pictura poesis* – contribute to the affirmation of the irreducibility of pictorial art, at least for a time and until they become a hindrance to this.) A genetic sociology should also include in its model the action of the producers themselves and their claim to the right to be the sole judges of pictorial production, to produce, themselves, the criteria of perception and appreciation for their products. Such a sociology should also take into account the way in which the artists' image of themselves and the image that they have of their production (and through this also their production itself) get generated and are affected by the image of themselves and their production that comes back to them through the eyes of other agents engaged in the field – other artists, but also critics, clients, collectors. (One can assume, for example, that the interest in sketches and cartoons shown by certain collectors since the quattrocento has only helped to contribute to the artist's exalted view of his own worth.)

Thus, as the field is constituted as such, it becomes clear that the 'subject' of the production of the artwork – of its value but also of its meaning – is not the producer who actually creates the object in its materiality, but rather the entire set of agents engaged in the field. Among these are the producers of works classified as artistic (great or minor, famous or unknown), critics of all persuasions (who themselves are established within the field), collectors, middlemen, curators, etc., in short, all who have ties with art, who live for art and, to varying degrees, from it, and who confront each other in struggles where the imposition of not only a world view but also of a vision of the artworld is at stake, and who, through these struggles, participate in the production of the value of the artist and of art.

If such is, in fact, the logic of the field, then one can understand why the concepts used to consider works of art and particularly their classifications, are characterized (as Wittgenstein has observed) by the most extreme indeterminacy. That is the case with genres (tragedy, comedy, drama, or the novel), with forms (ballad, rondeau, sonnet, or sonata), with periods or styles (Gothic, baroque, or classical), or with movements (impressionist, symbolist, realist, naturalist). One can also understand why confusion does not diminish when it comes to concepts used to characterize the work of art itself and the terms used to perceive and to appreciate it (such as the pairs of adjectives beautiful or ugly, refined or crude, light or heavy, etc.) which structure the expression and the experience of the work of art. Due to the fact that they are inscribed in ordinary language and that they are generally used beyond the aesthetic sphere, these categories of judgements of taste which are common to all speakers of a shared language do allow an apparent form of communication. Yet, despite that, such terms always remain marked – even when used by professionals – by an extreme vagueness and flexibility which (as has been noted again by Wittgenstein), makes them completely resistant to essentialist definition.[10] This is probably because the use that is made of these terms and the meaning that is given to them depend upon the specific, historically and socially situated, points of view of their users – points of view which are quite often perfectly irreconcilable.[11] In short, if one can always argue about taste (and everyone knows that confrontations regarding preferences play an important role in daily conversation) then it is certain that communication in these matters takes place only with a high degree of misunderstanding. That is precisely so because the *common-places* which make communication possible are the same ones that make it practically ineffective. The users of these topics each give different, at times diametrically opposed, meanings to the terms that they oppose. Thus it is possible for individuals, holding opposing positions within a social space, to be able to give totally opposing meanings and values to adjectives which are commonly used to describe works of art or mundane objects. The example of the adjective '*soigné*' comes to mind. It is most frequently excluded from 'bourgeois' taste, probably because it embodies the taste of the petit-bourgeois.[12] Situated within the historic dimension, one could go on drawing endless lists of notions which, beginning with the idea of beauty, have taken on different, even radically opposed meanings in the course of various periods or as a result of artistic revolutions. The notion of 'finite' is one example. Having condensed into one the closely linked ethical and aesthetic ideals of academic painting, this notion later found itself banished from art by Manet and by the impressionists.

Thus the categories which are used in order to perceive and appreciate the work of art are doubly bound to the historical context. Linked to a situated and dated social universe, they become the subject of usages which are themselves socially marked by the social position of the users who exercise the constitutive dispositions of their habitus in the aesthetic choices these categories make possible.

The majority of notions which artists and critics use to define themselves or to define their adversaries are indeed weapons and stakes in the battle, and many of the categories which art historians deploy in order to treat their subject are nothing more than skilfully masked or transfigured indigenous categories, initially conceived for the most part as insults or condemnations. (Our term 'categories' stems from the Greek *kathegoresthai* meaning to accuse publicly.) These combative concepts gradually become technical categorems upon which – by grace of the amnesia of genesis – critical dissections, dissertations, and academic theses confer an air of eternity. Of all the methods of entering such struggles – which must be apprehended as such from the outside in order to objectivize them – the most tempting and the most irreproachable is undoubtedly that of presenting oneself as a judge or referee. Such a method involves settling conflicts which in reality are not settled, and giving oneself the satisfaction of pronouncing verdicts – of declaring, for instance, what realism *really* is, or even, quite simply, of decreeing (through decisions as innocent in appearance as the inclusion or exclusion of so-and-so from a corpus or list of producers) who is an artist and who is not. This last decision, for all its apparent positivistic innocence, is, in fact, all the more crucial, because one of the major stakes in these artistic struggles, always and everywhere, is the question of the legitimate belonging to a field (which is the question of the limits of the world of art) and also because the validity of the conclusions, notably statistical ones, which one is able to establish apropos a universe depends on the validity of the category apropos of which these conclusions were drawn.

If there is a truth, it is that truth is a stake in the struggle. And although the divergent or antagonistic classifications or judgements made by the agents engaged in the artistic field are certainly determined or directed by specific dispositions and interests linked to a given position in the field, they nevertheless are formulated in the name of a claim to universality – to absolute judgement – which is the very negation of the relativity of points of view.[13] 'Essentialist thought' is at work in every social universe and especially in the field of cultural production – the religious, scientific and legal fields, etc. – where games in which the universal is at stake are being played out. But in that case it is quite evident that 'essences' are norms. That is precisely what Austin was recalling when he analyzed the implications of the adjective 'real' in expressions such as a 'real' man, 'real' courage or, as is the case here, a 'real' artist or a 'real' masterpiece. In all of these examples, the word 'real' implicitly contrasts the case under consideration to all other cases in the same category, to which other speakers assign, although unduly so (that is, in a manner not 'really' justified) this same predicate, a predicate which, like all claims to universality, is symbolically very powerful.

Science can do nothing but attempt to establish the truth of these struggles over the truth, while trying to capture the objective logic according to which the stakes, the camps, the strategies, and the victories are determined. Science can attempt to bring representations and instruments of thought – all of which lay claim to universality with unequal chances at success – back to the social conditions of their production and of their use, in other words, back to the historical structure of the field in which they are engendered and within which they operate. According to the methodological postulate (which is constantly validated by empirical analysis) of the homology between the space of the positions taken (literary or artistic forms, concepts and instruments of analysis, etc.), and the space of the positions held in the field, one is led to historicize these cultural products, all of which claim universality. But historicizing them not only means, as one may think, relativizing them by recalling that they have meaning solely through reference to a determined state of the field of battle; it also means restoring to them their necessity by removing them from indeterminacy (which stems from a false eternalization) in order to bring them back to the social conditions of their genesis, a truly generative definition.[14] Far from leading to a historical relativism, the historicization of the forms of thought which we apply to the historical object, and which may be the product of that object, offers the only real chance of escaping history, if ever so little.

Just as the oppositions which structure aesthetic perception are not given a priori, but are historically produced and reproduced, and just as they are inseparable from the historical conditions which set them in motion, so it is with the aesthetic attitude. The aesthetic attitude, which establishes as works of art objects socially designated for its use and application (simultaneously extending its activity to aesthetic competence, with its categories, concepts and taxonomies), is a product of the entire history of the field, a product which must be reproduced, by each potential consumer of the work of art, through a specific apprenticeship. It suffices either to observe the aesthetic attitude's distribution throughout history (with those critics who, until the end of the nineteenth century, have defended an art subordinated to moral values and didactic functions), or instead observe it within society today, in order to be convinced that nothing is less natural than the disposition to adopt toward an artwork, and more so, toward any object, the sort of pure aesthetic posture described by essentialist analysis.

The invention of the pure gaze is realized in the very movement of the field toward autonomy. In fact, without recalling here the entire demonstration, one could maintain that affirmation of the autonomy of the principles of production and evaluation of the artwork is inseparable from the affirmation of the autonomy of the producer, that is, the field of production. Like pure painting which, as Zola wrote apropos Manet, is meant to be beheld in itself and for itself as a painting – as a play of forms, values, and colours – and not as a discourse, in other words, independently from all references to transcendent meanings, the pure gaze (a necessary correlate of pure painting) is a result of a process of purification, a true analysis of essence carried out by history, in the course of successive revolutions which, as they do in the religious field, always lead the new avant-garde to challenge orthodoxy – in the name of a return to the rigour of beginnings – with a purer definition of the genre. One has thus observed poetry purify itself of all its accessory properties: forms to be destroyed (sonnet, Alexandrine), rhetorical figures to be demolished (simile, metaphor), contents and sentiments to be banished (lyricism, effusion and psychology), and all that, in order to reduce itself little by little, following a kind of historical analysis, to the most specifically poetic effects, like the break with phonosemantic parallelism.

In more general terms, the evolution of the different fields of cultural production toward a greater autonomy is accompanied by a sort of reflective and critical return by the producers upon their own production, a return which leads them to draw from it the field's own proper principle and specific presuppositions. This is firstly because the artist, now in a position to rebuff every external constraint or demand, is able to affirm his mastery over that which defines him and which properly belongs to him, that is, the form, the technique, in a word, the art, thus instituted as the exclusive aim of art. Flaubert in the domain of writing and Manet in painting are probably the first to have attempted to impose, at the cost of real subjective and objective difficulties, the conscious and radical affirmation of the almightiness of the creative gaze, capable of being applied not only (through simple inversion) to lowly and vulgar objects as was the aim of Champfleury's and Courbet's realism, but also to insignificant objects before which the 'creator' is able to assert his quasi-divine power of transmutation. 'Ecrire bien le médiocre.' This Flaubertian formula, which also holds for Manet, lays down the autonomy of form in relation to subject matter, simultaneously assigning its fundamental norm to cultured perception. Attribution of artistic status is, among philosophers, the most generally accepted definition of aesthetic judgement, and, as could be proved empirically, there is no cultured person today (which means, by scholastic canons, no one possessing advanced academic degrees) who does not know that any reality, a rope, a pebble, a rag peddler, can be the subject of a work of art.[15] Everyone knows, at the very least, that it is wise to say that such is the case, as an avant-garde painter, an expert in the art of confounding the new aesthetic doxa, made me observe. In fact, in order to awaken today's aesthete whose artistic good will knows no limit, and to re-evoke in him artistic and even philosophical wonder, one must apply a shock treatment to him à la Duchamp or à la Warhol, who, by exhibiting the ordinary object as it is, manage to prod in some way the creative almightiness that the pure aesthetic disposition (without much consideration) confers upon the artist as he has been defined since Manet.

The second reason for this introspective and critical return of art unto itself is the fact that, as the field closes upon itself, the practical mastery of the specific knowledge – which is inscribed in past works, recorded, codified, and canonized by an entire body of professional experts in conservation and celebration, along with literary and art historians, exegists and analysts – becomes a part of the conditions of access into the field of production. The result is that, contrary to what is taught by a naive relativism, the time of art history is really irreversible and that it presents a form of cumulativeness. Nothing is more closely linked to the specific past of the field, including subversive intention – itself linked to a state of the field – than avant-garde artists who, at the risk of appearing to be 'naive' (in the manner of Rousseau or of Brisset) must inevitably situate themselves in relation to all the preceding attempts at surpassing which have occurred in the history of the field and within the space of possibilities which it imposes upon the newly arrived. What happens in the field is more and more linked to the field's specific history and to it alone. It is therefore more and more difficult to deduce it from the state of the general social world at the given time (as a certain 'sociology', unaware of the specific logic of the field, claims to do). Adequate perception of works – which like Warhol's *Brillo Boxes* or Klein's monochromatic paintings, owe their formal properties and their value only to the structure of the field and thus to its history – is a differential, a diacritical perception: in other words, it is attentive to deviations from other works, both contemporary and past. The result is that, like production, the consumption of works which are a product of a long history of breaks with history, with tradition, tends to become historical through and through, and yet more and more totally dehistoricized. In fact, the history that deciphering and appreciation practically put into play is gradually reduced to a pure history of forms, completely eclipsing the social history of the struggles for forms which is the life and movement of the artistic field.

This also resolves the apparently insoluble problem that formalist aesthetics (which wishes to consider only form in the reception as well as the production of art) presents as a true challenge to sociological analysis. In effect, the works that stem from a pure concern for form seem destined to establish the exclusive validity of internal reading which heeds only formal properties, and to frustrate or discredit all attempts at reducing them to a social context against which they were set up. And yet, in order to reverse the situation, it suffices to note that the formalist ambition's objection to all types of historicization rests upon the unawareness of its own social conditions of possibility. The same is true of a philosophical aesthetics which records and ratifies this ambition. What is forgotten in both cases is the historical process through which the social conditions of freedom from regard to 'external determinations' get established; that is, the process of establishing the relatively autonomous field of production and with it the realm of pure aesthetics or pure thought whose existence it makes possible.

NOTES

1   A. Danto, 'The Artworld', Journal of Philosophy, 61 (1964), 571-84; G. Dickie, Art and the Aesthetic (Ithaca, NY, Cornell University Press, 1974).
2. See P. Bourdieu, 'The Philosophical Establishment', in A. Montefiore (ed.), Philosophy in France Today (Cambridge, Cambridge University Press, 1983), pp. 1-8.
3   See P. Bourdieu, 'L'ontologie politique de Martin Heidegger', Actes de la recherche en sciences sociales, 5-6 (November 1975), 183-90.
4   One should show, following the same logic, how Nietzsche furnished Foucault with 'screening' concepts. (I am thinking, for example, of the notion of genealogy functioning as a euphemistic substitute for social history.) These concepts have allowed Foucault to accept, by way of denial, modes of thinking which are typical of a genetic sociology, and to generate acceptance for them. He thus renounces the plebian methods of the social sciences, but without forfeiting them.
5   I have demonstrated elsewhere, apropos an analysis by Derrida of Kant's Critique of Judgement, how and why 'deconstruction' goes only halfway. (See P. Bourdieu, 'Postscript: Towards a 'Vulgar' Critique of 'Pure Critiques', in Distinction [Cambridge, Mass., Harvard University Press, 1984], pp. 494-8.)
6   Without calling forth all the definitions which are merely variants of Kantian analysis (such as Strawson's view that the function of the work of art is to have no function, see 'Aesthetic Appraisal and Works of Art', in Freedom and Resentment [London, Methuen, 1974], pp. 178-88), one could simply recall an ideally typical example of the essentialist constitution of the aesthetic through an enumeration of the traits which characterize an aesthetic experience, which is nevertheless very clearly situated within social space and historical time. Such an example is Harold Osborne, for whom the aesthetic attitude is typified by the following: a concentration of attention (it separates – frames apart – the perceived object from its environment), a suspending of discursive and analytical activities (it disregards sociological and historical context), impartiality and detachment (it separates past and future preoccupations), and indifference towards the existence of the object. See H. Osborne, The Art of Appreciation (Oxford, Oxford University Press, 1970).
7   On the disconcertment, even confusion, which the lack of minimal mastery of the instruments of perception and of appreciation (in particular labels and references like names of genres, of schools, of periods, artists, etc.) visits upon the culturally deprived museum-goers, see P. Bourdieu and A. Barbel, L'Amour de l'art, Les musées d'art européens et leur public (Paris, Ed. de Minvit 1966); P. Bourdieu, 'Eléments d'une theorie sociologique de la perception artistique', Revue internationale des sciences sociales, 20, no. 4(1968), 640-64. See also Danto, 'The Artworld'.
8   The concept of habitus, a dispositional 'structured structuring structure' is elaborated at great length in P. Bourdieu, Outline of a Theory of Practice (Cambridge, Cambridge University Press, 1977), and in Distinction.
9   Sociological analysis allows one to escape the dichotomous choice between subjectivism and objectivism, and to reject the subjectivism of theories of

aesthetic consciousness (*äesthetisches Bewusstsein*). Such theories reduce the aesthetic quality of a natural thing or of a human work to a simple correlate of a deliberate attitude of consciousness, an attitude which, as it confronts the thing, is actually neither theoretical nor practical but rather purely contemplative. Sociological analysis rejects these theories without falling, as does the Gadamer of *Truth and Method*, into an ontology of the work of art.

10 See R. Shusterman, 'Wittgenstein and Critical Reasoning', *Philosophy and Phenomenological Research*, 47 (1986), 91–110.

11 An acute awareness of the situation in which he is positioned could lead the analyst to rather insurmountable 'aporia'. Especially since even the most neutral language appears inevitably – as soon as naive reading makes it a part of the social game – as a stand within the very debate which he is only trying to objectify. Thus, for example, even if one replaced an indigenous word such as 'province', a word which is too charged with pejorative connotations, with a more neutral concept such as periphery, then the opposition between the center and the periphery which is used to analyse the effects of symbolic domination becomes a stake in the struggle within the field that is being analysed. For example, on the one hand there is the wish of the 'centrists' to describe the positions taken by those who occupy the peripheral sites as an effect of a delay, and on the other hand the resistance of the 'peripherists' against their lowered status implied in this classification, and their effort to convert a peripheral position into a central one or at least to make of it a willed gap. The example of Avignon illustrates the fact that the artist cannot produce himself as such – here as an alternative capable of effectively competing for the dominant position – unless he does so in relationship with his clients. (See E. Castelnuovo and C. Ginsburg, 'Domination symbolique et geographie artistique dans l'historie de l'italian art', in *Actes de la recherche en sciences sociales* 40 [November 1981], 51–73.)

12 See Bourdieu, *Distinction*, p. 194.

13 In other words, in proposing an essentialist definition of the judgement of taste or in granting the universality required by a definition which (like Kant's definition) is in accord with his own ethico-behavioural dispositions, the philosopher distances himself less than he imagines from ordinary modes of thinking and from the propensity toward making the relative absolute which typifies them.

14 Contrary to the dominant representation which claims that by relating each manifestation of taste to its social conditions of production sociological analysis reduces and relativizes the practices and representations involved, one could claim that sociological analysis does not in fact reduce and relativize the practices, but rather removes them from arbitrariness and absolutizes them by making them both necessary and unique and thus justified in existing as they exist. One could in fact posit that two people whose habitus are different and who have not been exposed to the same conditions and stimulations (because they construct them differently) do not hear the same music and do not see the same paintings and cannot, therefore, arrive at the same judgement of value.

15 See Bourdieu, *Distinction*, pp. 34–41.

9

The Eclipse and Recovery of Analytic Aesthetics

Joseph Margolis

Memory is mischievous and facile and demands a smug slogan. If we ask ourselves to explain the eclipse of analytic aesthetics, the short answer is ready: time has overrun all its entrenched positions. I speak with some authority as a partial victim at least, spared (if that is the term) only by running before the flood. Nevertheless, to admit this much is hardly to judge what has been gained and lost and not quite to say where the high ground will eventually reappear.

The best way to catch the change is to note its effects on acknowledged exemplars; and the best economy is to link these effects jointly to the principal themes of analytic philosophies of art and analytic philosophy in general – for they should be the same. They are indeed the same, and with only negligible exception the essential themes may be drawn from the work of relatively influential members of the 'analytic' community of philosophers of art.[1] I select four specimens and four themes: Monroe Beardsley, Nelson Goodman, Arthur Danto and Joseph Margolis (myself); and, not coordinately, empiricism, extensionalism and nominalism, physicalism and (what already in an alien idiom is termed) presence. All of this will need to be explained of course. But by the economy intended, what has happened to these four theorists effectively marks what has happened to analytic aesthetics over a period of somewhat more than one (the last) generation. Each has made tell-tale adjustments, whether primarily in aesthetics or in philosophy in general, that signify accommodations favouring themes substantially subverting whatever may be fairly taken to belong to the analytic canon.

There is no explicit canon of course, but there can be little doubt that 'analysts' have always been strongly disposed to subscribe to one. Also, each of the four theorists mentioned has proceeded in a way that suggests an entirely natural enlargement and shift in their respective views: so that although analytic aesthetics has been effectively subverted, the changes favoured in the views of each hardly justify a straightline application of that finding to each of them. In fact, with the exception of Beardsley, the theorists in question have clearly evolved as frank and vigorous opponents of certain themes distinctly favoured in the analytic camp. It needs to be said, also, that if we do not concede within analytic aesthetics a penchant for the canonical, there would be little point in speaking of its eclipse. Since this cannot fail to be a quarrelsome matter, there is bound to be a touch of fiction about the manner of reporting here favoured. Two caveats need to be mentioned. For one, both the substantive themes indicated and the disciplined manner of working that the analysts favour have come under severe fire – precisely because they are so intimately related. For another, the recovery of something not very distant from the canon is promisingly joined with options linked to the critique of the original themes. The truth is that the original analytic themes and the assured 'method' of analysis were always contested within the practice of analytic philosophy – and within analytic aesthetics. So the admission of the eclipse of analysis is already part of its anticipated recovery.

These are cryptic remarks no doubt. But they may explode the fiction that we are facing the imminent collapse of a monolithic philosophical programme because of essential mistakes that ineliminably define the dogmas of the entire movement. There are no such dogmas. In fact, *none* of the themes attributed to the canon was ever permitted to run uncontested; and no one can rightly claim to formulate *the* canonical method of analysis. Certain themes and methods have of course dominated the movement. Their distinct pretensions were regularly punctured by the best and most powerful practitioners of that movement; but then, of course, those same practitioners went blithely on with their own favoured projects – against their own instruction. To lose sight of the fact is to exaggerate the meaning of the 'eclipse'. To insist too casually on its 'recovery' is to miss the extent of the transformation required. To yield up the executive standing of extensionalism, nominalism and physicalism, the unity of science is, quite simply, to recover forbidden (or at least officially opposed or discouraged) conceptual fruit. And yet, the effective subversive strategies are all traceable, in an admittedly thin way, to the central work of Anglo-American analytic philosophy itself. Their recovery – and the recovery of analysis – signifies the need for a frank rapprochement between Anglo-American and Continental philosophical currents. For it is clearly among the latter that such themes as the historicist, the hermeneutic, the preformational, the structuralist and post-structuralist, the deconstructive, the genealogical, the praxical have been consistently and productively favoured; and it is only by quite openly accommodating those themes (and the varieties of conceptual strategy that addressing them must subtend) that analytic philosophy and analytic aesthetics *can* be recovered at all. So the truth is that the analytic tradition has tended to impoverish itself by a kind of increasing suicidal neglect of the leading themes of cultural life – *a fortiori*, of the leading themes that inform the world of the arts. It is also to neglect the subterranean possibilities of its own best world. The irony remains that, with regard to the *pre*-analytic period, both in philosophy in general and in the philosophy of art, the themes of intentionality, historical tradition, preformative history, discontinuity and incommensurability, the impossibility of conceptual closure, the symbiosis of the individual and the societal, the denial of cognitive transparency, the critique of critique, the emergence of human culture, the priority of practices, interpretive indeterminacy and consensual tolerance, and a thousand related themes had already been in place and had already been most vigorously dissected. The hegemony of the analytic has, quite unpardonably, done as much as it could to dismiss the full complexity of these matters in its zeal to install its own executive vision. And many, notably the specimen theorists of art who by their own interest should have been alert enough to have resisted that tendency, have often been coopted by it and, on occasion, have been quite pleased to lead compliant troops over the philosophical cliff.

So the point of the recovery is clear. The 'analytic' represents a measure of discipline that, at least saliently, at least with regard to the work of the formal and physical sciences (and whatever could fairly be associated with such work within the study of language, history, practice, art and psychology), clearly succeeded in displacing what was perceived to be the incompetence, confusion, informality and sheer error of pre-analytic philosophy. In aesthetics, the chief villain was idealism.[2] But it *was* (and it still is) unpardonable to have impoverished the field of analysis as unconscionably and as carelessly as the vanguard of analytic philosophy was prepared to do – and did do. Now, the matter haunts its progeny, and, now, many of that progeny are simply too fixed in their own prejudices to reopen the case.

So the current philosophical scene offers the spectacle of subversive talents drawn chiefly from outside the analytic tradition, that specialize in demonstrating or insinuating the inadequacy, irrelevance, unresponsiveness, sheer ignorance of a great body of *analytic* philosophy when applied to the palpable issues of any number of different sectors of bona fide interest. The disquieting truth is that many of the current critics of analytic practice are reasonably well informed regarding its best work: *they* cannot be easily counted among the *pre*-analytic innocents that the best analytic work of the early twentieth century bid fair to replace. There is a deeper innocence, now pretty well exposed, in the pioneer work of Russell and Moore in England, of the pragmatists in America, of the transplanted rigour of the positivists and logical empiricists and unity-of-science theorists of Berlin and Vienna, and of the later formal semantics of Quine and Tarski and of the followers of Quine and Tarski and Frege and Peirce and Wittgenstein, and of those attracted to ordinary-language analysis (Austin) and intuitive conceptual analysis (Ryle). None of that work is lost, nor need be lost. Some of it includes the best work philosophers have ever done. But all of it is now under fire – capable perhaps of being recast in terms more responsive to the latest attacks on both the themes and analytic strategies of the movement we are tracing (focused both within and without the tradition). These attacks are clearly too insistent to be ignored and much too compelling and too savvy to be met by old defenses.

Having said this much by way of a preface, two small warnings need to be added. First of all, the issue at stake is an eccentric and technical one, the intersecting careers of general analytic philosophy and analytic aesthetics. Since the weaknesses of analytic aesthetics are due largely to the persistence of certain entrenched commitments drawn from analysis at large, the discussion that follows may seem at times rather indifferent to the more local questions of aesthetics. Secondly, since we are primarily concerned with the threat to the future of analytic aesthetics posed by those entrenched commitments, the philosophies of art reviewed in what follows are treated essentially diagnostically. The result, frankly is that they are not particularly sympathetically described. There is something thankless about the effort, but it has its use and it invites a certain directness.

I

The most general picture of the span of analytic philosophy of the entire century – certainly of the past twenty-five years – is reasonably fixed by the conceptual linkage between W. V. Quine's well-known theory of the indeterminacy of translation and Richard Rorty's notorious recommendation that 'epistemology-centered philosophy' is (or ought to be) at an end.[3] This is not to say that either Quine or Rorty had pursued his own theme in the most perspicuous or most irresistible way. Actually, neither one has – which complicates the tale to be told. It is rather to say that what is most tenable in the accounts of each symbiotically entails that of the other, and that, at their peril, analytic philosophers of art have (until recently) tended to ignore the implied lesson. The 'eclipse' of analytic aesthetics may fairly be said to depend on ignoring that lesson; its 'recovery' depends on accommodating it. The irony is that, both in general philosophy and in aesthetics, the incompleteness of Quine's and Rorty's arguments – their frank prejudices and disinclination to explore the options they themselves have very nearly prepared – promises to enrich both analytic philosophy and analytic aesthetics in ways that could not be easily foreseen from their own exertions.

Quine is essentially a holist, a pragmatist who rejects all forms of cognitive privilege, who treats distributed claims as functioning within the space of the preformative parsings of societally entrenched 'analytical hypotheses' – hypotheses that are themselves reflexively specified only by way of more attenuated such 'hypotheses'.[4] From this and Quine's profound demonstration that there is no principled disjunction between analytic and synthetic truths, between distinctions of meaning and distinctions of fact,[5] the indeterminacy thesis ineluctably follows:

> There can be no doubt that rival systems of analytical hypotheses can fit the totality of speech behaviour to perfection, and can fit the totality of dispositions to speech behaviour as well, and still specify mutually incompatible translations of countless sentences insusceptible of independent control.[6]

The trouble is that Quine never satisfactorily explained how 'sentence', 'behaviour', and 'fit', between sentence and behaviour could be managed or reconciled with his own severe theory; or, what might be the *non*-behavioural evidence of 'incompatible translation' fitting behaviour 'to perfection'; or, what 'truth' might mean under such circumstances; or, indeed, what constraints within holism itself might reasonably be proposed to facilitate the comparative assessment of rival analytical hypotheses. On all of these matters Quine is disappointingly silent – even though it is plain that he favours physicalism, favours the rejection of intentionality, favours extensionalism, behaviourism, and a general empiricist bent congenially but loosely committed to something like the unity-of-science programme. The bearing of Quine's work on aesthetics rests with the double theme: (a) that analytic aestheticians (influenced by the tendencies Quine has spawned and nourished) have themselves tended to favour physicalist, extensionalist and behaviourist strategies with respect to puzzles about art and criticism; and (b) that those strategies proved to be peculiarly vulnerable in aesthetics because they were never satisfactorily secured in analytic philosophy in general and because they hobbled the chances of formulating any adequate analytic philosophy of art.

Rorty is more radical about the radical import of having taken Quine's lesson (and Wilfrid Sellars's lesson) to heart – even against the 'failure' of those two worthies to understand that the traditional philosophy of the West is at an end as a direct result of their own labours:

> To drop the notion of the philosopher as knowing something about knowing which nobody else knows so well would be to drop the notion that his voice always has an overriding claim on the attention of the other participants in the conversation [of mankind]. It would also be to drop the notion that there is something called 'philosophical method' or 'philosophical technique' or 'the philosophical point of view' which enables the professional philosopher, *ex officio*, to have interesting views about, say, the respectability of psychoanalysis, the legitimacy of certain dubious laws, the resolution of moral dilemmas, the 'soundness' of schools of historiography or literary criticism, and the like – I do not know whether we are in fact

at the end of an era – perhaps a new form of systematic philosophy will be found which has nothing whatever to do with epistemology but which nevertheless makes normal philosophical inquiry possible.[7]

Quine does not offer an explicit or satisfactory account of how we proceed with the distributed claims of any disciplined inquiry *within* his own holism; and Rorty does not satisfactorily explain what is entailed *in* his favouring the work of the sciences or other inquiries within that same constraint. Quine does not concede that *his* extreme holism disqualifies philosophy in the least; Rorty argues that it does but never shows us why. And we, caught between these two lines of argument, insist on saving whatever may be saved of the empirical sciences and other first-order inquiries we believe deserve an innings. But we too need to explain what we have salvaged in salvaging that.

Quine simply disallows programmes of analysis that go against the elimination of intentionality, for instance, as in his well-known attack on Brentano:

> In the strictest scientific spirit we can report all the behaviour, verbal and otherwise, that may underlie our imputations of propositional attitudes, and we may go on to speculate as we please upon the causes and effects of this behaviour, but so long as we do not switch muses, the essentially dramatic idiom of propositional attitudes will find no place.[8]

But if anything is clear about the theory of art, it is clear that we cannot make sense of the structure of artworks, their cultural status, their history, the detection and interpretation of their properties without featuring intentionality. Analytic aestheticians either have actually tried to restrict themselves to a de-intentionalized idiom (Monroe Beardsley, for instance) or have been drawn in a distinctly divided way toward and against physicalism, toward and against an idiom congenial to the unity-of-science idiom (Arthur Danto, for instance). Quine's influence is unmistakable here.

Once we see matters this way, the radical incompleteness of Quine's programme and the radical arbitrariness of Rorty's stare us in the face. Their joined claims, that is, the claims for which they are now regularly made the totemic bearers – holism with respect to the analytic penchant for rejecting transcendental arguments, for naturalizing epistemology, for promoting physicalism and extensionalism (Quine); and holism with respect to repudiating the viability of all epistemology and metaphysics, but for favouring in first-order discourse an inherited physicalism and extensionalism (Rorty) – signify what is popularly perceived as the 'eclipse' of analytic philosophy (*a fortiori*, the eclipse of analytic aesthetics). On the other hand, the perception of the incompleteness and arbitrariness of their respective programmes signifies the beginning of the best programme for the 'recovery' of analytic philosophy (and, of course, of analytic aesthetics). Rorty's claim – hardly restricted to analytic aesthetics – is that 'epistemology-centered philosophy', philosophy in the Western tradition, analytic philosophy as it has been canonically practised, is now doomed. On the Rortyan line, Quine's programme of analysis is best reinterpreted as a contribution to a supposedly radically different model of philosophy, the model of the *'conversation* [of mankind] as the ultimate context within which knowledge is to be understood.[9]

But what does that mean? Certainly, it means that *any* inquiry – scientific, philosophical, critical, interpretive, historical – must: (i) give up the pretence of the transparency of reality with respect to human cognition; (ii) admit the preformative and pluralized historical contingency of the conditions of understanding under which the members of any society make inquiry; (iii) concede the impossibility of drawing from the holist conditions under which we appear to dwell in the world and survive as a species any direct, distributed consequences affecting the truth of particular claims made within the space of those conditions; (iv) recognize that our critical speculations about the enabling conditions under which the sciences and other distributive inquiries prosper are themselves subject to the same tacit preconditions as are those very claims; and (v) acknowledge that our philosophical inquiries cannot be apodictic, cannot be known to be universally binding, synthetic a priori, or formulated for all conceivable conditions. To accept constraints (i) to (v) is to embrace what is convincing and common to Quine's and Rorty's views all right – to embrace what is common to pragmatism and analytic philosophy. It is also to embrace, of course, what is common to the best work of Hegel, Marx, Nietzsche, Husserl, Heidegger, Peirce, Dewey, James, Merleau-Ponty, Foucault, Derrida, Wittgenstein. *But it is not tantamount to disallowing an 'epistemology-centered philosophy' at all* – as Rorty's mentors (including Quine, Sellars and Davidson) have either implicitly grasped or at least never denied.[10]

To embrace (i) to (v) is, effectively, to disallow what has disapprovingly been called the philosophy of 'presence'.[11] But it is not – certainly it need not be – to disallow philosophy *tout court*, to disallow epistemology, metaphysics, transcendental argument in particular. It is only to insist that philosophy must henceforth confine itself within the terms of (i) to (v) or within the terms of other corollary constraints of the same sort. The point is that Quine nowhere supposes it is impossible to do so, and Rorty nowhere shows that it *is* actually impossible; *and* it may be argued both that it *is* possible and that pursuing philosophy thus offers a rational benefit, particularly conceding the destabilizing loss of privilege that (i) to (v) entails. The recovery of analytic philosophy, *a fortiori* the recovery of analytic aesthetics, is simplicity itself: merely proceed as before, or proceed as would now be congenial to how one proceeded before, under the 'new' constraints.

They are not really new constraints: they are only the old implicated constraints freshly perceived – perhaps perceived compellingly for the first time. Once grant (i) to (v), one sees at once *why philosophy cannot be abandoned*: first, because science and philosophy are continuous, incapable of principled disjunction; second, because first- and second-order inquiries make no sense without the other and because the distinction between them is itself a second-order distinction; third, because holisms of the pragmatist sort are not intended to disqualify science, or other first-order inquiries but only to disallow any privilege regarding their cognitive standing; and fourth, because to wish to secure the continuing practice of a rigorous science (or of any other first-order discipline) is, effectively, *to* secure epistemology and metaphysics. Quine certainly concedes all this. All the pretended demonstrations favouring the abandonment of philosophy – offered by Rorty, the poststructuralists, the postmodernists, the deconstructionists, the genealogists, the anarchists, the nihilists, the sceptics – are simply manifestations of a profound *petitio*, regardless of the persistence of the disordered thinking critics of these sorts have managed to expose in the received tradition and regardless of the important differences there may be among them in exposing their own favoured offenders.

The trick is to see that embracing (i) to (v) makes possible an indefinitely large, even unpredictable, variety of philosophical claims that could not have been favoured under the aegis of an epistemology and metaphysics that implicitly favoured privilege. Rorty makes the mistake, however, of concluding that there are no forms of epistemological, metaphysical, transcendental, second-order, legitimative inquiry *that are not inherently privileged*. But both the Anglo-American and Continental traditions (he favours) straightforwardly show *that* it is indeed possible to proceed epistemologically after having abandoned all epistemic privilege.

Analytic philosophy – *a fortiori*, analytic aesthetics – certainly has its work cut out for it. Under the radical limitations of (i) to (v), for instance, there may be no convincing reasons for preserving physicalism or extensionalism, for endorsing the rejection of intentionality, for insisting on bivalence or *tertium non datur*, for disallowing moderate or extended incommensurabilism or conceptual discontinuity, for opposing historicism, relativism, hermeneutic pluralism, the symbiosis of realist and idealist approaches to science or to any other forms of disciplined inquiry. But the whole notion of the sheer end of philosophy – hence the end of analytic philosophy, hence the end of analytic aesthetics – is nonsense, a self-inflicted wound utterly uncalled-for by the welcome philosophical epiphany of rediscovering the end of privilege. In its best form, the apparent lesson could be little more than a hoax by which to expose the easy deception of an army of grateful, self-sacrificing philosophers.

There are two distinct sorts of leverage that must be secured. They service at one and the same time the recovery of analytic philosophy in general and the recovery of analytic aesthetics. The first, of course, is the redemption of a viable and disciplined idiom that is not restricted to extensionalism, physicalism, behaviourism and the rest (in Quine's manner); and the second is the demonstration that the rejection of privilege does not entail the 'end of philosophy' (in Rorty's manner). Rorty's project, which is clearly having increasing influence on the theory of art and criticism, is peculiarly pernicious because it both fails to vindicate the 'end of philosophy' and because, in promoting that doctrine, it somehow insinuates the adequacy at (what would normally have been called) *the first-order level* of a physicalism, extensionalism and behaviourism congenial to Quine's, Sellars's and Davidson's own projects. What needs to be grasped, *contra* Rorty, is that (1) assertive or constative practices of discourse are clearly ineliminable and not in any significant respect different at first-order levels (science and literary criticism, say) and at second-order levels (philosophy and legitimation, say); (2) the offending doctrine of cognitive privilege cannot be derived merely from (1), on pain of eliminating science and criticism, in eliminating philosophy; (3) there can be no first-order work without second-order work; and (4) part of the concern of philosophy is, precisely, to clarify how the legitimation of methodological, ontological, epistemological, normative and related matters can be salvaged and fruitfully pursued under the constraints of historical existence, the loss of cognitive privilege, cultural preformation, moderate incommensurabilities and the like.

In a strange way, there is really no counter-argument needed against either Quine or Rorty. Quine is completely candid about the arbitrariness of his prejudice against intentionality, though it is true that he is entirely sanguine about the reduced idiom he prefers. Rorty simply offers no argument at all to show that (4) is not a possible or worthwhile project or in fact a project that his own mentors have regularly favoured and still favour. There are indeed arguments to show that Rorty's finding is a complete *non sequitur*: that, having shown that much of traditional philosophy does secure transcendental, legitimative, epistemological, metaphysical, normative arguments by illicit privilege, Rorty overhastily concludes that there is no alternative to that sort of failure. But we cannot pause here to track down that complex issue.[12]

We may, however, offer as a metonymic but entirely characteristic clue the following remarks by Rorty regarding the theory of truth:

> a pragmatist theory about truth . . . *says* that truth *is not* the sort of thing one should expect to have a philosophically interesting theory about. For pragmatists, 'truth' is just the name of a property which all true statements share. It is what is common to 'Bacon did not write Shakespeare', 'It rained yesterday', 'E equals mc^2', 'Love is

better than hate', '*The Allegory of Painting* was Vermeer's best work', '2 plus 2 is 4', and 'There are nondenumerable infinities'. Pragmatists *doubt* that there is *much* to be said about this common feature.[13]

These opening line of Rorty's *Consequences of Pragmatism* convey the mixed impression that the philosophical analysis of truth has been convincingly shown to be fruitless, that all pragmatists agree about this, *and* (also) that they only have doubts about its fruitfulness and have seen little or nothing to encourage the contrary impression. There is not, in all of Rorty's work, a straightforward resolution of this wobbling or a single demonstration that the theory of truth – even pragmatist theories of truth (even Peirce's or James's or Davidson's or Putnam's theory of truth) – are not fruitfully, even essentially, connected with the fortunes of first-order inquiry (say, regarding the direction of science and literary criticism). That is to say, there is no demonstration that the dialectical rebuttal of any of these and similar theories *is not* itself philosophically productive, not merely a self-consuming argument that shows (therapeutically) the point of abandoning philosophy. The nagging proof of this is very neatly tied to the fact that Rorty's recommendation to abandon philosophy still means to leave in place something like Quine's ulterior programme *at the first-order level* and to deny there any reasoned basis for critical review (inevitably second-order) of the adequacy of such an idiom – say, for the fortunes of the criticism and appreciation of the arts. But that is preposterous.

Now, the interesting thing is that a great deal could be cleared up in philosophy in general (and in aesthetics in particular) by pursuing the import of the 'recovery' of philosophical analysis under the threat of philosophy's coming to an end. It is really a question of using the old joke of Chicken Little in order to remind ourselves of the conditions under which we live and think. The argument regarding science and philosophy is embarrassingly elementary: the courage and acumen wanted bear rather on what is to be salvaged beyond the joke, and on what new directions might bear the weight of our appetite for philosophical inquiry. The argument is simply this. We cannot consider the truth of anything without the use of statements, propositions, affirmations, constatations, claims and the like. Cognitive concerns of every kind are caught up with them. So it must be the case that science and philosophy need not presuppose or entail privilege or transparency merely in taking a constative form. There is no large practice of natural language that, in permitting us to affirm this or that as true, fails to provide for the reference or identification of that about which we speak, or fails to provide for predications or attributions regarding what is thus identified as marking what we take to be true of it; and *that* must be true, at least as far as formal considerations go, for both first- and second-order discourse. Furthermore, *if*, as both Quine and

Rorty hold (however different the motive of each may be), that distributed truth-claims function and are confined within the space of some
holist adjustment to the actual world – but relative to which we can never
hope to exit to ensure the least measure of distributed privilege – then it is
doubly clear that philosophy, concerned as it is with the conditions and
legitimation of knowledge and distributed truths, *cannot possibly pretend
to recover privilege or transparency* (cannot possibly affirm the philosophy of 'presence') *merely by attending to second-order questions.* Philosophy, rather like science and literary criticism, must proceed in an
'internalist' way, in a way that is entirely internal to the cognitive
resources of a particular historical era reflexively identified and refined
under the same circumstance. But why not? That's all there is to it. Rorty
has missed the essential lesson.

One may well wonder how all of this bears on analytic aesthetics. I shall
say in a moment. But to collect the import of all that has been said so far, I
offer the following summation: (a) our confidence that the whole of
human inquiry takes a realist form is suitably in touch with the actual
world cognitively, is a *holist* theme to which all theories converge but
without requiring distributed (therefore privileged) cognitive grounds and
without directly yielding distributed (therefore privileged) truths; (b) the
admission of (a) justifies – indeed, is meant to locate properly – practices
internal to that holist assurance, in accord with which distributed truth-
claims are and may be assessed and confirmed in realist terms; (c) the
practices of (b) need make no principled distinction between *first-order*
(scientific) and *second-order* (legitimative or transcendental or
epistemological) claims; and (d) disputes about the truth of distributed
claims within (c) may be construed in realist terms despite the *loss of*
(distributed) *transparency* and therefore despite the impossibility of precluding *incommensurabilities, relativistic divergences, artefactual discontinuities* within the space of such disputes. *It is the prospects of elaborating (d) that count as the future of analytic philosophy and analytic
aesthetics, and it is just those prospects that invite (and require) a
rapprochement between Anglo-American and Continental philosophical
currents.* Shorn of philosophy's 'accustomed' privilege, we are now *more*
dependent than before on the good legitimative (second-order) guesses we
are able to construct. Since there is no assured logic of discovery, there is
actually an ineliminable need for transcendental speculation.

II

Turn, now, to our exemplars. All four may fairly be said to have mani-
fested more than a touch of 'objectivism' (or 'naturalism') in that sense in
which Husserl had throughout his career attempted to refine the critical
function of phenomenology *vis-à-vis* the presumed fixity and reliability of

the cognitive relationship between subject and object (self and world).[14] Analytic aesthetics has characteristically never shown much accommodation of the critical Husserlian theme of the preformative conditions of 'subjectivity' within which the *historically and psychologically contingent relationship of (cognizing) subject and (cognized) object emerges* – what Husserl ultimately cast in terms of the preformational, tacit, incompletely fathomable function of the encompassing *Lebenswelt* in which 'naturalistic' scientists and inquirers come to rely on their empirical resources.[15] Husserl himself, of course, pursued the delusive goal of an apodictic (phenomenological) science that his own better followers were disposed to modify along the lines of imaginative conceptual experiments that might yield, however provisionally *and* within the constraints of one's own *Lebenswelt*, some sense of an asymptotic approximation to conceptual invariance. The hopelessness of this line of (Cartesian or apodictic) speculation is, it is fair to say, the precise point of Derrida's early critique of Husserl.[16]

We are not concerned, here, to render a full and reasoned account of each of our four specimen figures; and we are not concerned (except in the way of offering a clue about the convergence of Anglo-American and Continental philosophy) to vindicate Husserl or the work of his somewhat less than completely loyal followers. Our interest lies rather in gauging the viability of analytic aesthetics in the face of certain philosophical challenges that appear to threaten its continued effectiveness – coming mainly from Continental sources and condensing in what (it may be hoped) we now see to be the pointless extravagance of Rorty's dismissal of analytic epistemology and metaphysics.

There can be little doubt that Monroe Beardsley is, of the four, the most devoted objectivist. This is the entire point of Beardsley's most widely discussed book, *The Possibility of Criticism* – which is committed to the rejection of intentionalism in criticism, the rejection of relativism in interpretation and the affirmation of the stable objective presence of literary artworks (and, of course, of artworks in general) on the admission of which depends the very 'possibility' (in the Kantian sense) of a discipline of critical reading that could be said to function as a fair analogue of the characteristic work of the empirical sciences.[17]

Beardsley never wavered in these commitments, though it is true that his own candor and inventiveness led him, first, to admit 'we can never establish . . . decisively [what is] "in" or "out" [of a given literary work]'[18]; and, secondly, to incorporate into his analysis of a poem a speech act model that installed the strong intentionalism of speech acts themselves, although Beardsley clearly hoped that the device of illocutionary acts would ultimately be dropped from his account.[19]

'If there were no principles involved in criticism,' says Beardsley, 'I do not see how it could be kept from collapsing into something purely intuitive and impressionistic.'[20] Apart from the questionable use of the phrase 'purely intuitive and impressionistic', this admirably fixes the sense in which Beardsley was a straightforward naturalist or objectivist (in Husserl's sense); it marks the point of his quarrels with E. D. Hirsch (about author's intentions) and with Joseph Margolis (about relativism in interpretation). Those two theorists, of course, may also be said to have exhibited a similar sort of objectivism, even if they disagreed with Beardsley's line of argument.[21] The essential challenge to a strong analogy between artworks and physical phenomena construed as *objects* suitably stable and determinate for the purposes of description, interpretation, criticism, and explanation (wherever and in whatever way pertinent for the disciplines in question) rests largely with the bearing of the puzzles of intertextuality on the determinate identity and intentional structure of artworks. *If* artworks cannot be fixed as referents for continuing critical discourse stable enough that their reidentification entails that their internal structure remains relatively fixed and finitely bounded through the very process of critical interpretation, then Beardsley's project must fail and the extension of something like the unity-of-science model to criticism is doomed. The theme of intertextuality, perhaps most floridly flaunted by Roland Barthes in the notorious manifesto, 'Every text, being itself the intertext of another text, belongs to the intertextual',[22] has by this time largely undermined any simple objectivism of Beardsley's sort in the practice of literary criticism. Whatever may be the ultimate fate of Yale deconstructive views (notably, Harold Bloom's) or reader-response theories (notably Wolfgang Iser's) or of such maverick theorists as Stanley Fish, it is precisely the intentionality and historicized existence of artworks, both opposed by Beardsley, that have forced a radical revision in the conception of the methodology of criticism.[23] In any case, although Beardsley pursued, particularly toward the end of his life, all the principal currents of Continental and Continentally inspired aesthetics, he never saw the need to modify the strong objectivism he favoured, an objectivism that clearly approached (however informally) the extensionalist severities of Quine's programme and of programmes associated with the unity of science.[24] Nevertheless, as we have already implicitly noted, Quine's notion of 'analytical hypotheses' is itself a thin pragmatist counterpart to Husserl's major theme of preformation – the key philosophical theme that eventually yielded increasingly radical notions of intertextuality.

We must be clear that the limitation of Beardsley's form of analytic aesthetics is a dual one: it is partly the consequence of an excessively optimistic empiricism in the face of intentional, historical, interpretive, productive complexities that have taxed the ingenuity of his New Critical orientation beyond its apparent resources; and it is partly the consequence, *via* those complexities, of his never having come to terms with the preformational, intransparent, conceptually discontinuous, incommensurable features of discourse about art and culture (and, by extension, about science itself) or, indeed, the deep indeterminacies of the very ontological structure of artworks. Analytic aesthetics (like analytic philosophy) can no longer pursue such simplifications if it is to survive. That texts and artworks are *not* suitably similar to physical objects, that their intentional structure obliges us to reflect on what it means to affirm or deny that artworks *have* determinate or completely determinate structures, is certainly the single most important theoretical issue confronting all philosophies of art at the present time as well as all practices in history and criticism. The bare question makes no sense in terms of Beardsley's framework – nor, indeed, in terms of any first-order work drawn from Quine's orientation.

But, having said that, it is crucial to understand that, once the apodictic pretensions of Husserl are disallowed, there remains no effective disjunction between naturalistic and phenomenological strategies. On the contrary, *non*-phenomenologized naturalisms *are* fairly dubbed 'objectivist' in Husserl's pejorative sense; and *non*-naturalized phenomenologies *are* cognitively pointless and empty. This is, in fact, the shared discovery of Heidegger and Merleau-Ponty, who ultimately refused to support Husserl's rather mad extremes.[25] But in more general terms it is the theme common to naturalistic forms of critique (as in the Kantian, Marxist, Frankfurt School and Freudian modes) and to non-naturalistic forms of critique (as in the phenomenological, existential, deconstructive, genealogical and postmodernist modes). The pivotal issue is the one already identified, namely, that *every* form of discourse must accommodate the constative functions of reference and predication; that such discourse cannot be committed for that reason alone to some form of cognitive privilege; and that no holism (whether naturalistic or phenomenological) makes any sense if it does not provide for distributed truth-claims servicing the sciences and any other form of critical discourse (literary criticism, moral debate, for instance) that we wish to preserve. The upshot is that Beardsley's philosophical pursuit of *objectivity* is *not* a disabling weakness of his 'analytic' aesthetics: it is only his particular way of securing it (inspired by empiricism and the unity of science) that is indefensible.

In many ways, Goodman's aesthetics, particularly when qualified along the lines of his *Ways of Worldmaking* and *Of Mind and Other Matters*,[26] appears to bridge the divide between the two sorts of strategy. It does afford the possibility of an opening, but Goodman hardly has that in mind. Again, as with Beardsley, questions need to be raised about Goodman's substantive views regarding the arts as well as about the general philosophical orientation of his most recent publications. The truth is that there is no clear way of reconciling the peculiar fixities – bordering on essentialism – of *Languages of Art* with the so-called 'irrealism' of *Ways of Worldmaking*;[27] and those fixities are themselves particularly doubtful on internal grounds.

The most noticeable oddity about Goodman's general philosophy, which remains pretty constant from *The Structure of Appearance* and *Fact, Fiction, and Forecast* to the latest books (despite the incompatibility between the visions of the two pairs), is that Goodman's entire effort is centred on epistemological puzzles, although he never actually engages those puzzles in explicitly epistemological or epistemologically informed methodological terms. For instance, he raises the question of the viability of nominalism;[28] but then he both treats the matter in purely formal terms, without the least attention to biological and cultural constraints on the effective, spontaneous use of discriminated resemblances and general terms in natural-language contexts, and converts the nominalist issue into an exclusively logical matter regarding the (ontological) eliminability of nonindividual entities.[29] Or, he poses the seemingly methodological question of projectibles within the context of induction,[30] but he nowhere pursues it in cognitive terms. That theory depends inescapably on an account of 'entrenchment' – which is clearly an epistemological matter and, as such, is clearly nowhere discussed in Goodman.[31] Furthermore, although the notion of entrenchment reappears in Goodman's later writings (in fact, in the context of his aesthetics[32]), Goodman's handling of it is utterly irreconcilable with the notion developed in *Fact, Fiction, and Forecast*, remains completely undeveloped in epistemologically pertinent terms now so urgently required by his irrealism (that is, by the proliferation of plural, made, actual worlds) and is clearly at odds with the rather strong essentializing tendencies of *Languages of Art*. The matter is complicated and takes a little patience to get clear about. But it can be shown to bear in a decisive way on the structure of Goodman's aesthetics.

The clue may be grasped by reminding ourselves of the stern once-and-for-all application of the (intended) testing of would-be projectibles in a world that (once) seemed to be so steady and orderly that Goodman's well-known new riddle of induction actually appeared to capture the methodological practices of the sciences. Entrenchment seemed so palpable and straightforwardly recoverable (then) that Goodman could afford to announce:

> The obvious first step in our weeding-out process in determining (true) projectibility is to eliminate all projected hypotheses that have been violated. Such hypotheses, as already remarked, can no longer be projected, and are thus henceforth unprojectible. On similar grounds, all hypotheses having no remaining unexamined instances are likewise to be ruled out. However, neither the violated nor the exhausted hypotheses are thereby denied to have been projectible at an earlier time.[33]

Of course, all of this was meant by Goodman to be read in terms of 'the passing of the possible': 'Possible processes and possible entities vanish. . . . All possible worlds lie within the actual one.'[34]

All of this is now forgotten, swept away, or reduced to an utter shambles inasmuch as (pertinently for his theory of art) Goodman now affirms:

> Irrealism does not hold that everything or even anything is irreal, but sees the world melting into versions and versions making worlds, finds ontology evanescent, and inquires into what makes a version right and a world well-built. . . . How, then, are we to accommodate conflicting truths without sacrificing the difference between truth and falsity? Perhaps by treating these versions as true in different worlds. Versions not applying in the same world no longer conflict; contradiction is avoided by segregation. A true version is true in some worlds, a false version in none. Thus the multiple worlds of conflicting true versions are actual worlds, not the merely possible worlds or nonworlds of false versions. So if there is any actual world, there are many. For there are conflicting true versions, and they cannot be true in the same world.[35]

There is, however, no explanation, in Goodman, of how to individuate worlds or world-versions, or what it means to say that something is true in one (actual) world but not in another, or what it means to say that what is false is false in all actual worlds (despite the fact that what is true in one world may be in 'conflict' with what is true in another), or what it means to say that *we* can sort such different worlds. All of this amounts to a complete abandonment of the epistemological questions of entrenchment.

Goodman has found a way of *suggesting* that he is accommodating anti-analytic attacks on objectivism in the most ramified way. But it is extremely difficult to find any such accommodation and it is equally difficult to make the case that his theory remains coherent in this regard;[36] *and*, whatever its motivation, it is quite impossible to draw out of it – or reconcile with it – the salient claims of *Language of Art*. The essential point is this: Goodman's irrealism and apparent historicizing of the construction of plural worlds (in *Ways of Worldmaking*) are *never* intended to make any concessions in the direction of radically intentionalizing the world of art (or the world of science for that matter); it is simply a device for avoiding palpable contradictions in a Quinean-like unitary world governed by a nominalist and extensionalist canon. Goodman uses the device of plural actual worlds in order to make nominalism and extensionalism work *in the domain of art and culture*. This is why it is important to note that Goodman fails to address the (apparently) *historicized* puzzle of entrenching projectibles in epistemic terms. If he had, he would not have been able to avoid the problems of textuality or of intentionality or of the limits of nominalistic models.

There can be little doubt that *Languages of Art* is written in a straightforwardly objectivist spirit. There is nothing in it that manifests the slightest qualm along phenomenological or deconstructive or genealogical lines – that is, concerns about preformational forces. On the contrary, apart from the extremely important development of a semiotic idiom for the handling of philosophical issues about the arts – which certainly can and ought to be redeemed by an analytic aesthetics – Goodman is peculiarly intransigent about the *nature* and *properties* of the arts, a matter that might seem at odds both with his nominalism and his (later or at least more explicit) irrealism. Two doctrines are of particular importance. In one, he contrasts in the strongest disjunctive sense what he calls allographic and autographic arts.[37] That is, he not only introduces the formal distinction, he surveys the arts and finds that music and literature are (it seems, essentially) allographic.

The ulterior reason for the distinction may escape one's notice: it is simply meant to bring discourse about the arts into a satisfactory alignment with an extensionalist model. The autographic arts are ones in which 'even the most exact duplication of an original does not thereby count as genuine'.[38] So intentional complexities are disallowed by ensuring uniqueness of reference. The allographic arts are ones in which all apparent discrepancies, variations, differences (as of performance and printing) may be tolerated (and discounted) as far as numerical identity and individuation are concerned, provided only that the individuating marks preserved satisfy completely extensional scores or notations. Goodman struggles manfully with the notational informalities of the history of music; but he never quite comes to terms with its profoundly historical and intentional nature. He is ultimately driven to the obviously unnecessary (even intolerable) conclusion:

> The innocent-seeming principle that performances differing by just one note are instances of the same work risks the consequence – in view of the transitivity of identity – that all performances whatsoever are of the same work. If we allow the least deviation, all assurance of work-preservation and score-preservation is lost; for by a series of one-note errors of omission, addition, and modification, we can go all the way from Beethoven's *Fifth Symphony* to *Three Blind Mice*.[39]

If Goodman had but found 'ontology evanescent' enough, he might have allowed intentional informalities to flower, or at any rate cognitive fixities to go more informal. For example, if one concedes that the numerical identity of a dance (as in re-identifying one and the same dance in different performances) is a function of its *stylistic* features, and if its stylistic features are profoundly intentionalized, historicized, *incapable* of being captured by any strict extensionalized notation, then it may well be that all so-called allographic arts are ineluctably autographic – and, in being autographic, irreconcilable with the severe nominalism and extensionalism Goodman means to favour.[40] The truth is that Goodman nowhere actually analyses the stylistic *properties* of artworks (with regard to their intensional complexity) – or the predicates purporting, in a logically relaxed way, to designate such properties; he never goes beyond merely insisting that any and all such properties *are* capable of being extensionally regimented. Clearly, the collapse of that claim would place Goodman's sort of analytic aesthetics in serious jeopardy.

The other large issue that Goodman addresses – tied to the present one because there is, in Goodman's work, no actual discussion of the structure of artworks – concerns the notion of exemplification. It concerns the nature of artistic expression and so borders once again on the complexities of intentionality. Goodman's key is given by the following:

> Expression [in a work] is not, of course, mere possession [by the work of the putatively expressive property]. Apart from the fact that the possession involved in expression is metaphorical, neither literal nor metaphorical possession constitutes symbolization at all. . . . [But] an object that is literally or metaphorically denoted by a predicate or the corresponding property, may be said to exemplify that predicate or property. Not all exemplification is expression, but all expression is exemplification.[41]

Once again, the essential point remains that Goodman treats expression (semiotically) as metaphorical, *because* to treat the expressive property *of* an artwork as 'literally' possessed by it would entail serious complications *for any extensional treatment of art* – hence, for the autographic/ allographic distinction as well. Nevertheless, Goodman nowhere justifies the *metaphorical* ascription:[42] he literally *has* no ontology of art; and he nowhere provides a suitable clue about how philosophical inquiries regarding the arts should proceed. He has no genuine analytic aesthetics.

That is, Goodman practises a variety of analytic aesthetics, but he nowhere entertains questions about the nature of philosophical strategies in the large. As a result, it is impossible to gain from Goodman's work a clear idea of how analytic aesthetics should meet the challenge of anti-analytic currents; although it remains both true and provocative that Goodman's notion of worldmaking has been seen – for instance by the phenomenologically and hermeneutically minded French philosopher Paul Ricoeur – as promising a new view of 'fiction' (Ricoeur is thinking of Goodman's symbol systems: quite another matter) as a sort of 'productive imagination' by which we 'make and remake reality' in ways that would obviously defeat any straightforwardly objectivist stance.[43] But whether Goodman would, or could, accept Ricoeur's adventurous suggestion is difficult to say. In fact, the essential irony is just that *Ricoeur* favours Goodman's view of worldmaking because he, Ricoeur, sees this as a powerful concession in the direction of historically preformative forces that lay a proper foundation for the admission and treatment of the intentional or hermeneutic features of artworks; whereas Goodman's motivation is to extricate a strongly anti-hermeneutic (that is, a formal semiotic) conception of artworks *for* his own favoured extensionalism. There could not be a more curious marriage of ideas.

Of our four specimen analysts, Arthur Danto affords the most detailed sense of adjusting a theory of art to the actual phases of the history of contemporary art – chiefly painting. He is particularly attentive to modernist, postmodernist and especially so-called conceptual art. For that reason, he is sensibly disinclined to specify any essentialist definition of art. For instance, he is suitably brief regarding George Dickie's institutional conception of art,[44] and he ultimately dismisses Goodman's thesis of expression as metaphorical exemplification with the rather nice piece of tact: 'It would be unfortunate to conclude that expressive predicates are never literally true of works of art.'[45] He is also noticeably hospitable to Hegelian and broadly phenomenological currents. Nevertheless, it is quite clear that his general philosophical orientation is uneasily – and unsatisfactorily – divided between his appreciation of the complexities of cultural phenomena, particularly historicity and intentionality, and his residual commitment to a relatively inflexible physicalism and extensionalism. In fact, in his discussion of the issue of expression, which in the context of the rhetoric of art occupies Danto's principal attention, he actually concludes: 'The philosophical point [of the discussion of some of Cezanne's paintings and other artworks] is that the concept of expression can be reduced to the concept of metaphor, when the *way* in which something is represented is taken in connection with the subject represented.'[46] By this device, Danto recovers what Goodman does not quite accommodate – but in an ingenious way that preserves his ulterior convergence with Goodman's extensionalism and tendency toward physicalism.

This is a large and rather complicated matter, not easily grasped or conceded. Our intention here, one must remember, is to draw the thread of analytic aesthetics from a number of its principal champions in order to weigh the prospects for its continuing force. Let it therefore be said of Danto's work (in the philosophy of art) that its fatal weakness lies with Danto's failure to have resolved the analysis of what he himself had memorably identified as 'the 'is'' of artistic identification'.[47] The point to grasp is that Danto's difficulty with the 'is' of artistic identification (not, of course, a difficulty Danto himself feels) is both the mate of similar difficulties that surface in all of his philosophical work – in his theory of history and in his theory of action, for instance[48] – and a clue to his essential philosophical strategy. But it needs to be said, of course, that most readers of Danto do not sense the conceptual strain in his aesthetic simply because they do not take seriously enough the bearing of the 'is' of artistic identification on *all* of his otherwise most perceptive discussions of artworks. That is, *most* readers accept Danto's straightforward account of the complexities of art without attempting to reconcile his critical and appreciative remarks with *his fundamental philosophical orientation*. It is not that Danto embraces the empiricism, physicalism, nominalism, extensionalism, unity-of-science orientation so characteristic of the analytic tradition: it is rather that his theory is fatally encumbered by the traces of such affiliations, that he is divided in his heart regarding the adequacy of those doctrines and their disciplined application to the world of action, history, art, language and culture, *and* that he fails (for reason of that divided allegiance) ever to resolve the puzzle of the 'is' of artistic identification.

The objective of Danto's entire strategy (going well beyond aesthetics) is to marry two somewhat disparate projects: one, the articulation of an idiom ample enough for the entire span of cultural life – notably, art, history, action, knowledge; the other, adherence to an underlying ontology, more or less faithful to the inspiration of the unity-of-science programme and of a strong physicalism. *That* is what the 'is' of artistic identification is all about, and that explains why Danto takes such pains to distinguish it from the 'is' of (numerical) identity. *If*, however, *what* is *constituted* by the first 'is' *is* real as such, then the second 'is' *would* ineluctably apply to it. So the trick is that Danto manages to hold that artworks are 'constituted' as artworks by the 'is' of artistic identification all right, but that *that constitution does not yield an entity or real phenomenon about which it may be said that it is both real (in the ontological sense) and self-identical as such.* What is true of 'it' is held at arm's length from what is real, kept from capturing the actual properties of 'mere' physical phenomena (not quite the equivalent of what Danto calls 'mere real things').[49] But the motivation for that manoeuvre is still not too distant from Sartre's insistence that art is 'unreal', that is, superior to what is 'merely' real.[50]

All of this comes out reasonably clearly in Danto's recent objection to Susan Sontag's view of interpretation. Here is what he says:

> Hers [that is, Sontag's objections regarding the nature of interpretation] is against a notion of interpretation which makes the artwork as an explanandum – as a symptom, for example. My theory of interpretation is instead constitutive, for an object is an artwork *at all* only in relation to an interpretation. We may bring this out in a somewhat logical way. Interpretation in my sense is transfigurative. It transforms objects into works of art, and depends upon the 'is' of artistic identification. Her interpretations, which are explanatory, use instead the 'is' of ordinary identity. Her despised interpreters see works as signs, symptoms, expressions of ulterior or subjacent realities, states of which are what the artwork 'really' refers to, and which requires the interpreter to be master of one or another kind of code: psychoanalytical, culturographic, semiotical, or whatever. In effect, her interpreters address the work in the spirit of science. . . . Mine is a theory which is not in the spirit of science

but of philosophy. If interpretations are what constitute works, there are no works without them and works are misconstituted when interpretation is wrong. And knowing the artist's interpretation is in effect identifying what he or she has made. The interpretation is not something outside the work: work and interpretation arise together in aesthetic consciousness. As interpretation is inseparable from work, it is inseparable from the artist if it is the artist's work.[51]

Now, the transfigurative 'is' is meant to accommodate absolutely everything of interest that may be said about artworks, but it collects all of that only *in a relational way*. That is, it is initially the artist's intention *with respect to* a merely physical object (or, in a more relaxed, provisional sense, with respect to a 'mere real thing' that may even happen to be an artefact – a snow shovel or bottlerack, for instance); and it is subsequently, therefore, the viewer's (or aesthetic percipient's) recovery of *that* (or something like that) *constituting relationship* (the interpretation) that permits the viewer to 'see' it *as* an artwork: 'To see something as art requires something the eye cannot descry – an atmosphere of artistic theory, a knowledge of the history of art: an artworld.'[52]

This is the reason Danto is so comfortable in declaring (as we have seen) that 'the concept of expression *can* be reduced to the concept of metaphor', after having dismissed Goodman's version of a related thesis. *Danto* has a better way of holding on to all the complexity of art, while reaching for the same extensional and physicalist model Goodman is more explicitly attracted to. But it cannot be enough *if*, as seems plain, *human persons themselves*, the paradigms of culturally complex entities, are *not* similarly reducible (by the 'is' of identity) to mere physical bodies.[53] After all, if persons were thus reduced, then there would be no independent entities capable of *relating* to other physical objects by suitable interpretation or theory, in such a way that those 'objects' would be imaginatively 'transfigured' (but *not* ontically transformed) into artworks – or human actions or historical events or speech or the like. Otherwise, Danto would merely be the stock figure of a reductive physicalism (would hold that artworks just are – by the 'is' of identity – physical objects), whereas (in truth) he means to be a *non*reductive physicalist.[54] But he is never sufficiently clear, ultimately, about the relationship between the intentionally complex language of human culture and the language of physicalism – which is what the true physicalist (whether reductive or nonreductive) cannot permit to remain inexplicit. That is why his accounts fails. More than that, his endeavour fixes the plain sense in which, for all his considerable ingenuity and perceptiveness, his version of analytic aesthetics remains essentially bound to the objectivism that we noted at the start in Beardsley's very much simpler aesthetics.

Nevertheless, it would be churlish not to admit the finesse of Danto's sustained discussion of the historical and intentional complexities of art.

What Danto manages to show thereby – against his own intentions – is that, by a logically small adjustment, fatal to the older strains of analytic aesthetics, these exemplary observations could revive the analytic orientation by embracing just the kind of complication the older strains disallow. Danto is too well informed to disallow them; but he is also too loyal to those older strains to work out an explicit ontology fitted to the kind of critical remarks he himself regularly favours. Hence, he never skimps on the critic's role; but then he also never addresses the obvious theoretical pressure that it imposes on a realism essentially committed to the contraints of physicalism.

The fourth of our specimens, Joseph Margolis (myself, of course, if I dare speak in the third person), is the only one of the four to have attempted systematically to reconcile the strategies of analytic philosophy with the principal currents of anti-analytic philosophy – chiefly, with those that appear in Husserl, Heidegger, Derrida and Foucault, that is, with phenomenological and poststructuralist currents. Margolis's general argument insists that, first of all (as already remarked), there is no way to avoid the constative function of discourse; and, secondly, that all such discourse (whether first-order or second-order, whether intended to be descriptive of the world or intended to be legitimative with respect to what purports to be descriptive of the world – there being no way to disengage one from the other) must submit to some form of critique, that is, to some way of attending to the preformative conditions under which constative discourse functions as such.[55] This has the effect of 'phenomenologizing' naturalistic discourse or of 'naturalizing' phenomenological or deconstructive or genealogical discourse. For the absence of the first leaves the naturalistic blind, and the absence of the second leaves the phenomenological and the deconstructive pointless and empty; *and*, for that reason, *critique* may be either naturalistic (say, Marxist or Frankfurt School) or anti-naturalistic (say, Nietzschean or Heideggerean). The important point is that critique (in this sense) is entirely 'internalist' and viable as such, that is, restricted in the same way as any first-order inquiry (say, science and literary criticism). In short, though second-order and legitimative, it utterly eschews cognitive privilege.[56]

It is a very pretty and uncomplicated consequence that the postmodernist conception of philosophy – preeminently, Rorty's view – simply fails at a stroke, that is, fails in the sense that there are no professional practices of cognitive inquiry that can escape the need for second-order, legitimative reflection, even if (or precisely because) it is the case that the 'loyalty' we may manifest with respect to such practices 'no longer needs an ahistorical backup'.[57] Rorty's point is that the metaphysical, transparent, cognitively privileged, essentialist, correspondentist, mirrored, objectivist, transcendental, presenced, logocentric idiom of Kant and Descartes is neither necessary nor defensible. Fine. He offers two options: one, a historicized and naturalistic but *not* philosophical or epistemological source of reasons and arguments for the practices in question (which he regards as a naturalized Hegelian line); the other (the 'postmodernist bourgeois liberal', also 'Hegelian'), one that simply abandons the entire need *for* a justification of practices – contenting itself with the notion that: 'On a Quinean view, rational behavior is just adaptive behavior of a sort which roughly parallels the behavior, in similar circumstances, of the other members of some relevant community.'[58]

But this is simply intellectual bankruptcy. For, for one thing, we cannot eliminate (Rorty does not wish to eliminate) constative discourse. And for a second, the *practice* – any practice, the practice of any community of inquirers – must have a rationale *regarding how to go on to new cases not included in the paradigms learned in learning the original language or practice*. Therein lies the essential disability of Goodman's nominalism and of every nominalism construed in a cognitively pertinent sense; and therein also lies the defect and defeat of the postmodernist manoeuvre. For the problem is not merely one of how to go on extending the scope of complex predicates in new circumstances but also one of how to go on giving rational or critical redirection to any sustained and disciplined inquiry. The first is the *pons* of nominalism; the second, of post-modernism. If analytic aesthetics is to survive – if analytic philosophy or any philosophy is to survive, if any rational inquiry is to survive – then: (1) it must be possible to bridge the difference between naturalism and phenomenology and deconstruction and genealogy and the like, and (2) it must be possible to provide for second-order legitimative discourse that does not fail in the 'Kantian' manner Rorty is at such pains to dismantle. Margolis's entire philosophical effort is committed to working out the conceptual conditions for satisfying (1) and (2), with attention particularly to the metaphysics and epistemology of culture and art. This is at least a viable proposal regarding a *new* programme and orientation for analytic aesthetics – again, of course, considered here only in the spirit of tracing the prospects of analytic aesthetics. It would put into question all the older doctrines of objectivism, physicalism, nominalism, extensionalism and unity-of-science constraints; and it would embrace, at least as pertinent options, historicism, intentionality, preformation, intertextuality, relativism, cultural emergence, nonreductive materialism, critique, incommensurabilism, legitimation. The vista is large enough.

Through a marvel of innuendo but not argument, Rorty declares and insinuates at one and the same time: 'Analytic philosophy *cannot*, I suspect, be written without one or the other of these two distinctions: the "Kantian" distinctions (ambiguously) repudiated by Quine and Wilfrid Sellars respectively, namely, the 'necessary-contingent" distinction and the "given-interpretation" distinction'.[59] The juxtaposition of the italicized 'cannot' and the coy 'I suspect' permits Rorty to play the enormously pleasant game of agreeing with all his critics for the sake of the ongoing 'conversation' while at the same time cutting philosophy (and science and criticism) off at the knees. So he adds, catching up the point of what we took note of before:

> Behaviourism claims that if you understand the rules of a language-game, you understand *all* that there is to understand about why moves in that language-game are made. (All, that is, save for the extra understanding you get when you engage in various research programs which nobody would call epistemological – into, for example, the history of the language, the structure of the brain, the evolution of the species, and the political or cultural ambience of the players.)[60]

But that is just what one does not understand, unless one understands the rationale, the legitimative rationale, the second-order transcendental moves in accord with which we recommend – dialectically, historically, contingently, without foundations – how to go on rationally.[61] If we give up the 'Kantian' position, which we must, then we need second-order legitimative discourse more than ever – not less – because we need the best rational guess about what the conditions of inquiry and truth-claims are by which to guide ourselves in extending our practice. That is what philosophy is all about; and that is what no one has ever convincingly shown to be disposable. To be sure, 'rational' (like 'true' and 'false') also *has* a history, which complicates philosophy enormously. But it complicates it, it does not rule it out. Even Foucault rather wistfully acknowledges the point in reviewing the threatening incoherence of his own postmodernist efforts.[62] There *cannot* be a recovery of analytic aesthetics, now faced with its own stalemate, without a 'rational' second-order redirection of its energies. Rorty's is simply a counsel of despair or irresponsibility.

Margolis, then, has deliberately sought to reconcile what the objectivist and naturalistic idioms have correctly perceived – namely, that constative discourse is ineliminable and that first-order and second-order (legitimative) discourse are inseparable – with the best elements of non-naturalistic (in effect, non-'analytic') philosophy; while at the same time he abandons the objectionable logocentric or privileged discourse that the phenomenologists and poststructuralists have rightly perceived to be entrenched in most of analytic philosophy. This means that the famous 'subject/object' relationship that Husserl (and Heidegger and Derrida) so much inveigh against cannot be eliminated but, *once* placed in an appropriate preformational or critical context (*without*, then, reclaiming privilege on its own), the relationship affords a perfectly adequate and viable (and necessary) basis for recovering epistemological and metaphysical inquiry – in aesthetics as elsewhere.

It is true that Margolis has come to this rapprochement somewhat later than his characteristic accounts of the ontology of artworks, of the logic of interpretation and of relativistic judgements in general.[63] The result is that there *is* a distinct vestigial objectivism in these various discussions that needs to be exorcised. This is as it may be, a matter entirely local to Margolis's own efforts; and is of little consequence in the present context. In his more recent papers,[64] Margolis explores the ontic indeterminacies, the historicized openness, the lack of essential fixity artworks exhibit. But there is no question that all of this needs to be put into better form. That is not my present concern. The fact remains that the analysis of the nature of art and culture, of description and interpretation, of texts, of histories, of reference, of judgement, of relativistic and nonrelativistic truth-values is entirely congenial both with regard to the rapprochement sketched and the continuance of analytic aesthetics. In fact, Margolis's themes (even within a more naive epistemological framework drawn from a less developed non-foundationalist account of analytic philosophy than we are now suggesting) have characteristically been hospitable to the full recovery of intentional phenomena, the irreducibility of culture to nature, the inadequacy of both reductive and nonreductive physicalisms, the admission of emergence, the replacement of the unity-of-science programme, the abandonment of a comprehensive extensionalism, the acknowledgement of the complexities of historicism, the advocacy of ontic indeterminacies, of conceptual incommensurabilities, of divergent pluralisms, of relativistic values, the rejection of closed systems, the insistence on the symbiosis of the psychological and the societal, the symbiosis of realism and idealism, and the constructive nature of selves and world. These are all themes peculiarly favourably attuned to phenomenologizing naturalism and naturalizing phenomenology – meaning by that to accommodate all forms of critique (say, the Marxist as well as the Nietzschean) that seriously address the question of the pursuit of first- and second-order inquiry under contingently preformational conditions that, at the level of both first- and second-order discourse, we cannot fathom in a privileged way.

In short, analytic philosophy – and analytic aesthetics in particular – cannot be expected to prosper without recovering (at least selectively) these and related questions within the subtler space of an inquiry that avoids the older cognitive privilege or foundationalism, or without resisting altogether the siren attraction of a know-nothing postmodernism. But there is reason already to think that the imminent future will transform these implied recommendations into a prophecy – and a fulfilment. In any case, the best prospects of analytic aesthetics depend on two adjustments: (i) the pursuit of all the themes just mentioned, that go entirely counter to the canonical tendencies of analytic philosophy but are not at all incompatible with the native discipline of such philosophy; and (ii) the ability to steer a middle course between the older tendency toward ahistorical privilege and the newest tendency to disallow, within a historicized condition, suitably adjusted versions of philosophy's legitimate legitimative concern.

NOTES

1 I have attempted several summaries of this sort before. I trust the overlap will
   not seem excessive. The perspective keeps changing of course. See Joseph
   Margolis, 'Recent Currents in Aesthetics of Relevance to Contemporary
   Visual Artists', *Leonardo*, 12 (1979) 111–19; 'Recent Work in Aesthetics', in
   Kenneth G. Lucey and Tibor R. Machan (ed), *Recent Work in Philosophy*
   (Totowa, NJ, Rowman and Allanheld, 1983).
2 See, for instance, William Elton (ed.), *Aesthetics and Language* (Oxford,
   Basil Blackwell, 1954); and Joseph Margolis (ed.), *Philosophy Looks at the
   Arts* (New York, Scribner, 1962).
3 Richard Rorty, *Philosophy and the Mirror of Nature* (Princeton, NJ,
   Princeton University Press, 1979), p. 390.
4 W. V. Quine, *Word and Object* (Cambridge, Mass., MIT Press, 1960),
   pp. 15–16.
5 W. V. Quine, 'Two Dogmas of Empiricism', *From a Logical Point of View*
   (Cambridge, Mass., Harvard University Press, 1953).
6 Quine, *Word and Object*, p. 72.
7 Rorty, *Philosophy and the Mirror of Nature*, pp. 392–4.
8 Quine, *Word and Object*, p. 219.
9 Rorty, *Philosophy and the Mirror of Nature*, p. 389.
10 See, further, Joseph Margolis, *Pragmatism without Foundations:
   Reconciling Realism and Relativism* (Oxford, Basil Blackwell, 1986).
11 See Richard Rorty, 'Overcoming the Tradition: Heidegger and Dewey', in
   Consequences of Pragmatism: Essays 1972–1980 (Minneapolis, University of
   Minnesota Press, 1982).
12 I examine the recovery of certain key philosophical projects in *Pragmatism
   without Foundations*; see particularly, ch. 11.
13 Rorty, *Consequences of Pragmatism*, p. xiii; italics added.
14 A brief sense of the range of Husserl's criticism may be got from Edmund
   Husserl, *Phenomenology and the Crisis of Philosophy*, trans. Quentin Lauer
   (New York, Harper and Row, 1965). Lauer brings together two independent
   essays of Husserl: 'Philosophy as Rigorous Science' and 'Philosophy and the
   Crisis of European Man'.
15 See Edmund Husserl, *The Crisis of European Sciences and Transcendental
   Phenomenology*, trans. David Carr (Evanston, Ill., Northwestern University
   Press, 1970).
16 See Jacques Derrida, *Edmund Husserl's Origin of Geometry: An Introduction*, trans. John P. Leavey, Jr (Stony Brook, NY: Nicolas Hays, 1978); and
   Speech and Phenomena and Other Essays on Husserl's Theory of Signs,
   trans. David B. Allison (Evanston, Ill., Northwestern University Press,
   1973).
17 See Monroe C. Beardsley, *The Possibility of Criticism* (Detroit, Mich.,
   Wayne State University Press, 1980).
18 Ibid., p. 36.
19 Ibid., p. 14 and 'The Testability of an Interpretation' in the same volume.
20 Ibid., p. 14.
21 See E. D. Hirsch, Jr, *Validity in Interpretation* (New Haven, Conn., Yale

University Press, 1967); and Joseph Margolis, *The Language of Art and Art Criticism: Analytic Questions in Aesthetics* (Detroit, Mich., Wayne State University Press, 1965). The latter volume has been considerably re-worked and enlarged as *Art and Philosophy: Conceptual Issues in Aesthetics* (Atlantic Highlands, NJ, Humanities Press, 1980), though it exhibits much the same orientation.

22 Roland Barthes, 'From Work to Text', trans. Josue V. Harari, in Josue V. Harari (ed.), *Textual Strategies* (Ithaca, NY, Cornell University Press, 1979), p. 77.

23 For an overview of these and similar currents, see Joseph Margolis, 'What is a Literary Text?' in Herbert L. Sussman (ed.), *At the Boundaries: Proceedings of the Northeastern University Center for Literary Studies*, vol. 1, 1983 (Boston, Mass., Northeastern University Press, 1984), 47–73.

24 I may say, here, that Beardsley read Roland Barthes's *S/Z* as a straightforward, objectivist semiotics of literature and failed completely to appreciate the subversively deconstructive intent of Barthes's essay. That is, where he was able to assimilate the poststructuralist literature, he regularly read it as something like a continuation of New Criticism – which indeed it superficially resembles. Otherwise, just as Derrida serves as a straightforward (!) deconstructionist (*On Grammatology*), Beardsley serves as a straightforward and uncompromising New Critic.

25 See, for instance, Maurice Merleau-Ponty, *The Phenomenology of Perception*, trans. Colin Smith (London, Routledge and Kegan Paul, 1962); Walter Biemel, 'Husserl's *Encyclopaedia Britannica* Article and Heidegger's Remarks Thereon', in Frederick A. Elliston and Peter McCormick (eds), *Husserl: Expositions and Appraisals* (Notre Dame, Ind., University of Notre Dame, 1977). The rapprochement of naturalism and phenomenology and deconstruction is discussed at length in Joseph Margolis, *Texts without Referents: Reconciling Science and Narrative* (Oxford, Basil Blackwell, 1988).

26 See Nelson Goodman, *Ways of Worldmaking* (Indianapolis, Hackett Publishing, 1978); and *Of Mind and Other Matters* (Cambridge, Mass., Harvard University Press, 1984).

27 Cf. *Ways of Worldmaking*, p. x.

28 See, for instance, Nelson Goodman, 'Seven Strictures on Similarity', in Lawrence Foster and J. W. Swanson (eds), *Experience and Theory* (Amherst, University of Massachusetts Press, 1970).

29 See Nelson Goodman, *The Structure of Appearance*, 2nd edn (Indianapolis, Bobbs–Merrill, 1966), ch. 2.

30 See Nelson Goodman, 'Prospects for a Theory of Projection', *Fact, Fiction and Forecast*, 2nd edn (Indianapolis, Bobbs-Merrill, 1965).

31 Ibid., pp. 94–9.

32 Cf. Goodman, *Of Mind and Other Matters*, pp. 32–3.

33 Goodman, *Fact, Fiction and Forecast*, p. 83.

34 Ibid., p. 57.

35 Goodman, *Of Mind and Other Matters*, pp. 29, 31.

36 See Hilary Putnam, 'Reflections on Goodman's *Ways of Worldmaking,*' *Philosophical Papers*, vol. 3 (Cambridge, Cambridge University Press, 1983).

37 See Nelson Goodman, *Languages of Art* (Indianapolis, Bobbs-Merrill, 1968), pp. 113–22.

38 Ibid., p. 113.

39 Ibid., pp. 186–8.

40 See Joseph Margolis, 'The Autographic Nature of the Dance', in Maxine Sheets-Johnstone (ed.), *Illuminating Dance: Philosophical Explorations* (London and Toronto, Associated University Presses, 1984); and Nelson Goodman, 'The Status of Style', in *Ways of Worldmaking*.

41 Ibid., p. 52.

42 Cf. Margolis, *Art and Philosophy*, pp. 12–14.

43 Paul Ricoeur, 'The Narrative Function', *Hermeneutics and the Human Sciences*, ed. and trans. John B. Thompson (Cambridge, Cambridge University Press, 1981), particularly pp. 292–3.

44 Arthur C. Danto, *The Transfiguration of the Commonplace* (Cambridge, Mass., Harvard University Press, 1981), pp. 92–5.

45 Ibid., pp. 189–97, particularly p. 192.

46 Ibid., p. 197.

47 The notion first appeared, unanalysed, in Arthur Danto, 'The Artworld', reprinted in Margolis (ed.), *Philosophy Looks at the Arts*, 3rd edn (Philadelphia, Temple University Press, 1987).

48 This more ramified issue is explored in Joseph Margolis, 'Ontology Down and Out in Art and Science', *Journal of Aesthetics and Art Criticism*, 46 (1988). The relevant texts include: Arthur C. Danto, *Narration and Knowledge* (New York, Columbia University Press, 1985) – the enlarged second edition of Danto's *Analytical Philosophy of History* (1964); and *Analytical Philosophy of Action* (Cambridge, Cambridge University Press, 1973).

49 Cf. 'Works of Art and Mere Real Things', in *Transfiguration of the Commonplace*.

50 See Jean-Paul Sartre, *The Psychology of Imagination*, (Secaucus, NJ, Citadel Press, n.d.); also, Arthur C. Danto, *Jean-Paul Sartre* (New York, Viking, 1975), ch. 1.

51 *The Philosophical Disenfranchisement of Art*, (New York: Columbia University Press, 1986) pp.44–5.

52 Danto 'The Artworld', p. 162.

53 The nature of this difficulty is explored in Joseph Margolis, 'Constraints on the Metaphysics of Culture', *Review of Metaphysics*, 39 (1986), 653–73.

54 The most ingenious version of nonreductive physicalism is developed in John F. Post, *The Faces of Experience* (Ithaca, NY, Cornell University Press, 1987). Post's book is examined at some length in Margolis, *Texts without Referents*, ch. 6.

55 Cf. Margolis, *Pragmatism without Foundations*, ch. 8; and *Texts without Referents*, pt I.

56 On 'internalist' strategies, see Margolis, *Pragmatism without Foundations*, ch. 11.

57 Richard Rorty, 'Postmodernist Bourgeois Liberalism', *Journal of Philosophy*, 80 (1983) 583–89; reprinted in Robert Hollinger (ed.), *Hermeneutics and Praxis* (Notre Dame, Ind., Notre Dame University Press, 1985); the material quoted appears on p. 216 (in Hollinger's edition).

58 Ibid., p. 217.

59 Richard Rorty, 'Epistemological Behaviourism and the De-Transcendentalization of Analytic Philosophy', *Neue Hefte fur Philosophie*, 9 (1978); reprinted in Hollinger, *Hermeneutics and Praxis*, pp. 95–6. Rorty professes to follow Lyotard, of course, in characterizing his own view as postmodern. Cf Jean-Francois Lyotard, *The Postmodern Condition: A Report on Knowledge*, trans. Geoff Bennington and Brian Massumi (Minneapolis, University of Minnesota Press, 1984).
60 Rorty, 'Epistemological Behaviourism', p. 98; italics added.
61 I have tried to formulate a fresh interpretation of transcendental arguments along these lines, in *Pragmatism without Foundations*, ch. 11.
62 See, for instance, Michel Foucault, 'Questions of Method: An Interview with Michel Foucault', trans. Alan Bass, *Ideology and Consciousness*, 8 (1981); reprinted in Kenneth Baynes et. al. (eds), *After Philosophy: End or Transformation?* (Cambridge, Mass., MIT Press, 1987).
63 For instance, in *Art and Philosophy*; also, in *Culture and Cultural Entities* (Dordrecht, D. Reidel, 1984), ch. 1.
64 See, particularly, Joseph Margolis, 'What is a Literary Text?', (ed.), *At the Boundaries* p. 47–73; 'The Threads of Literary Theory', *Poetics Today*, 6 (1986) 75–110; 'How to Theorize about Texts at the Present Time: Deconstruction and Its Victims', in Peter J. McCormick (ed.), *The Reasons of Art* (Ottawa, University of Ottawa Press, 1985), pp. 98–111; 'Opening the Closure, and Vice Versa', in Mark Neuman and Michael Payne (eds), *Self, Sign, and Symbol* (London and Toronto, American University Press, 1987), pp. 34–44; 'Puzzles of Pictorical Representation', in Margolis (ed.), *Philosophy Looks at the Arts*, 3rd edn., pp. 338–57; 'Reference as Relational: *Pro and Contra*', *Grazier Philosophische Studien*, 25/26 (1985/6), 327–57.

10

Changing the Subject

Catherine Z. Elgin and
Nelson Goodman

I INCARCERATION

'Art aspires to beauty; science, to truth. Art is creative; science, descriptive. Art appeals to emotion; science, to reason.' Convenient clichés segregate the arts from the sciences, expressing the widespread conviction that each would be contaminated through association with the other. Philosophy long sustained popular opinion, demarcating purportedly impenetrable boundaries between domains. But border crossings were common; and neither art nor science suffered for them.

Only philosophy suffered. Strangled by its own strictures, it could not explain the interanimation of aesthetic and scientific concerns. Moreover, the domestic affairs of a discipline are inextricably tied to its foreign relations. So philosophy's failure filtered inward, spreading confusion throughout aesthetics and the philosophy of science.

Traditional aesthetics conceives of works of art as artefacts, the aesthetic attitude as a form of receptivity, aesthetic experience as the satisfaction derived from the appreciation of aesthetic value. It thus frames its problems in terms of the familiar duality of subject and object. The conception of a problem directs and circumscribes efforts to solve it. So traditional philosophy of art takes its task to be delineating the essential properties of the subjects and objects in its realm. It searches for shared features that qualify objects, attitudes, experiences and values as aesthetic. Failing to find them, it resorts to stipulation.

Convinced, for example, that aesthetic merit must derive from a single property common to all good art, it calls that property *beauty*, conveniently overlooking the implausibility of claiming that Goya's *Disasters of War* and Botticelli's *Birth of Venus* are alike in being beautiful. The paradox of ugliness springs to life, born of the conviction that beauty is essential to great art.

The pattern recurs. Under their normal interpretations, terms fail to mark the requisite distinctions. Redefinition is always an option, but stipulative definitions are uninformative. The 'pleasure' derived from both *Medea* and *The Magic Flute*, like the 'beauty' shared by *The Disasters of War* and *The Birth of Venus*, is so denatured it is unprojectible. Neither affords a basis for classifying undecided cases.

Any work has many properties. A painting is a risky investment; a sculpture, a doorstop; a classical ballet, an opportunity for a nap. But to perceive only these features is not to see the work *as art*. To do that allegedly requires an aesthetic experience of the work.

But what makes an experience aesthetic? Art often excites emotion. And emotion, by tradition, is antithetical to cognition. So aesthetic experience must be a feeling – a noncognitive reaction to works of art. Since we obviously value such experience, it must be a type of pleasure, enjoyment, or satisfaction. All this naturally follows from reasonable premises once the duality of cognition and emotion is granted. We need not investigate the apprehension of art to find these things out.

Subjectivism threatens. If feeling is decisive and knowledge irrelevant, ignorance does not discredit bliss. Moreover, if the pleasure a work produces determines its aesthetic value, popularity is the mark of great art.

Hardly a welcome conclusion. To avoid it, theorists construe aesthetic experience as a highly refined emotion, one the Philistine is too coarse to feel. Only appropriately situated, appropriately sensitive individuals are supposed to be susceptible to such fine feelings. Unsurprisingly, controversy surrounds the identification of the favoured subjects and objects. It is odd, though, to expect to escape subjectivism by taking *some* subjects' reactions to be determinative of merit.

Interpretation causes trouble too. Understanding is plainly cognitive. So the noncognitivist must choose between objectionable alternatives, concluding either that interpretation yields no understanding, or that the understanding it yields contributes nothing to the aesthetic experience of the work.

We thus come to overlook the interpenetration of cognitive and aesthetic concerns, settle for the lesser among evils in choosing criteria for interpretation and evaluation, and swallow any number of additional unpalatable consequences because they seem forced upon us by a seemingly natural and inevitable conception of aesthetics – one grounded in the dichotomies of subject and object, emotion and cognition, essence and accident. That these dichotomies are imposed a priori rather than derived from our encounters with with art makes them all the more unshakable. To elude such unwelcome results requires a reconception of the subject, resources, and objectives of aesthetics. This is what analytic philosophy provides.

II LIBERATION

With the analytic turn, philosophy abandons the attempt to police shifting and inconsequent boundaries. It reconceives philosophy's projects, recognizing that understanding neither begins nor ends with absolutes.

Instead of trying to explicate fleeting feelings and ephemeral ideas, analytic philosophy focuses on public manifestations. Thoughts are not trapped in the mind; they travel widely, borne on words and deeds. And however they may behave in private, when appearing in public, they are subject to canons of acceptable behaviour.

By identifying those canons and controlling for their contributions, analytic philosophy undertakes to determine what our words and deeds commit us to. Initially the task seemed simple: distill out convention, leaving content behind. But it soon became clear that convention and content are fused. Ideas are inseparable from their expressions; expressions, inseparable from their languages. Still, utterances can be analyzed, their meanings and referents disclosed. Logic and linguistics supply the tools of the analyst's trade.

Initially, analytic philosophy focused on literal descriptive language. Its contributions to aesthetics, though salutary, were slight. By attending to what we say about art, it revealed tensions between the theory and practice of art criticism. The principles we advocate often clash with the ones we employ; the reasons we endorse with the ones we adduce. The avowed aspirations of critical discourse frequently diverge from its actual endeavours. In short, analytic scrutiny showed that criticism is riddled with failures to practise what it preaches.

Still, talk about talk about art is not talk about art. Nor is understanding what we say about art understanding art, unless what we say about art is right. And metacriticism is powerless to determine *that*. So if analytic aesthetics is merely metacriticism, it is unable to address the main issue: It has nothing to say about art.

But analytic aesthetics need not end with metacriticism. For works of art refer, and thus are symbols. And the analytic techniques originally devised to explicate language can be extended and emended to apply to symbols of other kinds. One approach to this task is sketched below.

III ART AS SYMBOL

To construe a work as a symbol is to embed it in a language or symbol system. The system's syntax determines the identity of its signs; its semantics fixes their reference. One task of analytic aesthetics is to map out systems suited to art. Another is to determine how they resemble and differ from other systems.

Comparisons can be fruitful. Juxtapositions can reveal how the effects works achieve and obstacles they overcome derive from the (shared or separate) resources their symbol systems provide. Picasso's variations on *Las Meninas* illuminate not just Velázquez's work, but the possibilities open to painting as an art. And Alpher's musical variations on Picasso's variations carry aesthetic understanding across media.[1]

Interdisciplinary confrontations may be equally informative. We find that science scorns vague, ambiguous, and imprecise symbols; art welcomes them.[2] In science, symbols normally refer singly and directly; in art, reference is often complex, multiple and indirect. Scientific symbols are fairly attenuated; aesthetic ones, relatively replete.[3] Science thus seeks nearly invisible windows through which its objects can be clearly discerned. Art tends to focus on symbols themselves.[4] This is no accident. A discipline's aspirations and objectives shape and are shaped by the symbols it employs.

Nevertheless, science is not completely alien to art. For syntactic and semantic categories cross disciplinary lines. Syntactic density is common to scientific and artistic drawings; syntactic differentiation, to scientific and literary discourse. Proofs as well as poems literally exemplify their forms and may metaphorically exemplify properties like elegance, economy and power. In science and literature, metaphor bridges gaps, forging connections between remote realms.[5]

Delineation of kinships and contrasts is far from complete. Analytic philosophy provides sophisticated techniques and a suitable framework for investigating them. Instead of segregating the arts and the sciences, it integrates them, dismantling stifling stereotypes that denigrate both.

Contemporary analytic philosophy recognizes no Archimedean point, no position outside the fray from which to monitor or mediate the battle between the gods and the giants. And from within, there is no sign of pitched battle, only local squabbles. These are as likely to pit science against science, art against art, as they are to set a science against an art.

This reconception of aesthetics revitalizes arts education. If artistry is the fortuitous commingling of inspiration, creativity, and genius, education has little to offer. Receptivity to the muse can hardly be inculcated! But prospects for educational effectiveness improve when works of art are conceived as symbols in syntactically and semantically structured systems. Minimally, fundamentals can be taught. A student can learn the 'grammar' of a system and develop skill in manipulating its symbols. Fluency can be inculcated, even if eloquence cannot.[6]

Learning a language does not insure that a speaker will have anything interesting, insightful, or important to say. It provides him with the ability to say what comes to mind, and with conceptual categories for framing his thoughts. Mastery of other symbol systems yields similar benefits, supplying the rudiments of an art without which creativity would be illusory; genius, idle; inspiration, mute.

Through its study of symbols, analytic philosophy maps a common ground where the interests of art and science intersect. This enables us to investigate artistry and arts education scientifically. We can explore the physiological and psychological bases of symbolizing, and inquire into the efficacy of various teaching methods. We can study the mastery of a symbol system, learn whether it is enhanced or inhibited by mastering other systems, or by developing other skills. The value of controlled experiments here is plain. Noting, for example, that both computer languages and musical notation are digital, we might test for correlations between the ability to write programmes and the ability to write music. Answers are far from obvious; research, far from complete. But preliminary studies have already yielded promising results.[7]

This reconception might seem to anaesthetize art, to benumb aesthetics. But it does neither; for reason does not exclude passion. So aesthetic experiences may be at once cognitive and affective. Our revision of aesthetics displaces but does not disavow emotion. It takes the feelings work evoke, not as aesthetic ends in themselves, but as modes and means of understanding.[8] Refined emotions, like discriminating perceptions, are aesthetically valuable because they enable us to discern and distinguish subtle but significant aspects of a work.

Apprehension is not pure receptivity, but constructive engagement. Nothing is 'given' in sensation or reflection. The properties we find in a work of art and in our responses to it are products of experience, expectation, categorization, and skill. By altering the background, we modify the conditions that inform and structure a work. We discover different things in it, place different interpretations on it. Aesthetic acuity is not a natural endowment, but a synthesis of carefully honed skills. We learn to see what had been invisible; to hear what had been inaudible; to feel what had been insensible. By enriching our stock of categories, sharpening discrimination, augmenting knowledge, fine-tuning expectations, we deepen our understanding of art.

Even merit functions cognitively. Curiosity quickens when we learn that practically indistinguishable works differ in value. The news goads us to search for salient differences. Challenged to account for an unexpected evaluation, we discover what to look for, what to look at, what to overlook in works of a given kind.

So merit, like emotion, transforms from end into means.[9] We do not become connoisseurs to distinguish good art from bad; we learn to distinguish good art from bad to become connoisseurs – people who understand art, and through art their worlds.

IV   INTERPRETATION

Construing works of art as symbols transforms the task of interpretation. No longer an exercise in speculative psychology, it need not plumb the mind of the artist or the critic or the spectator. Interpretation is closer to cryptography – a matter of decoding signs whose makeup and meaning are not immediately evident. The signs are publicly available; and previously effective interpretive strategies may be called into play. But code breaking is not automatic. Precedents may be insufficient, and a work may belong to several systems at once. Our reconception thus yields no recipe for interpreting individual works. But it corrects common misapprehensions that often confound our endeavours.

It discredits the conviction that interpretation is inevitably subjective. Since a work is a symbol, its interpretation depends on the syntactic and semantic rules of symbol systems(s) it belongs to. These rules are intersubjective, even if discovering them is hard. We must glean them from their applications as a linguist gleans a grammar from observed language use.

Misinterpretations abound. We can no more tell what an unfamiliar work means 'just by looking' than we can tell what an alien utterance means 'just by listening'. To interpret a symbol correctly requires mastering its symbol systems(s). And mastery is not given in the apprehension of the symbol. So a work does not mean whatever anyone takes it to mean.

Nor does it mean whatever an elite cadre of critics contends. Even if their readings are usually right, expertise does not make for rightness. Like skilled translators, astute critics may overlook an ambiguity, slight a subtlety, neglect a nuance, and so misinterpret a work. Even an expert can err.

Despite the manifold opportunities for error, several interpretations of a work may be equally effective, each answering to and illuminating aspects of it. None is all-encompassing. So it would be dogmatic to insist that one is right, all others wrong. The best policy is to accept any interpretation that satisfies the highest interpretive standards. A work of art then admits of multiple right interpretations. Art is inexhaustible because no interpretation or collection of interpretations can claim to deliver the last word on a work. There is no last word.

V ANALYTIC AESTHETICS

Pluralism and open-endedness may seem antithetical to the analytic enterprise. For analytic philosophy is widely believed, by supporters as well as detractors, to promise algorithms that determine the meaning and reference of every symbol in its purview. Such a promise is not easy to keep. Still, prospects improve if we restrict our scope. So early analytic philosophy intentionally skirted aesthetics. It recognized the folly of expecting a rule to capture the meaning of a powerful aesthetic symbol. But it hoped to find rules for the simpler signs of science and everyday language.

By now we realize that not even literal, descriptive language admits of analysis by routine application of antecedent rules. No rule mandates: ' "Vegetable" literally means just this and nothing more; literally refers to just that and nothing else', any more than a rule mandates: 'The white whale means just this and nothing more; refers to just that and nothing else.' What a symbol means depends on its use, its context, and its history, as well as on the syntax and semantics of the languages or symbol systems it belongs to. Language is too wily to be snared by an abstract, general system of rules.

Once we recognize that we neither have nor need algorithms for the interpretations of literal terms, the absence of algorithms for interpreting other symbols looks less troubling. The strategies we employ to interpret literal, descriptive language can then be profitably extended to accommodate symbols of other kinds. And our understanding of nonverbal and nonliteral symbols can illuminate the workings of literal language.

Analytic philosophy no longer purports to deliver complete and final specifications of meaning. But it retains its emphasis on symbolization. To understand a discipline requires knowing how its symbols function. Pluralism and open-endedness do not exempt works of art from the analytic philosopher's scrutiny. They challenge him to construct techniques sensitive enough to disclose the richness and complexity of aesthetic functions. If the task is endless, he will never be unemployed.

NOTES

1   See Nelson Goodman and Catherine Z. Elgin, *Reconceptions* (Indianapolis, Hackett Publishing, 1988), ch. 4.
2   Israel Scheffler, *Beyond the Letter* (London, Routledge and Kegan Paul, 1979), pp. 6–7.
3   Nelson Goodman, *Languages of Art* (Indianapolis, Bobbs–Merrill, 1976), pp. 252–5; and *Ways of Worldmaking* (Indianapolis, Hackett Publishing, 1978), pp. 67–8.
4   Nelson Goodman, *Of Mind and Other Matters* (Cambridge, Mass., Harvard University Press, 1984), p. 137.
5   Catherine Z. Elgin, *With Reference to Reference* (Indianapolis, Hackett Publishing, 1983).
6   Goodman, *Of Mind and Other Matters*, pp. 150–7.
7. Howard Gardner and David Perkins (eds), *Art, Mind, and Education* (University of Illinois Press, forthcoming).
8. Goodman, *Languages of Art*, pp. 248–52.
9. Nelson Goodman, *Problems and Projects* (Indianapolis, Bobbs–Merrill, 1972), pp. 120–1.

Index